1,000,000 Books
are available to read at

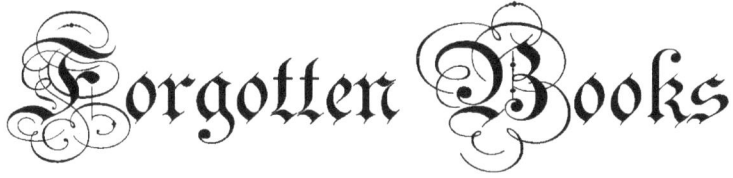

www.ForgottenBooks.com

Read online
Download PDF
Purchase in print

ISBN 978-0-259-86788-3
PIBN 10832623

This book is a reproduction of an important historical work. Forgotten Books uses state-of-the-art technology to digitally reconstruct the work, preserving the original format whilst repairing imperfections present in the aged copy. In rare cases, an imperfection in the original, such as a blemish or missing page, may be replicated in our edition. We do, however, repair the vast majority of imperfections successfully; any imperfections that remain are intentionally left to preserve the state of such historical works.

Forgotten Books is a registered trademark of FB &c Ltd.
Copyright © 2018 FB &c Ltd.
FB &c Ltd, Dalton House, 60 Windsor Avenue, London, SW19 2RR.
Company number 08720141. Registered in England and Wales.

For support please visit www.forgottenbooks.com

1 MONTH OF FREE READING

at

www.ForgottenBooks.com

By purchasing this book you are eligible for one month membership to ForgottenBooks.com, giving you unlimited access to our entire collection of over 1,000,000 titles via our web site and mobile apps.

To claim your free month visit:
www.forgottenbooks.com/free832623

* Offer is valid for 45 days from date of purchase. Terms and conditions apply.

English
Français
Deutsche
Italiano
Español
Português

www.forgottenbooks.com

Mythology Photography **Fiction** Fishing Christianity **Art** Cooking Essays Buddhism Freemasonry Medicine **Biology** Music **Ancient Egypt** Evolution Carpentry Physics Dance Geology **Mathematics** Fitness Shakespeare **Folklore** Yoga Marketing **Confidence** Immortality Biographies Poetry **Psychology** Witchcraft Electronics Chemistry History **Law** Accounting **Philosophy** Anthropology Alchemy Drama Quantum Mechanics Atheism Sexual Health **Ancient History Entrepreneurship** Languages Sport Paleontology Needlework Islam **Metaphysics** Investment Archaeology Parenting Statistics Criminology **Motivational**

THE WILKIE GALLERY:

A Selection of the best Pictures

OF

THE LATE SIR DAVID WILKIE, R.A.

INCLUDING HIS

SPANISH AND ORIENTAL SKETCHES,

WITH

NOTICES BIOGRAPHICAL AND CRITICAL.

LONDON:
PRINTED BY RICHARD CLAY,
BREAD STREET HILL.

List of the Plates in the Wilkie Gallery.

	PAGE
Portrait of Sir David Wilkie . *to face Vignette.*	
Vignette Title, Manse and Church of Cults, Birth-place of Wilkie.	
The Village Recruit	11
The Village Politicians	14
Alfred in the Neatherd's Cottage	16
The Blind Fiddler	17
The Rent-Day	20
The Card-Players	22
The Village Festival	24
The Jew's-harp	26
The Cut Finger	26
The Pedlar	27
The Rat-Hunters	29
Blind-Man's Buff	31
The Letter of Introduction	32
Duncan Gray	34
The Rabbit on the Wall	35
The Piper	37
Sir Walter Scott and his Family	38
Reading the Will	40
The Errand Boy	41
The Cottage Toilet	42
The Gentle Shepherd	44
The Parish Beadle	45
The Princess Doria washing the Pilgrim's Feet	51
The Portrait of Mrs. Young	73
Distraining for Rent	77
The Penny Wedding	79
The Clubbists	80
Guess my Name	81
The Highlander's Return	82
The Pifferari	83
The Gipsy Mother	85

The above list of Thirty-three Engravings comprises those which are introduced into the "Biographical Notice." The remaining plates, enumerated below, have separate descriptive text printed for each, and may be arranged to suit the taste of the owner; but the publisher would recommend the following order.

The New Coat.
The Breakfast-Table.
The Daughter of Admiral Walker.
The Broken China Jar.
A Turkish Courier relating the News of the Capture of Acre.
A Group of Figures entering Madrid.
A Group of Camels at Smyrna.
Chelsea Pensioners reading the Gazette of the Battle of Waterloo.
Three Greek Sisters at Therapia.
The Guerilla taking leave of his Confessor.
The Senoritta and her Nurse.
The Spanish Lady.
A Scene at Toledo.
The Wounded Guerilla.
The Duke of Wellington writing his Despatches.
Columbus at the Convent of La Rabida.

Saturday Night.
Guerilla Council of War.
The Hooka-Badar.
The First Ear-ring.
An Arab Sheik.
The Turkish Letter-Writer.
The Wardrobe ransacked.
Napoleon and the Pope at Fontainebleau.
Hebrew Women reading the Scriptures.
Reading the News.
Wilkie in search of Murillo.
A Persian Prince.
Death of Sir Philip Sidney.
A Circassian Lady.
Mother and Child.
Benvenuto Cellini and the Pope.
Dorty Bairn.
The Peep-o'-Day Boy's Cabin.

THE

WILKIE GALLERY.

BIOGRAPHICAL AND CRITICAL NOTICE.

DAVID WILKIE, the great painter, was the third son of the Rev. David Wilkie, minister of Cults, in Fifeshire, by his third wife, Isabella Lister, daughter of Mr. James Lister, of Pitlessie mill, in the same parish, and elder of the church there.

From both parents he appears to have inherited that seriousness, sagacity, and habitual spirit of self-control, which, besides being among the most honourable of the national characteristics, were peculiarly called forth by the circumstances of the Scottish clergy. The father of Wilkie was bred in the school of privation, the descendant of a family long possessed of a humble independence; but reduced to become tenants of their patrimonial estate of Ratho Byres, (a spot ever dear to the feelings of the painter,) it was not without difficulty that they could bear even the comparatively trifling expense of an university education in Scotland, necessary for the sacred profession to which they destined him. The slender allowance afforded from their narrow means, was increased by the trifling emoluments of a bursary to which he was honourably promoted, and by giving lessons to others in the studies which he himself long and zealously pursued. Years thus wore away in hopeless penury and the rigorous celibacy which it enforced, ere any prospect appeared of his attaining even the humble distinction and modest independence of a parish clergyman. And thus perhaps he might have continued to the autumn of life, but for the assistance of a kinsman, the Rev. William Wilkie, a man of some poetical celebrity in his day, and Professor of Divinity at St. Andrews, through whose kindly influence some rays of prosperity began to cheer the long-neglected and despondent student; but although his worth and learning were now brought to the light, yet it was by slow steps that he emerged from obscurity; for it was five years longer before he was promoted to the vacant manse of Cults.

In about two years from his induction, he married a woman, one of the most beautiful of the land, whose society, he might have fondly hoped, would have repaid him for the long years of youth passed in sordid celibacy; but this anticipated happiness fled like a dream, for only a few brief months elapsed ere he consigned this beloved partner to the tomb.

The serious duties of a parish minister at once forbid the long indulgence of selfish grief, and minister to its alleviation; and a sense of the propriety of his station probably induced the bereaved husband to marry, after a proper interval, his cousin, Miss Peggy Wilkie; but she also was snatched from him in less than two years. The twice stricken widower, now well past forty, had no child by either of his deceased wives, and the prospect of passing the lonely evening of life, now fast stealing on, in brooding over the past by his solitary hearth, led him a third time to enter into that state which had brought with it his highest happiness and his severest trials. But the storms of affliction had spent their force, and permitted his remaining years to pass away in undisturbed serenity. The third object of his choice was affectionate and prudent, and managed his narrow resources with admirable economy; and children were born to him, to sustain his declining years, of which, as before said, the great painter was the third.

The little Wilkie, from his earliest years, was remarked to possess the indications of a quiet, concentrated energy of character, and a subdued love of drollery. His words were few, in proportion to his inward mental activity; and less from the spirit of imitation, which is so powerful a motive in childhood,—for art, or artists, there were none in the neighbourhood, —than from a spontaneous impulse, he delighted in essaying to pourtray the objects that amused his childish fancy. It was a mile of rural road from the paternal manse to the school of Pitlessie; and here "with sauntering step and slow," he was accustomed to remark the characteristic figures that, unnoticed by any one else, arrayed themselves already in his mind as a succession of pictures, touched upon and heightened by the humorous cast of his perceptions. Enough there was too in that remote inland country nook to furnish matter for the development of his hidden talents. His mind was so preoccupied with the ruling impulse, that he was but a negligent scholar; and heedless of the tiresome confinement and irksome routine of school, he could not withhold himself, even under the eye of the master, from drawing on his slate by stealth the odd variety of physiognomy and expression afforded by his schoolfellows. The very kirk itself, serious as was his education and feelings, did not escape matter for humorous observation of character; and the walls and floors of the schoolroom at the manse were covered with imitative records. When about twelve years old, he began to commit to paper certain of the scenes and groups which had forcibly impressed him, some of which were the germ of his peculiar style. The love of art "grew with his growth, and strengthened with his strength;" he was restless unless engaged in his favourite pursuit, and it became evident to all his friends, that whether for good or evil, he had inwardly decided on painting as his profession, and was morally incapable of following to advantage any other path in life, particularly that of the church, to which the wishes of his relatives appear to have originally inclined.

Not without good reason, it must be admitted, could the worthy pastor of Cults have felt uneasy, when he perceived this unconquerable bias of his son's mind. In the pursuit of a regular profession he had himself fully experienced the bitterness of hope deferred, ere even a moderate competence could be attained; yet here uncertainty seemed certain, compared with the chances of an occupation accompanied by so many contingencies, where fame might never be reached, even after a long and arduous course of study, and the rewards that should attend upon it were so often utterly disproportioned to the risk and toil, and even insufficient to procure the means of existence, far less independence to its possessor. Brilliant exceptions there indeed were, but they were not numerous; and he might well hesitate at allowing his son to engage irrevocably in a career so fraught with peril and uncertainty; though, on the other hand, he could not fail to perceive that his devotion to art arose from no sudden impulse, but from the bias of Nature, who provides no less the power than the inclination to follow out her leadings with success. Neither could he have been without confidence and a secret pride in that settled, collected energy of purpose, and that quiet determination to overcome obstacles, which he must have felt that his son inherited from himself; nor was he uninfluenced by the counsels of his wife, who, with all a mother's tenderness, could not bear to see her son crossed in a pursuit in which his happiness was involved, and in which, with maternal hope and pride, she could not but augur his success. Thus, after much wise and anxious pondering, he came to the determination to overrule his own scruples, and the unwelcome bodings of friends, and to consent to allow his son to follow the bent of his inclination. It was not in the nature of the Wilkies to swerve from a purpose they had once advisedly formed; and thus the father of the young aspirant looked round at once for the best practical means of instruction, which his limited income would allow him to obtain. The famous seats of academical instruction were too distant for the purse, and probably for the feelings of the affectionate parents, who, even during the height of their son's brilliant career in London, appear ever to have been uneasy about his health and comfort, and who might naturally fear the neglect of both, in the absorbing mental excitement and ardent emulation of an opening career, in a scene too remote to enable them to bring succour in case of need. But Edinburgh was at hand, where an institution, called the Trustees' Academy,—founded, as it would seem, principally for the purpose of improving the taste of mechanics by the study of the models of art, and thus improving the designs of our manufactures,—yet afforded the means of elementary instruction in drawing to all who sought it, with whatever purpose; and accordingly, in his fourteenth year, the decisive step was taken, and young Wilkie, with his specimens and introductions, quitted the manse of Cults for a lodging in the Scottish metropolis. He first set up his easel at a small lodging in Nicholson-street.

The moment was fortunate in which the young student entered the Scottish Academy, not, as it would appear, without a previous rejection, on account of the crude and unartistlike character of his introductory specimens, wholly deficient in mechanical execution, and in which the secretary could hardly be expected to discern the germ of original excellence, though his scruples were overcome by the influence of an exalted patron, the Earl of Leven, and Wilkie was at length admitted. Hitherto the object of the teaching appears to have been principally limited and mechanical; but the appointment of a master imbued with original notions of art turned the scale in favour of a more liberal mode of study: emulation was kindled, much latent talent drawn forth; and when Wilkie took his place in the ranks of the Academy, he found among its aspirants several young men who have since attained high distinction, and in an honourable and friendly competition with whom his own powers were rapidly developed. The names of Allan and Burnet are scarcely less wide spread than that of the great painter himself; and this triumvirate would alone, were there no others, reflect high honour on the name of the enthusiastic and talented John Graham, who, single-handed, and in the midst of much warm opposition, converted a mechanical Academy into a nursery of immortal genius.

With firm resolve, untiring perseverance, and a resolute confidence in the result of his endeavours, derived from consciousness of the wealth of original materials long stored up, Wilkie commenced his academical career; and, as the first and most needful step,—conscious of his utter deficiency in drawing and anatomical knowledge of the figure,—he applied himself at once with the utmost diligence to the attainment of this indispensable preparation. He displayed none of the eccentric humour and fitful application of many great men, but kept up the routine of steady application, to such an extent, indeed, that it was to this attribute of dogged perseverance, rather than to the original impulse of genius, that he was accustomed in after-life to attribute the eminence he had attained. His progress was rapid in mastering the elements of art, in proportion to his power of discerning the true character and expression of the casts he was engaged in copying; he sought not merely to execute a smooth and correct, and well-handled resemblance of the antique fragment, whether foot, or hand, or torso, which was placed before him, but to seize and bring out the proper and pervading expression; nor was it long before the combined efforts of untiring industry and acute perception overcame mere mechanism, and he began to feel the ability to work out with the hand the original conceptions over which he had long brooded. Allan Cunningham has remarked, that it was well for him, perhaps, that he had no picture to lead him from the path of his own originality, and no one of influence enough to overrule or misdirect his studies. Nature had indeed led him by a path of her own, and marked him out for one of her finest interpreters. Endowed with the best characteristics of his native country, he was the more fitted to bring them out and embody them on canvass. The superior intelligence of the Scottish peasantry, their devout spirit, inward enthusiasm, honourable thrift, and acute forecast, "their dry humour, sedate glee," he himself possessed: from childhood he had been accustomed to remark the expression of these qualities, in the unsophisticated varieties of character, which abounded in the remote and primitive region in which he was born and bred; nothing had escaped his silent observation, and he was taught by a fine instinct how strikingly suitable they were for picturesque, no less than moral effect. He knew by heart all the old familiar figures of lowland life—the wandering beggarman, as Scott has finely depicted him; the broken soldier; the travelling tinker, or pedlar; the time-honoured elder of the village; the barefooted lassie by the burn-side. He could enter into the rich humours of the fairs and local amusements of his people, and well felt, too, their serious habits and customs. These he was qualified to express, in all their native simplicity, without the exaggeration and caricature which might have accompanied the efforts of any but an artist, who was "native and to the manner born;" and it is to be regretted that he was ever withdrawn by the requirements of patronage from this his chosen and natural walk in art, or he might have produced, with the same inimitable excellence, a still greater variety of truly national masterpieces.

Hitherto Wilkie had seen but few pictures, neither did Edinburgh furnish a large collection. But etchings from the works of Rembrandt and Ostade—masters with whose style and subjects he had a natural and corresponding sympathy—were well pondered, and had no doubt their measure of influence upon the style and arrangement of the pictures he meditated.

As yet he had brought to pass nothing beyond desultory sketches. The first impulse to the production of distinct and finished compositions appears to have arisen from the small prizes offered by the ardent Graham, for the best oil-studies from a given subject or poem; and although they did not always happen to be such as were calculated to draw forth the original powers of Wilkie, he was still occasionally successful in gaining the premium. These initiatory efforts accustomed him to the mechanism of painting, and his progress now was become so surprisingly rapid, that his wondering compeers could not fail to perceive that he would ere long astonish the world.

With all the encouragement he received, and a consciousness of the anticipations of his friends, the young painter was in no wise puffed up; neither did he abate a jot of the persevering course of study which he had laid down for himself. He must indeed, even thus early, have felt an inward joy and pride, that the sacrifices which his family were making were not likely to be ultimately fruitless, and that the tender interference of his mother, which probably turned the scale in his behalf, would be repaid by the joy of witnessing his success. The thoughts of Wilkie, when not bent upon the now fast-maturing conceptions which were hereafter to be so finely realised, appears ever to have been at home, at the manse of Cults. The first-fruits of his exertions, a small premium gained at the Academy, was devoted to the purchase of a trifling present for his mother; and the fine moral nature of the man, and his right training, are seen in this, that the intoxication of success never drew him aside, though at a distance, and amidst the blandishments of the world, from this true home of his affections. In his solitary lodging in Edinburgh he revolved the sacrifices of his family, the hopes of his parents, and the forebodings of friends: in the midst of temptation, cut off from all but the bare necessaries of his position,—although with a fair and promising dawn of success,—he was yet well aware of the many difficulties he must encounter ere he could attain the goal of fame and competency; and he had staked his all upon the issue of the course, as well as the feelings and the means of those no less dear to him than himself. He was confident, not rash—less in word than thought; so imperturbably kindly and good-humoured, among the little freaks and jealousies of his fellow-students, that his gentle nature overcame all opposition, and seated him in the hearts even of his rivals in the pursuit of fame. "When his fellow-students," says Mr. Cunningham, "followed him into his two-pair-of-stairs study in Nicholson-street, they found all in keeping, they said, with his demeanour in the Academy. The Bible and 'The Gentle Shepherd;' a sketch or two on the wall: a table and a few chairs; with a fiddle, whose strings, when he grew tired with drawing, he touched to a favourite air, were the chief articles. Neither lay-figures covered with silk, nor easels of polished mahogany were there: a few brushes, and a few colours, and a palette made by his own hands, may be added. The fiddle was to him then, and long after, a useful instrument; its music, he said, not only soothed himself, but put his live models, who sat for his shepherds and husbandmen, into the sort of humour which he desired; nay, he often pleased so much, that one of them, an old rough mendicant,

'Whose wallets before and behind did hang,'

to whom he had played a welcome air, refused the pence when offered, and strode down the stair, saying, 'Hout! put up your pennies, man! I was e'en as glad of the spring as ye were!' He sometimes too, in a land where living models of any other part save the head or hand are difficult to be obtained for either love or money, made himself into his own model, and with a bared foot, a bared ancle, or a bared knee, would sit at the looking-glass till he confessed that he was almost benumbed by exposure. Nor did he desist when a friend knocked: he would say, 'Come in;' nor move from his posture, but deliberately explain his object, and continue to draw till he had made the sketch."

Even before he had reached his eighteenth year, or quitted the Trustees' Academy, Wilkie had begun to paint portraits, and had dashed out roughly the first bold idea of the subject, afterwards wrought up into the fine composition of "The Village Politicians," and a picture from the finest pastoral poem of his nation, "The Gentle Shepherd" of Allan Ramsay. He returned to his home at Cults, having already realised enough to justify his confidence in his own talents, and by his quiet unassuming deportment acquired the respect both of his teacher and fellow-students.

Like so many other aspirants of original genius in painting, who have not been so favoured by fortune as to be in a condition to follow out their own wishes, Wilkie, checked at the outset by "poverty's insuperable bar," hesitated whether to choose the doubtful path of fame, or turn his attention to the more sure resources of portrait painting. For a while he hovered between the two plans; but, though he obtained a few sitters, and might reasonably have looked forward to the attainment of a position and affluence like that of Raeburn and Ramsay, could he have exclusively devoted himself to this branch of art; still the strong bias of his mind would make its way, and he was soon led to project works in which he might hope to display his peculiar talent and win fame, if even at a loss of time and money; or at least enjoy that inward delight and satisfaction, as the growth of his own creations kindles under his hand, which never fails to indemnify the true worker with nature, for outward privation and the world's neglect. With this view he began to look around the neighbourhood for materials, and, hesitating for a while between the grave or the humorous characteristics of the people, he decided at length on a subject which should embody the latter—the fair at the old familiar village of Pitlessie. Nothing could have been more happily chosen to draw him out. All the varieties of rural life of the country were there. The market-people swarming from the surrounding hamlets filled the picturesque old village street; quack-doctors, blue-gowned beggarmen, pedlars, and ballad-singers and fiddlers, as they ply their several vocations, mingle their voices in harsh and ludicrous contrasts. The recruiting-serjeant flames in scarlet and gold in the midst; the roll of his drum predominates over these minor discords, as he seeks to entrap the dazzled or discontented idler; while the magnates of the village pass among the shifting throng, awake to everything, and slyly relishing the fun, though maintaining the while an inflexible gravity of demeanour. Such a scene afforded infinite scope for the peculiar talents of the painter. For the first time he was ambitious in the dimensions of his canvass, intending to omit nothing of the humours of the place; and, after sketching in the general distribution of the groups, he proceeded to select such rustic figures as the neighbourhood furnished for sitters; and slyly obtained the characteristic traits of those recusants of the higher class, who stood upon their dignity, and declined to sit, by hastily jotting them down as they reclined dozily in the midst of the congregation. This, it must be confessed, was rather too bad for the son of the minister himself; and when the picture was finished, and when these worthies found that they figured in spite of themselves, and probably in a ludicrous light, among the profane vulgar, and the means by which this was effected came to light, as might have been expected, many and grievous were the complaints against the profane temerity of the artist. That he should have ventured on such an expedient shows, indeed, the force of the ruling passion, for Wilkie, with all his love of humour and drollery, was no less a man of much inward and profound seriousness of mind. No less than one hundred and forty figures were grouped in this curious piece of local portraiture, infinitely varied in character: and though too minute in detail and desultory in general arrangement, it brought out the painter at once, and showed to the world, as well as to himself, what he *could* do, and what might be expected, when this display of rich exuberance of material should be chastened by taste and animated by a pervading sentiment. Wilkie himself, on seeing it again, after he had painted his finest works, declared that it had more subject and more entertainment in it than any other three pictures he had since produced.

Another effect too was wrought by the exhibition of this picture. The domestic circle of Cults, who had been watching the issue of the first experiment at Edinburgh with no small anxiety, were not only relieved of their fears, but gratified with the praises bestowed on their son; the prophets of evil things were silenced; and those who had hesitated, in order to watch the result, at length discovered that the silent, reserved, and eccentric lad, had more in him than they had first imagined, and were ready to take the credit of prognosticating a success which they could not fail to perceive was now inevitable. Young Wilkie began to obtain much honour even in his own country, but so little profit withal, that he was driven to paint portraits for bread; and after setting up his easel in the surrounding towns, and exhausting the few sitters of a poor provincial district, whom vanity might tempt to incur so unwonted an expense, he began to perceive, perhaps not reluctantly, that he must seek a wider stage for the display of his talents, where the love of art, and the power to patronise it, existed; in short, that he must repair to London—great as might be the comparative expense of living, and still greater, in that vast crowd of competitors for fame, the difficulty of making an impression, or even of attracting notice. There too he could alone hope to supply his deficiencies, and improve his style, by a better course of academical drawing, and by the study of the works of the great ancient and modern masters, of which advantages Scotland was comparatively destitute. Accordingly in May, 1805, he took his passage at Leith.

With all his sober enthusiasm, the young painter must have felt nervous at being committed to the chances of a hard and doubtful struggle for fame, in the heart of that great Babel of strife, clamour, and pretension, where small reputations are soon swept away, or forgotten for others; and nothing short of surpassing excellence can hope to win lasting attention. The talents which had surprised the little circle of Cults, might here remain unnoticed, till neglect and want might compel the poor student to retrace his steps, disappointed and heart-broken, from the arena where he had hoped to win the high rewards of his profession, back to the narrow circle which had already proved insufficient to provide him even with bread. He might with reason too have been alarmed at the expense of living in London, which, with all the self-denial and frugality of his habits, required, for the maintenance of the mere decencies of his position, double the sum that sufficed for his student life in Edinburgh. His first lodgings were at No. 8, Norton-street, Portland-road.

His worldly vantages were but small; a few pictures, some introductory letters, such as could be obtained, but none of them to persons of great influence, and a small stock of money, sufficient, with rigid economy, to bear his expenses for a few months, made up the sum. Should this be exhausted ere a fresh supply could be obtained, his position would be truly critical; and not the least painful part, the necessity of revealing it to his beloved parents, and of thus exposing the failure of his ardent hopes, and his need of that assistance which he could as little bear to ask as they could refuse out of their poverty to bestow. These contingencies must have been deeply felt by the sensitive mind of Wilkie, though he was accustomed to master and conceal his inward emotions, and in writing home to put the best face he could on his position and prospects; and with his characteristic energy and perseverance to be "up and doing," with a cool estimate of the difficulties that beset his path, and a firm resolution to overcome them. His first step was to seek out a dealer's, where he could exhibit the pictures he had brought with him, and try their effect upon the public, while he hoped, through the introductions he had brought, to obtain some commissions for portraits, and thus maintain himself, while he entered upon a rigorous course of academical drawing, and with new light and improved style of execution, carried out some new works by which he might hope to fix the attention of the public. Notwithstanding his anxieties, Wilkie appears to have greatly relished the new life he was introduced to in the metropolis; he liked the comfort, and even the living, upon which he dwells in his letters with gusto, but principally the society and new circle of artists, whose example and success wrought emulation, and inspired ambition, while the treasures of ancient and modern art to which he had access, shewed him in what he had hitherto been deficient, and supplied the best models for study. He lost no time in entering himself a student of the Royal Academy, which he diligently frequented. Here he met with Haydon, then in all the spring-tide ardour of that ambitious and troubled course which had so melancholy a termination. There was a curious contrast between the two men: the English student, fired with the example of the great masters of high expression, Raphael and Michael Angelo, attempted, with irregular and ill-directed powers, at more than he could accomplish; wrapt up in the unattainable ideal, all else seemed unworthy of attention or praise; while Wilkie, with an enthusiasm no less, but better regulated, instead of idly grasping at the shadow of past greatness, was sedulously engaged in cultivating his own peculiar talent; and while he increasingly appreciated the great examples of the Italian painters, sought only how he might elevate his own style, without renouncing its distinctive originality. As might be expected, many were the contests between two minds so oppositely framed; yet this did not prevent them from contracting a lasting friendship. Jackson, too, whose portraits are perhaps the finest of our modern school, was also among his contemporary aspirants. The provincial reputation of Wilkie had in some measure preceded him, and all perceived that he would ere long do honour to the English school; while his kindly, though reserved manners, and the absence of all jealousy, rendered him a favourite among all but the more loquacious and envious of his fellow-students. He was introduced to several of the Academicians, of whose works he speaks with admiration, but dwells particularly on Morland, whose natural and original style had more charms for him than the classical compositions of painters of higher pretensions.

Time fled rapidly in these new occupations and pleasures, but with it fled too the fast-failing means of Wilkie. As yet, too, he had derived little or no benefit from the introductions he had brought with him: some of the parties were absent, others coldly civil, but none called to see his pictures, or sit for portraits, on which for the present he wholly depended. He had sold one or two small subjects at low prices, but still he could find no remedy for the rapid consumption of his purse. His anxieties must have been cruel at this period, though he speaks, in his letters home, with assumed confidence, that he might not wound the feelings of those who followed his every step with the deepest anxiety. He confesses, however, to another relative, " that he was uncertain how long he might remain in London; that he could stay no longer than his money lasted, and that he had no opportunity of increasing it by portrait painting, as his time was wholly taken up in study; therefore it was probable that he would be obliged to return to Scotland by the end of October, and fall to his old trade." In this state of miserable incertitude he remained, watching the occurrence of the smallest opening, with which he never failed to cheer the sympathising circle at Cults. Their love ever followed the absent adventurer; they appear even less anxious about his success, than fearful of the decline of his health, under the combined influence of hard study and intense anxiety. "We are pleased," says his venerable parent, "to hear that you have got a room to your mind in the west end of the city: be careful to attend to your diet, and do not fatigue yourself too much by either walking or work. You have, no doubt, seen much in your art already; and it is proper that you should be introduced to as many respectable characters as you can. I need not desire you to be careful of your expense." There was, indeed, little occasion to warn the anxious student on this head; for as at Edinburgh his first earnings were applied to the purchase of a present for his mother, so, here too he appears to have looked forward to a little patronage, in the hope of presenting his sister Helen with a pianoforte, of a better description than could be obtained in Fifeshire. There is no doubt that he practised the most severe economy: he could black his own boots, and make a model, when too poor to purchase one, of his own bared leg or arm; and yet he confesses afterwards to his father, when prospects began to brighten, and he could venture to speak of his past privations, "that he had become quite inured to the difficulties of living in London, for he had been several times reduced within the bounds of the last half-guinea, and had been under the necessity of living upon credit." Conscious of the pain which it would occasion his son to return to Scotland for lack of means, when brighter prospects might be about to dawn upon him, the

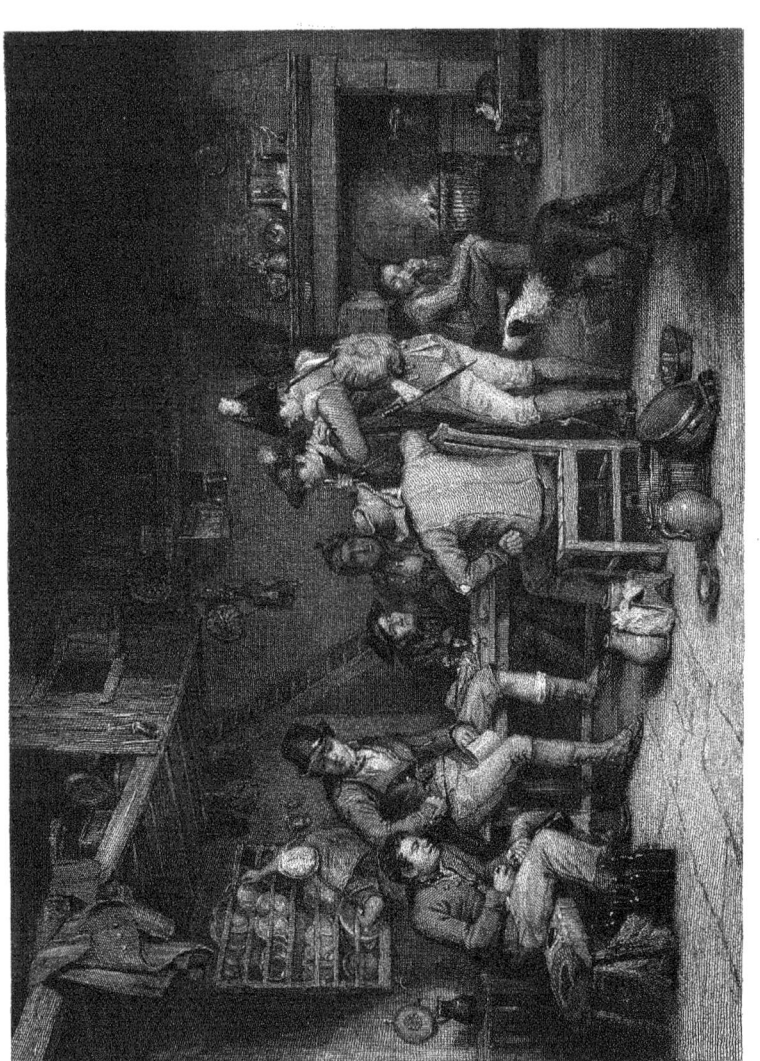

simple, kind-hearted parent, notwithstanding his sense of independence, his own means of assistance being exhausted, says, " As you mention your wish to continue in London during the most part of winter, and have some hope of success in your line, I have had it in my mind for some time of applying to Lord Crawford for the loan of a few pounds—*fifteen or twenty;*—which, if he lends, I would transmit to you, in case you found that such assistance was necessary to continue in London for a certain time." But this the honest pride of the painter, and respectful consideration for his father's position, would not for a long while suffer him to consent to.

In fact the clouds which beset his path were beginning to lift a little, and some few rays of encouragement relieved the heaviest pressure upon the mind of "the pale, thin student," who still kept fighting on, steadily frequenting the Academy, and staving off despondency by confidence in his own genius, and determined industry. The turning-point in his fortunes occurred through the friendly patronage of Stoddart, the eminent pianoforte maker, who having married a Wilkie, welcomed the painter to his house, sat for his portrait, and recommended him to friends, which put a few guineas into his exhausted purse, and enabled him, though not without a little assistance from Cults, to continue his studies and keep himself in the way of further encouragement. But a still more important service rendered him by this worthy man, was an introduction to the Mansfield family. It happened that the picture of "Pitlessie Fair," which the painter had sent for from Scotland to retouch, was at the house of the Stoddarts when the Countess of Mansfield called, who desired that it might be sent home with her, to show some friends, and thus spread the reputation of the painter over a wider and more influential circle.

The Earl of Mansfield now sought out the study of Wilkie. "Pitlessie Fair," full of the national characteristics, came home to him at once, and he looked round the walls for some study from which he might obtain a finished picture of similar truthfulness; and fixing at once on the powerful sketch of "The Village Politicians," he left with the delighted artist a commission for this subject, in which he felt that he could put forth all his powers to the best advantage, with the certainty of awakening that attention which he desired.

The intensity of mind that Wilkie threw into this first great work, was proportioned to the belief he could not have failed to entertain, that a decided success in this picture would open at once the door of the temple of fame, and work a total revolution in his prospects; happily, too, he was not labouring, as he was sometimes afterwards compelled to do, on a subject he could not feel, but upon one which he might stamp with his own power. Great was the astonishment and delight of his fellow-students at his progress; the feeling of rivalry seemed lost in irrepressible admiration of his native, original excellence, and they spread his fame far and wide among the circle of their brethren and the patrons of art.

Among the latter it "chanced one day that Sir George Beaumont and Lord Mulgrave were praising the Dutch school; when Jackson, who was present, said that if they would come with him, he would find them a young Scotsman, who was second to no Dutchman that ever bore a palette on his thumb." "We must go and see this Scottish wonder," said Sir George, and they followed him to Wilkie's abode, where they found "The Village Politicians" all but finished.

No introductions could have been so fortunate as these—both gentlemen were as devoted to art, as generous in its patronage. Sir George Beaumont, himself a landscape painter of no mean skill, refined in all his tastes, the friend and ardent admirer of Wordsworth, was well capable of appreciating original excellence of whatever kind, and rejoiced in the opportunity of drawing it forth. He was won also with the native and modest simplicity of the man, equally remote from that vulgarity and servility, on the one hand, and conceited presumption on the other, with which his knowledge of the world of artists must have rendered him unpleasantly familiar; and from that moment he never ceased to treat him with friendly confidence and delicate generosity to his life's end. His kindly warmth of manner must have cheered the feelings of the young painter, and the expressions of admiration of his talents by such a judge must have been truly gratifying—substantiated as they were by a commission to paint a picture at a price, which, although small, perhaps, in consideration of the time and study required, was yet far higher than any he had hitherto obtained.

It was in good season that this encouragement came to cheer up a little the struggling painter, for he was at this time labouring under the depressing consciousness of debt. He had striven hard to keep the wolf from the door; but his London expenses were unavoidably heavy, and the prices at which he was exhausting health and spirits were utterly insufficient to procure him bread. Even the more liberal payment for his new commissions would barely cover the expense of their production. With this, and with its wasting influence on his health, his family became acquainted, and their tenderness was justly alarmed. His father wrote to urge with warmth his return to Scotland. "In the manse," he said, "you will find a home while I am afoot;" and warns him not "to put too much faith in hope, which, rainbow-like, eludes our grasp, and glitters but to deceive our eyes:" urges besides the bad state of his finances, and assures him of encouragement for a while in his own neighbourhood, and informs him, as a still more powerful inducement to return, of his own bad health, and that of his beloved mother.

Wilkie was every way moved by this paternal appeal, yet how could he return home at the moment when he had sent his picture to the Exhibition of the Royal Academy, waiting, with mingled hope and fear, to see what its effect would be upon that public, from whose unbiassed suffrages alone he must expect the meed of fame? He had not indeed long to wait, like some, the refined merit of whose productions has been more gradually appreciated: crowds besieged his picture—for it was happily of that class which appeals as powerfully to the sense and feeling of the common observer, as to the judgment of the educated artist or amateur:—the dramatic vigour with which the story is told, and the inimitable character came home to the former, as much as the fine grouping, masterly arrangement of light and shade, and breadth of style satisfied the critical requirements of the latter. Wilkie was placed at once first in the public estimation as the painter of life, and every new picture from his hand was looked for as a public feast. The press enthusiastically echoed his praises; nor were the more sober Academicians unmoved; and all recognised the fact, that a great and original genius had sprung up to redeem the correct platitudes and classical inanities which so largely prevailed. Some indeed had, or pretended to have, their concern and misgivings lest this style, "pauper" in subject, as they ventured to term it, though not in manner, should spread and become fashionable; and warned the young painter to beware of the direction of his powers. But all this, as well as the intoxicating applause of the public, Wilkie bore with his usual quiet indifference of manner, abating nothing, though suddenly lifted into fame, of that unassuming and modest deportment which had won the hearts of his fellow-students and aristocratic patrons.

But his heart might well have swelled with honourable pride at the attainment of that fame for which he had so long laboured in privation and discouragement, and a glow of sweeter and deeper feeling have thrilled through his attenuated frame, as he thought upon the joy which the news of his success, fast flying on the wings of public fame and private congratulation, would diffuse through the beloved circle at Cults. When they learned that their long-neglected son was no longer pining in obscurity, but that the talented and wealthy vied in paying him honour, and inviting him to their splendid hospitality, and found that these attentions were even reflected on themselves, they must have felt richly repaid for their sacrifices. Though to have seen him at home at such a moment would have been a cordial to their infirmities, his father now fully concurred in the propriety of his remaining awhile in town, to profit by his new-born reputation. "As to your return to Scotland," he writes, "if attention to your mother and me be your principal motive, that need no longer influence you; we must not interfere between our son and his success, but endure the accidents of life in the best manner we are able." He tells him, too, "that he cannot imagine how great a fervour of admiration the accounts of his picture had produced in his own neighbourhood; in particular that gentleman for whom he had painted pictures the year before affirms that each of them is worth an hundred guineas." So altered was their estimate. The Wilkie who sought for fame and bread among the towns and straths of Fife, and who was regarded with cloudy brows by the pious of Cults, for presuming to trace their faces as they slumbered in their pews at church, and the Wilkie whom high-born earls were proud to employ, and whom the first-born of the realm courted to come to their country-seats, seemed different persons. He was first spoken of in the North as an ingenious young man; for the Scotch are slow in saying all they think; then the mercury of their praise rose a few degrees, and he was a very clever painter of humble subjects; and, finally, he became, without excelling far his first productions, "our distinguished countryman, and our own immortal Wilkie."

The picture of "The Village Politicians,"—which at once lifted its painter into public favour; though it originated in the stormy days of the French Revolution, when the sudden outburst of long pent resistance to the rights of man, and the promulgation of new and sweeping doctrines, carried away in its might the deep-rooted institutions of society, no less than their superficial abuses, and spread its ferment and agitation into the remotest nooks of our own land,—is one which, in its true and human expression, will probably be applicable enough to all time. The scene is laid in a strange old Scottish clachan, picturesquely combining the attributes of parlour and kitchen, with its array of mutchkins, pint-stoup, gridirons, hams, and salted herrings; the walls and rafters are dusky with smoke; and the light streaming into the centre of the room falls upon a most marvellous group, inimitable at once for its variety, and its unity of expression. The collected senatorial gravity and amusing consciousness of importance diffused over the whole figure of that old man, the Nestor of the village, as he calmly cherishes his chin, and weighs with judicial impartiality, unmoved by the din, the merits of the respective arguments, his jug, grave and weighty as himself, deposited on the floor the while, contrasts finely with the figure of the ardent young ploughman, intoxicated with the new light of liberalism, and who, with an intensity proof against all interruption, is propounding some strange doctrine, which he himself seems scarcely able to comprehend, to the decision of this calm umpire. Aided by the potent stimulus of a mutchkin of mountain-dew, he has apparently reached the very climax of his argument, which he is establishing triumphantly, wholly rapt and deaf to the clamorous exceptions of his antagonists, who are unable to edge in a single syllable. One of these, provoked at the utter enormity of the doctrine thus put forth, has sprung to his feet, and with swelling veins, and eyes protruding with all the fury of contradiction, is hurling at the young enthusiast some tremendous, unanswerable objection; to which his gourmand comrade, his attention a moment diverted from the cheese, with suspended knife, appears to be directing the attention of their opponent, but in vain—the young enthusiast heeds neither. The sentiment of this central party is greatly heightened by contrast with the vacant apathy of the group of village idlers collected around the fire, and the listless Highland drover, with his wild, hungry dog, which, profiting by the abstraction of all around, seems about to make forcible seizure of the oat-cake of a wee frightened bairn, scarce higher than himself; while another keen-eyed tyke is making the most of the golden

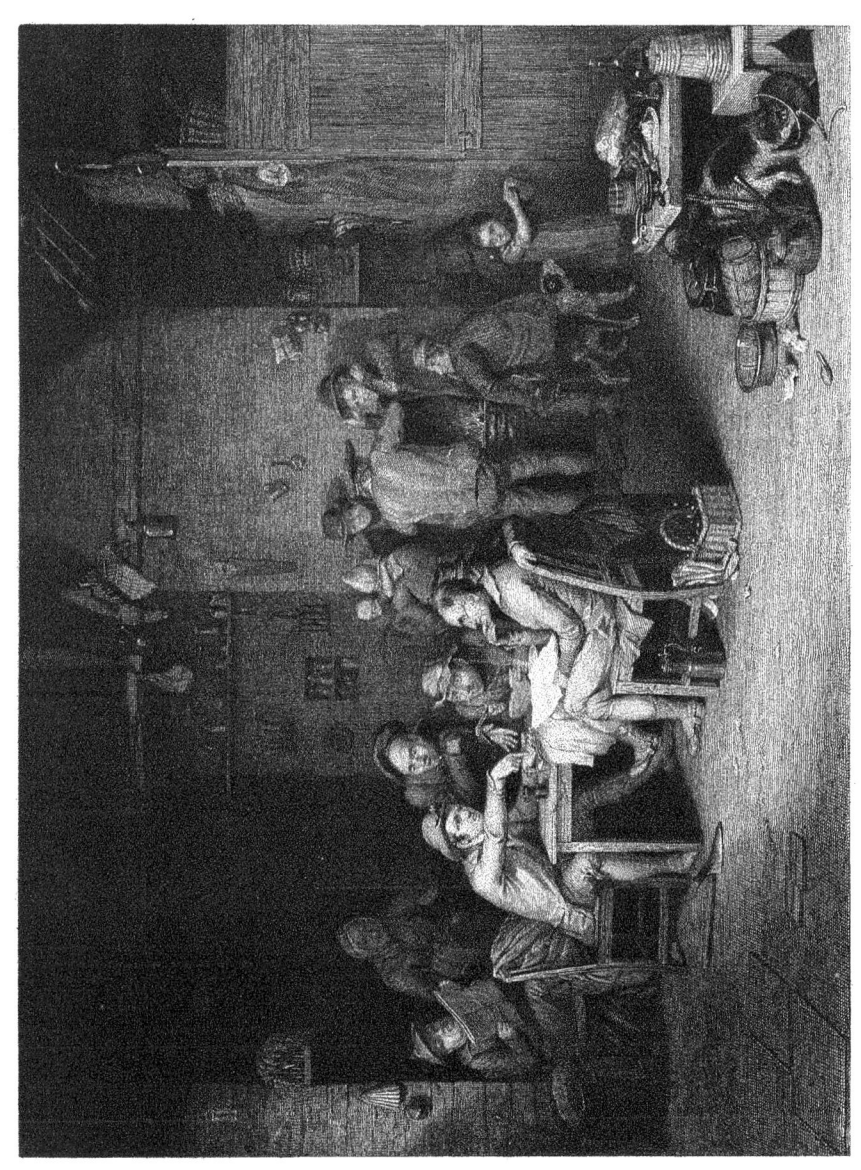

opportunity among the flesh-pots in the foreground. Most amusing too is the old man, seated near the window, who, remote from the arena of strife, with spectacles on his nose and mouth half open, is absorbed in puzzling out the sense of some article in the Gazette; whilst the quiet, sly old dame is emerging from the cellar, well pleased at the thirsty character of the debate, and bringing with her wherewithal to relieve the drought and animate the vigour of the combatants. All these varieties of expression are given with wonderful dramatic force, and proper subordination, untinctured by a particle of exaggeration: every figure too has a striking individuality; the accessories separately studied from nature, have also the closest national and local truth, and by the management of consummate art, they assist, without overcrowding the composition, or distracting attention from the main expression of the subject. The arrangement of the groups, and distribution of the light and shade, are not less inimitable than the other merits of the picture.

Fame the painter had thus at length attained, even to his heart's content, but as far as present results were concerned, it was somewhat dearly purchased. The noble patron at whose instance the picture, with the merits of which the world rung, had been painted, was, it seems, less moved thereby to any injudicious display of generosity, than wisely tenacious of his right to possess it for the sum named by the painter in the day when he could not have foreseen the value it would ultimately reach. *This sum was fifteen pounds,* at which price the Earl of Mansfield now claimed to be proprietor of the picture. Wilkie was at first inclined to demur, having received more than one offer of an hundred; moreover, it was his impression that the Earl had never distinctly closed, even with this modest stipulation; but on the Earl's declaring on his honour that he had intended to do so, the point was gracefully conceded by the artist. That it was purely, however, on Wilkie's account that this munificent nobleman had insisted on the fulfilment of the contract, "it being," to use his own words, "his conviction that it would be advantageous to him to have it in his power to say, that, notwithstanding the success of his picture, and the offers which were made to him, he adhered to his original engagement," he proved to the satisfaction of every one, by generously presenting the painter with no less than *thirty* guineas, instead of the original fifteen. Poor Wilkie! another such victory would indeed have been his ruin.

The painter's position was now totally altered. Men of wealth and taste delighted to honour him; and we find him not long after the exhibition of his picture a guest at the house of Mr. Whitbread and at Mulgrave Castle. At this time too commences his correspondence with Sir George Beaumont, one which is perhaps unique between painter and patron, both for its critical value to the artist, and also for the expression of that friendly cordiality on the part of Sir George—a man of true nobility of mind—which henceforth knew no interruption, and which was ever responded to by Wilkie, with feelings of grateful regard.* The criticism of this enlightened patron was of the greatest value to Wilkie at this period, as he himself ever loved to admit, while his generosity too was always steady and considerate : he was well acquainted with the painter's circumstances, and wishes him, yet with every expression of delicacy, to anticipate the payment for "The Blind Fiddler," should it in the least degree be desirable to him to do so. Wilkie was now advancing rapidly with this picture, and at the same time with another, "Alfred in the Neatherd's Cottage," painted for Mr. Davidson, as one of a series to illustrate English history. This was a subject somewhat out of Wilkie's line, wholly ideal, and of which the difficulties were great; for, while confined to the literal truth of the scene, he had to paint up to that heroic and imaginative feeling with which we love to invest the "lights of the world and demigods of fame." At a later period, when his mind had become imbued with the grandeur of Italian art, he would have treated this subject in a more elevated manner; as it is, he produced a strikingly picturesque composition, without any extraordinary elevation of style or sentiment. The story is well, if not powerfully told. The rude comfort of the Saxon cottage, in the depth of the woodland, like that of an American log-hut, is well imagined and represented. In the centre of the homestead is seated the disguised monarch; his harp and bagpipe are slung above the door-post; a dead rabbit is at his foot, with his bugle and bow-case, and he is employed in polishing a tough bow, to use against his Danish enemies. Absorbed in melancholy reveries upon his fallen estate, and meditating his plans for its recovery, he has forgotten the care of the cakes, which are burning on the hearth among the embers of the wood fire, which the neatherd and his dame are just entering the cottage with a load of fagots to replenish. At the sight and smell of the scorched eatables the dame waxes indignant at the carelessness of her guest, and is roundly reproaching him for it; while the neatherd, (a capital figure,) betrays alarm lest his disguised sovereign, startled from his self-possession by the reproaches of the careful housewife, should betray his disguise, and risk thereby the failure of all his plans. The figure of Alfred is easy, natural, and dignified; an expression of care and dejection is on his countenance; but he exhibits no anger at the irritating invectives of his hostess; as being too magnanimous, or sunk too deep in painful preoccupation of mind. This is well imagined; and yet perhaps the whole picture would have gained in dramatic effect had Wilkie represented the king as startled, and on the point of betraying himself, as suggested by Sir George Beaumont.

All the accessories are excellent—the girl, who hastily withdraws the burning cakes from the hearth; and the quiet scene of rustic courtship going on in the background.

His next picture will ever be considered one of his happiest; and, despite the somewhat

---

* For this, and Wilkie's general correspondence, which will be perused with the greatest interest, the reader should consult the *only* work which contains it,—Allan Cunningham's Life of Wilkie, published by Murray.

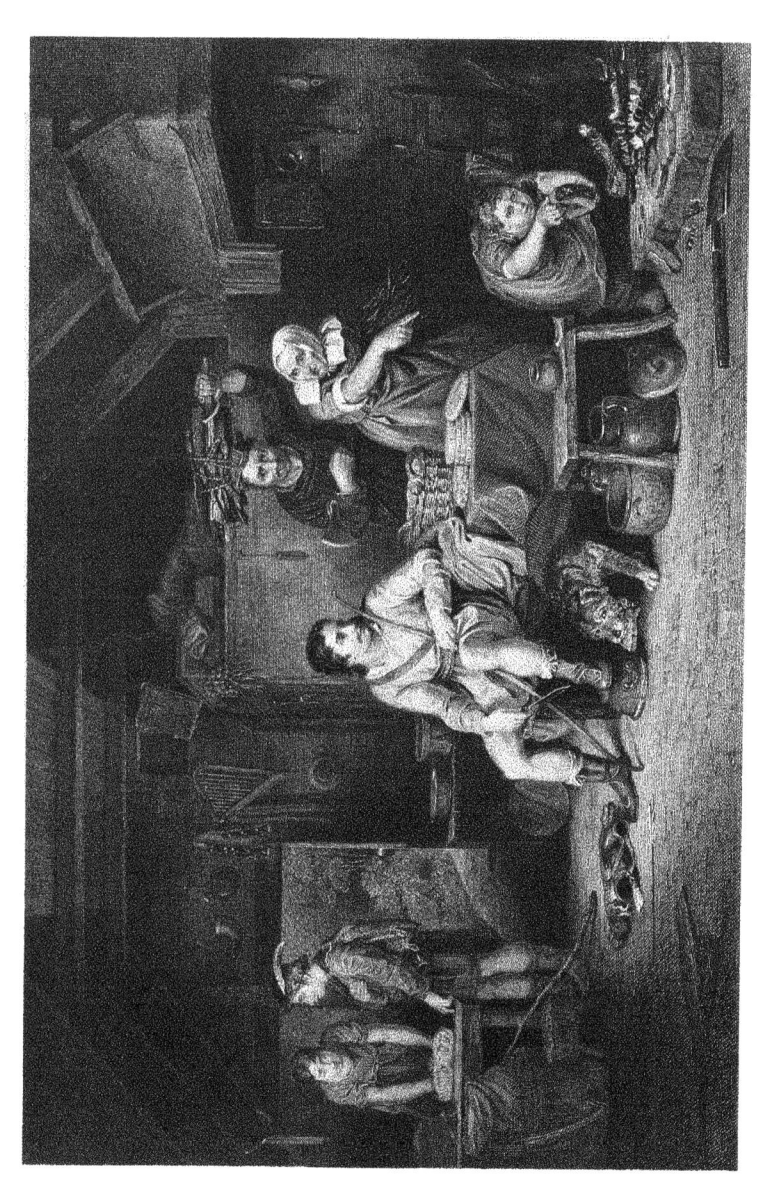

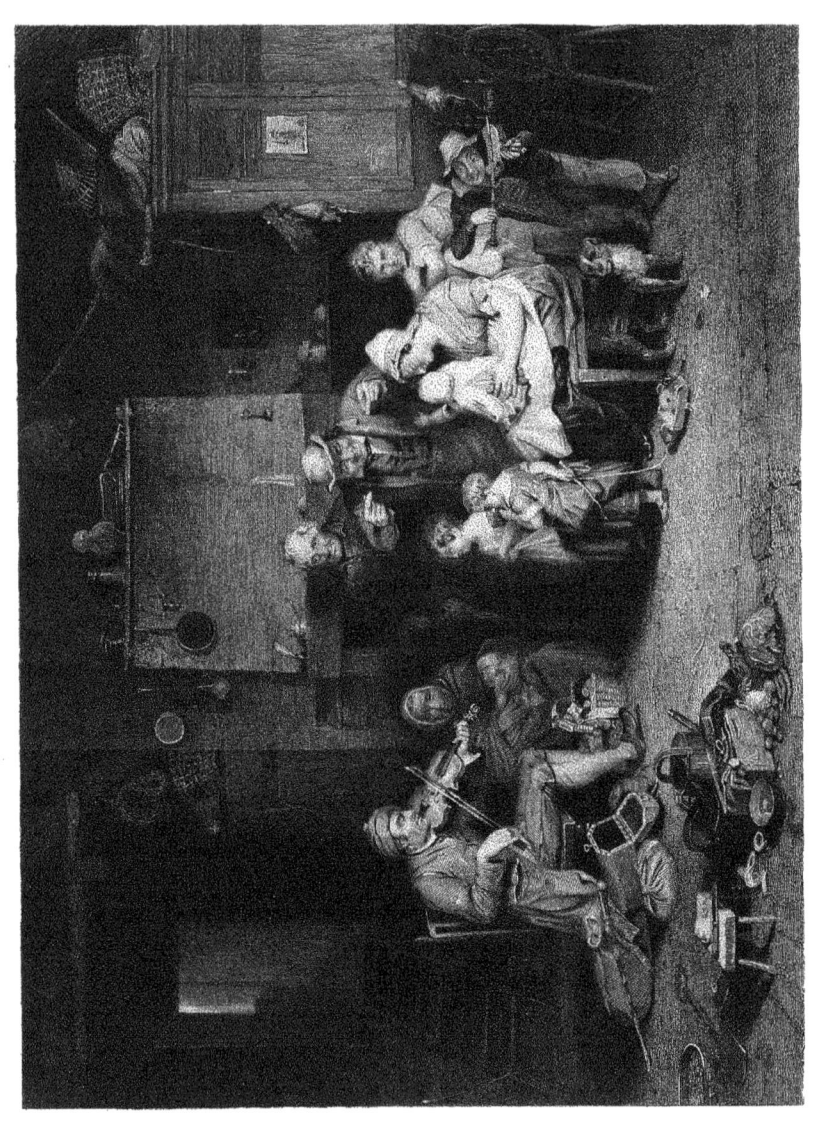

too cold and metallic colouring of the original, (a defect not observable in the engraving,) will perhaps, with a large class of his admirers, be deemed his very finest work. The discriminating patron for whom it was painted hailed its appearance with delight, as a decided advance even upon "The Village Politicians."

We are within the cottage of a shoemaker: it is a cold, raw day; old and young gather to the peat fire: there are two groups almost painfully contrasted—the family of the honest Crispin, thriving and well to do in the world, in their humble way, well fed and neatly clad; the other, houseless, homeless wanderers. There is a pathos about that gaunt old fiddler, lank and weatherbeaten; his face is worn and sad; his hands wiry and shrunken; he seems acquainted with hard weather, and harder fare: he has laid down his staff and bundle, drawn forth his fiddle from its case, and is mechanically plying it to some stirring march perhaps, which he accompanies for effect with the beat of his weary foot. His huckster wife, cold and hard featured, seems indifferent to the old-accustomed sound, and anxious only to get food, warmth, and shelter for herself and babe. Not so the inmates of the cottage: they are all alive to the merry strain; and exquisitely has the painter discriminated the varied effects of the music upon the auditors, from infancy to hoary hairs. The infant pet of the family, seated on the knee of its buxom mother—delighted more with her babe than even with the music, and whose neat shoe displays the triumph of her husband's skill—screams wildly, as the father merrily cracks his thumbs in time; the child of three years old has stopped his miniature waggon, and listens in unmixed wonder, while the face of his sister, elder by a year, is radiant with open delight; the eldest boy, rife with fun and mischief, is imitating the musician with all the glee of his age; the white-headed grandfather, with his back to the fire, through whose old veins the blood flows in a half-frozen current, seems calmly pleased, but no more; a servant girl, her spinning suspended, seems carried away by the tune into a world of curious fancies or associations of her own; the very dog stands suspended and tickled by the lively strain. No wonder that this inimitable production went, even more than "The Village Politicians," to the public heart; for there is in it a feeling, and a sense of beauty, of which the other picture did not admit: it was, in fact, opening a new and more pathetic and exquisite, though less humorous vein, and showed the marvellous variety, as well as originality, of the painter's powers. The nature is so deep and truthful as to hide the exquisite art; it seems as though the original conception in the mind had been suddenly breathed upon the canvass, rather than wrought out by the toils of study and thought; yet here the critical artist is no less delighted at the subtle skill with which the groups are arrayed, without being too scattered or crowded, at the picturesque varieties of form, the fine effects produced by judicious contrasts, and the admirably graduated and varied expression, while at the same time unity of purpose and sentiment is preserved more successfully, perhaps, than in any other of the painter's productions.

The fame of Wilkie was now fully established, yet the prices received for his works were utterly inadequate. For "The Blind Fiddler" he had received only fifty guineas; but this sum Sir George Beaumont subsequently, in fact, doubled. He began therefore seriously to revolve the project of publishing engravings from his pictures. In this he had a twofold object. "He could not but feel how valuable to a great painter a great engraver was: while the canvass itself remained fixed as fate in some rich man's gallery, and only known to the fortunate few who had influence to open the reluctant doors, the impressions from the graver flew lightly over the world, and carried into the cabin of the cotter, as well as into the hall of the lord, the same shape and sentiment and feeling (we had almost said the same colour) which charmed us in the original. The painter who disregards this auxiliary of art seems willing to lose the influence of half of his own power, because he keeps the world in ignorance of his strength; and he foregoes the honourable fruits of his own genius, because he has as fair a right to share in the profits of the engraving, as the hand has which directs the graver." It was fortunate that Wilkie should have met with professors of the sister art capable of entering into the peculiar humour and character of his works, and of retaining the inimitable expression, and rich racy touch and handling. In his fellow-student, Burnet, and in Raimbach, he found what he sought; and there is perhaps no instance of the works of a fine painter being so completely rendered. The large original engravings have enabled the world at large to participate in an enjoyment little less than that of witnessing the originals themselves.

The time was now come when Wilkie might venture for a while, without injury to his prospects, to pay his long-deferred visit to the affectionate circle who so ardently desired to have him among them again. He had not been neglectful, as his means improved, of numerous kind offices to them; and his sister Helen had received the promised piano. Impatient to arrive, he stayed but to get a glance at the Academy exhibition; and early in May went down by sea to Scotland, under circumstances widely different from those which not long before might have driven him back there, a baffled, impoverished, and disappointed man; having now won that fame which was reflected from himself to his friends, and caused them to rejoice in his joy. All his old friends gathered around him. His early patrons took pride in having been the first to perceive and draw forth his talents. "Neither did those older and graver persons whom he had introduced in his 'Pitlessie Fair,' hesitate, it is said, to call and forgive him for having handed them up to fame in the lasting colours of the pencil." These were the happiest days of the painter's life, and they might well repay his previous anxiety and the dark and cloudy days through which he had passed. But his health—undermined by these causes, and by the over-excitement, perhaps, of a sudden lift almost from concealed despondency to the intoxication of triumph, and the returning gush of tenderness after unwonted absence—at length gave way, and in the midst of the endearments of home he was laid up with protracted illness, which yielded at length to youth and the tender care of his nurses. His captivity was soothed by letters of the most cordial kindness from his attached friend Sir George Beaumont; and as his convalescence permitted, he replenished his portfolio with a new stock of studies from nature, to be wrought into his future compositions. After five months' absence, he took leave of his family, and, accompanied by his mother to Edinburgh, sailed again from Leith Pier, to resume his studies and his triumphs in the Great Metropolis.

Wilkie's position, at this period, as to patronage and emolument, may be best gathered from his own words, in a letter to his brother:—" You will very naturally conclude, from the accounts you have most likely heard of the fame that I have acquired, that I must be rapidly accumulating a fortune. It is, however, I am sorry to say, very far from being the case. What I have received since I commenced my career has been but barely sufficient to support me, and I do not live extravagantly either. Indeed, my present situation is the most singular that can well be imagined. I believe I do not exaggerate when I say that I have at least forty pictures bespoke, and some by the highest people in the kingdom; yet, after all, I have but seldom got anything for any picture I have yet painted."

This is a sad fact, that works which were the result of years of observation and study, and that in their actual composition and execution occupied so much time, should have been thus repaid: and that the painter should have been obliged to turn his attention to portraits, and to resort, at a later period, to the doubtful speculation of exhibiting his works. Tempted as he must have been, by the inadequate return for his labours, to shorten the time required for the production of his pictures, and to hit upon a style more rapid and superficial, which would *pay* better, he had yet too much of the true artist about him to give way; but even, to the surprise of some, continued sedulously, at a period when his fame might seem to have dispensed with it, to draw at the Academy, especially from the living model, continually endeavouring to improve his style by a closer study of nature. This constant aim of Wilkie at further refinement of style, seems, at a not much later period, to have been, and not without reason, a source of no small uneasiness to his best admirers, who feared lest he should overshoot the mark, and lose somewhat of his racy native vigour in the search after qualities of secondary importance. Sir George Beaumont reminds him, while admirably discriminating his peculiar walk in art, that "there is in the first feelings of a man of genius a simplicity and truth, which, as he advances in practical skill, will, without constant attention, be very apt to be lost in the struggle to excel: simplicity," he continues, " is the vital principle of the line you have chosen. Deep pathos, although I think you are quite equal to it, you do not appear to aim at; satire and broad humour are not, perhaps, congenial to your feelings; what remains then is the amenity of humble life, dashed with a proper proportion of comic pleasantry. In this line—in 'The Blind Fiddler,' &c.,—you have succeeded to the admiration of the world. I only wish to caution you," &c. There was as yet however, little to fear; for the painter still continued to pour forth from the rich stores of his mind fresh compositions, which, as regards, at least, still greater *variety* of character and incident, surpassed those by which his fame had already been established, and put to flight the envious carping of some of his brethren, who affected to doubt whether his "pauper" vein were not already exhausted. They erred in their estimate, for Wilkie had drank deep at the fountain-head of inspiration. Of life, as it had fallen under his observation, and was viewed by his peculiar and original cast of mind, he continued to reproduce the image upon his canvass, with no diminution of his original felicitous power. Of this "The Rent-Day" gave ample proof. The scene and subject were totally different from his previous subjects, and yet equally true to nature. We have no longer the interior of the Scottish clachan or the rustic cottage, but are introduced to a more important, if less picturesque, scene of action,—the comfortable steward's room, in the mansion of his noble master, where preparations have been made to receive the rents of his humble tenantry, and to feast them well when the business is concluded. The box containing their deeds and leases is open; while tables are spread with the means of luxurious refreshment, rarely or never partaken of but on this important occasion. Varying from stalwart youth to asthmatic infirmity, the tenants all appear of the humble class, clad alike in the frieze coat and clouted shoe, familiar with the plough-handles; yet they appear not to have come equally well provided to the scene of reckoning; for while the countenances of some are calm and assured, others appear blank and despondent: and death too appears to have been busy since the last rent-day, in calling in his debts; for among the circle sits a young widow, whose hearth has been thus rendered desolate, and her children orphans. A pathetic, almost painful, feeling pervades this group: here, exquisitely blended by the painter's art, the lights and shadows of a humble class of Scottish life are cast upon the canvass with subtle skill and profound feeling, and we read in their varied expression, "the short and simple annals of the poor." At a table in the foreground is seated, in his padded chair, the self-important functionary, " every inch a steward;" a world of care and responsibility is on his close-knit brows; shrewdness in his eye, and in the keen and somewhat selfish lines of his face, the lower part of which indicates withal the well-fed, pampered inmate of a luxurious house. Before him stands a figure perfectly primitive and patriarchal in the simplicity of his aspect and costume; one who has grown gray, and bent under the toils of his humble life. His broad-brimmed hat and staff are laid on the floor, while he pays his rent; and, being no orator, he has devolved upon a young man, perhaps his son, the office of reclaiming some portion: his placid and patient manner contrasts curiously with the generous warmth of the young man, who, with looks persuasively bland and much ingenious acuteness, is pleading his cause to the important arbiter, who seems half puzzled, half angry, at the nature of the application, and little

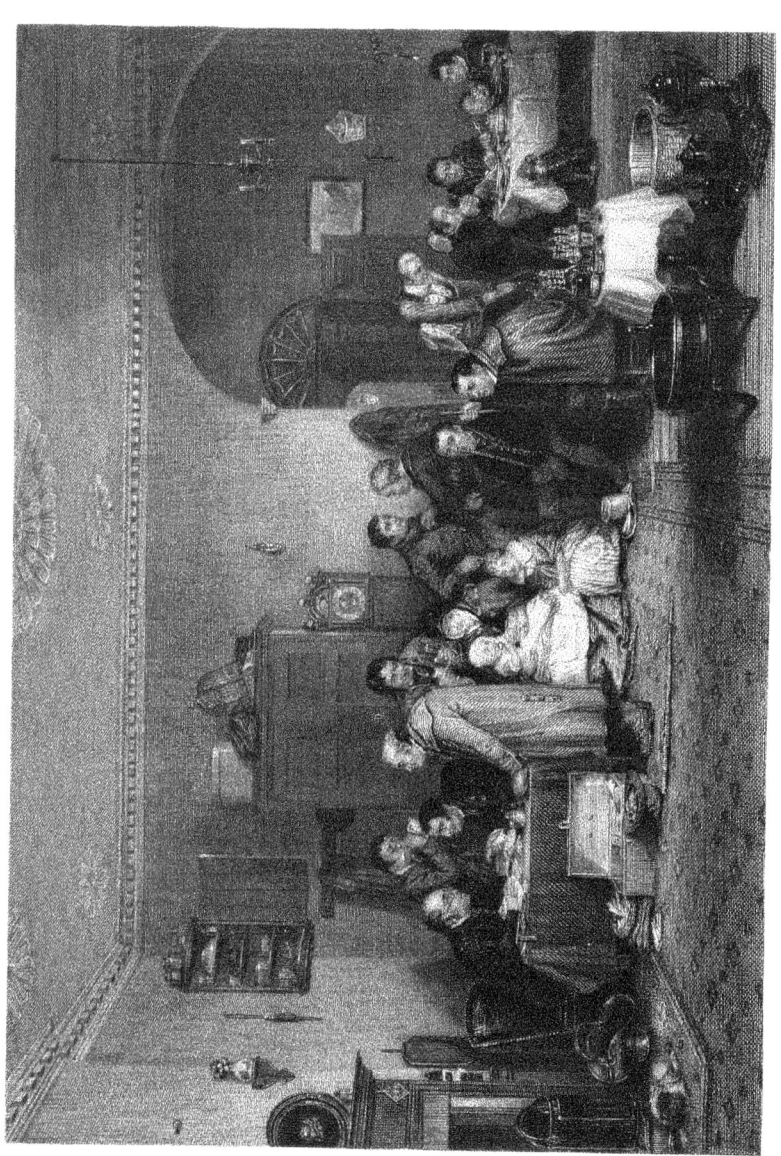

disposed to admit it, if the letter of the lease, as seems the case, will bear him out in his hard exaction. Behind these are two farmers whose business is settled, and whose inimitably comic expression relieves the darker shades of the picture—the one on the left, who appears to have paid somewhat in too great a hurry, is going over the items afresh; and the conclusion that he has been overreached is just dawning upon his face, full of ludicrous consternation and incipient fury. The other appears to be, like Cassio, " no arithmetician,' and is carefully and slowly working his way upon his finger-ends through some intricate calculation, with a curious abstraction that would provoke a smile " under the ribs of death." Next comes the sweet widow, upon whose pretty gentle face sorrow appears to have cast the first traces, attired with modest neatness; her babe playing unconsciously with the key that once opened all the joys of a home of which she is no longer tenant: her elder child sits by her—a group pleasingly painful, as we anticipate in idea the distresses that too probably await those who have hitherto been living in the lap of affectionate security, from which their bereavement has driven them. Two more farmers are seated; one, whose fallen countenance tells of unavailing struggles with misfortune; he gnaws the head of his staff, as, with listless dejection, he awaits his turn to be called; the other is convulsively coughing, as though he would burst a blood-vessel, perhaps with exaggerated emphasis, to bespeak compassion and indulgence for a short-coming payment. Behind them stand two more: one of them seems well to do in the world, to whom his fellow, holding him tight by the button, seems to be detailing a whole catalogue of agricultural disasters.

The painter has wisely consigned to the background a display of gluttony, which, while it completes the character of the picture, would be repulsive but for the still broader humour which he has thrown over it. Around a well-spread table a few of the tenants who have paid their rents are making the most of an opportunity that comes but once a year; as though, by their desperate efforts, they could recover some portion of the money they had reluctantly parted with, or were determined to take away with them as large a discount as possible. A jovial butler, well amused at their voracity, is drawing corks with all his might, to keep pace with the drought of the party. There is a dogged seriousness about their half-choking visages, which is intensely ludicrous, and which *absorbs*, so to speak, all the grossness of the exhibition.

Wilkie was now at the zenith of his fame, and the lovers of art in every class were delighted to honour him. His journal,* commenced about this period, shows us his daily life, and abounds in notices of the characters he mixed with. His course of study was unintermitting; he painted steadily on, in the midst of many interruptions from aristocratic patrons, in whose society he mixed freely. Among these the most constant and valuable were Lord Mulgrave and Sir George Beaumont, who watched with

* Contained in Cunningham's Life.

interest the course of that brilliant genius they had delighted to welcome. Wilkie's principal companions among the artists were still Haydon and Jackson, though his journal records the visits of Newton, Leslie, and Mulready, and men of kindred talent and feeling.

The closeness of his application was occasionally relieved by dinners with his patrons in town, and visits to their country houses. Wherever he went, he was on the watch for incident and character : " A peculiar turn of the head, a particular motion of the body, a face in which he beheld something nationally true, either in beauty or expression, were treasured in his memory or his sketch book." About this time he received a commission from Mr. Angerstein, who wisely left price and subject to his option, and for whom he subsequently painted " The Village Festival." He was now engaged on three pictures, " The Sick Lady," " The Jew's Harp," and " The Cut Finger."

Wilkie had removed from Sol's Row to Great Portland-street, to the house of Mrs. Coppard, with whom he ever remained on the most friendly footing, and whose family appear to have done everything to promote his comfort. His sphere of acquaintance widened every day: we find him now on intimate terms with Dr. Baillie, and his sister, the celebrated Joanna Baillie, who were ever among his warmest friends and admirers. He paid a visit to Lord and Lady Lansdowne, at the old Castle of Southampton, where they maintained a fanciful and half-baronial state He sat for his picture to Sir W. Beechy—he was a pretty constant attendant in town upon the preaching of the celebrated and witty Sidney Smith : we find him too, with feelings of envy, dining with Godwin, Wolcot, and Liston, a curious triumvirate ; to Jack Bannister, the celebrated comedian, he owed the happy suggestion of " The Reading of a Will " as a fitting subject ; Leigh Hunt too appears on his list of friends, which seems to have been a truly catholic one, in which kindred wit, genius, good-humour, and refinement were the attracting principles. With the numerous calls upon his time, occasioned by this spreading fame, he continued his usual industrious course, frequented the Academy, and attended Sir Antony Carlisle's lectures on anatomy. He began also to sketch out his first ideas of the picture of " The Village Alehouse."

From this time it would appear that Wilkie began to travel a good deal, a taste which grew upon him as he advanced in life; and his health required change of air and scene. He made a pilgrimage with Haydon to the birth-place of Sir Joshua Reynolds, at Plympton, in Devonshire; and in the autumn went down to Coleorton Hall, the seat of his steadfast friend, Sir George Beaumont. This was a visit long held in pleasing remembrance. The place combines the magnificent and tasteful luxury of our aristocratic family seats, with the romantic beauty dear to the poet and the painter : the hand of refined taste had adorned, without spoiling, its natural advantages ; heightening, but not invading, the beauty and contemplative stillness of its ancient woods and glades.

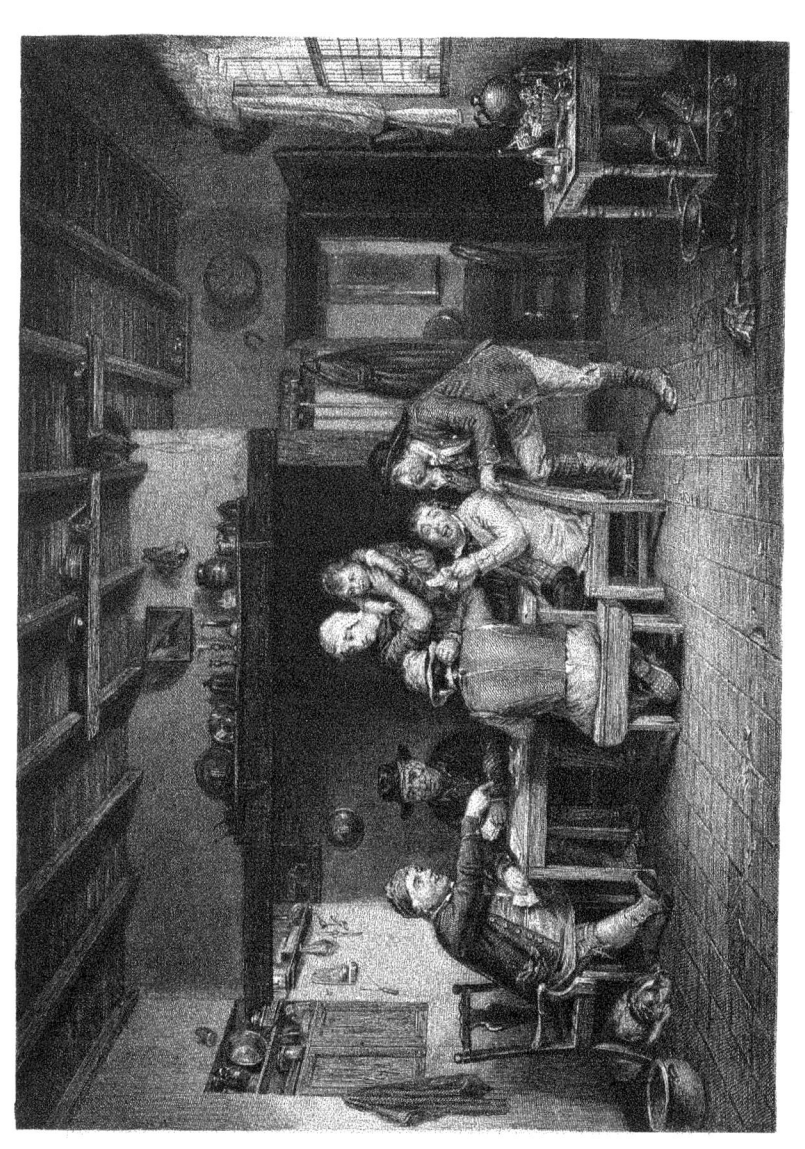

And never was such a scene tenanted by an owner better able to appreciate it, or who could so well increase its enjoyment to the intellectual circle which he loved to assemble around him, by the amenity of his manners and the elegance of his pursuits and pleasures. Here Wilkie passed his time after his own heart, in sketching from the surrounding scenery, or from any remarkable groups he could obtain, varied by walks with Sir George and Lady Beaumont, and agreeable conversations on art or poetry; while in the evening Sir George often read to the circle selections from our poets and essayists, which proved the justness of his taste. In all this Wilkie was well qualified to bear his part: for over and above his distinction as a *painter*, his letters abundantly display his general intelligence and refinement as a *man*; and the attentions he had received from the great, far from inspiring the vulgar presumption of many, had produced no other effect than that of "polishing his simplicity and his natural good manners." Nor were his generous entertainers less gratified than himself. "The pleasure," says Sir George, "which your visit gave us, will not soon pass from our minds; and I cannot but look forward with pleasure to the time when you are to paint a picture here. I hope you will not defer it too long, for at my time of life, and with my constitution, it would be presumptuous to promise myself many years; as long, however, as it pleases God to spare my life, I shall be happy to see you. I hope you have finished your *task*, and are proceeding with the work of your *heart*." This concluding remark has an allusion to two pictures then in hand—one a group of family portraits, which appears to have consumed much of his time; and the long-projected and carefully considered "Village Alehouse," in which he intended to put forth all his powers, and show the advances he had made in colour, harmony, and richness, from the sedulous study of the great masters of the Dutch school, Rembrandt, Ostade, and Teniers.

While this picture was on the easel, Wilkie became an Associate of the Royal Academy. This was, it is true, a superfluous distinction for one whose popularity was based upon public sympathy and the admiration of the best judges; but still he had been accustomed to aspire to it as an honorary distinction, and felt perhaps that it was his due. However, with his customary modesty, he did not take the initiative; and it was not till various members of the Academy had advised him to put his name down for the vacancy, that he was induced to do so, and to go through those formalities which are usual on such occasions. It is hardly necessary to say that he was successful; his election dates November 6th, 1809.

He was now at work in earnest upon Mr. Angerstein's commission of "The Village Alehouse:" and from the entries in his journal, recording the numerous sittings of his models, his repeated alterations, and the suggestions and criticisms of his friends, no picture that he ever painted appears to have been so deeply considered, or so laboriously wrought up to perfection. He was here in the new field of out-of-door life; hitherto he had painted interiors, requiring strong concentration of light and shade, but he had now to diffuse over his composition the brightness and the joyous clearness of open daylight, and to paint in a background of landscape and sky, matters as yet quite foreign to his style, and in which he ran some risk of comparative failure. Sir George Beaumont, who watched his progress with interest, and influenced him much by his judicious advice, remarks, "All that part which would be impossible to others, you will execute with ease; I am only afraid, from want of practice in these things, the sky and background may cost you some trouble." Here he had an able adviser in Callcott, who looked over his labours, which he suspended from time to time, to occupy himself with smaller pictures, and the irksome but needful task of portraiture, without which he could not have found means to carry on his larger works. The more generous of his patrons reproached him with the extreme moderation of his charges, advising him to raise them, which advice Lord Mulgrave enforced by sending him double the price, he had put upon a picture executed for him. Had all acted thus, Wilkie might have continued in his proper walk of art without interruption; but those who were ready to reproach him with leaving it, were not always equally disposed to prevent his doing so by the exercise of needful liberality.

Of the smaller pictures, one painted at this period was the jeu d'esprit of "The Man with the Girl's Cap." This he sent to the Exhibition, but so inferior to his other works did it seem to the "hanging" committee, that in an indirect manner they advised him to withdraw it. To such an intimation his ardent and high-spirited friend, Haydon, would have opposed a feeling of indignant defiance; but Wilkie, whatever might have been his private feeling on the subject, submitted to the wish of the committee with becoming resignation. Indeed it may be reasonably doubted whether the taste of this picture is altogether equal to its happy execution; certain it is, at least, that though none but a Wilkie could have painted it, it would never alone have obtained for him his high reputation, nor would such a class of works have long sustained it. Yet it is a pleasing morceau enough.

He had now at length finished and placed in the exhibition the picture of "The Village Festival," on which he had bestowed more than usual study. Though this is a very beautiful picture, we may be allowed to doubt whether it is equal either in truth or veracity of character to the finest of Wilkie's works; yet so picturesque is the composition, and so delicious its tone and colour, so fine the management of the broad transparent shadows, and the rich well-concentrated lights, that it is only on a closer inspection that we perceive its comparative want of interest, both as regards the subject and the limited range of character exhibited. The figures, too, are not Scotch, whose every peculiarity Wilkie excelled in representing, but English; and they do not bear, with one or two exceptions, to our thinking, the same unequivocal national fidelity. "Indeed, he con-

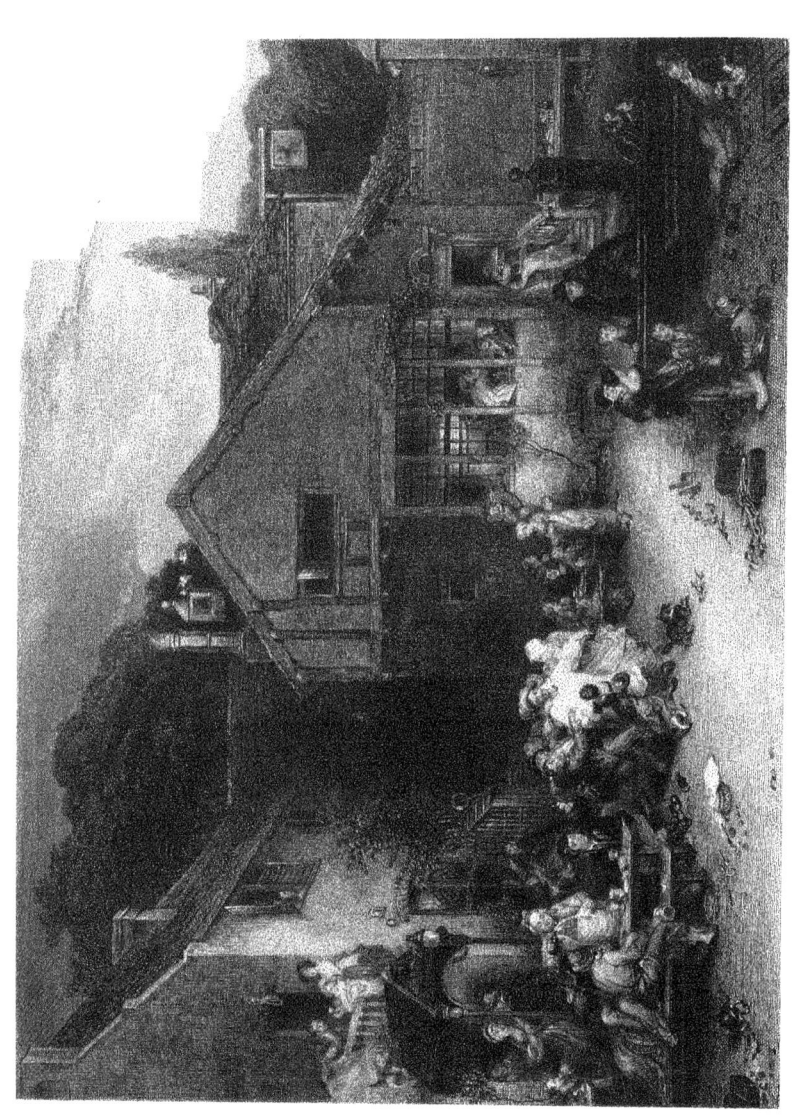

fessed," says Mr. Cunningham, "that he never could enter into the spirit of English fun, as he could into the peculiar glee of Scotland. "There is a sort of muddiness of intellect about all who drink *ale* in the pictures of Wilkie: see how different are the heroes of his 'Whiskey Still;' their heads are clear, their eyes like stars, and humour flows improved from their lips." So charming is the picture as a whole, that this may be deemed, however, somewhat hypercritical. The scene is an old village alehouse, with its timber beams and gabled roof, with additions of more modern date; the tall elms of old England cluster richly above it. Within and without all is redolent of joyous hilarity, fast passing into riotous uproar, under the potent influence of the landlord's ale, which circulates around in bottles and flagons, jugs and glasses, till, at length, with spilth and overflow, "even the very table itself looks drunk."

At a table near the tavern porch stands the portly Boniface, with clean white cap and apron, a capital and characteristic figure. His round rosy face expands in benevolent satisfaction; and in the happy consciousness of increase to his till, he pours forth from a black bottle an irresistible glass of ale, creaming and foaming and sparkling over the brim, as does England's best in the light of a summer-day—to all other potations far superior. The gleaming cascade catches the eye of a smock-frocked ploughman, who has had some drop too much already; getting more drouthy as he drinks, he finds his power to leave the scene of temptation fast abandoning him. He is the object of contention between a party of his roystering companions, still further gone than himself, who are determined to make a finish of it, and will have no sneaking off, and his poor wife and daughter, who are endeavouring to get him home while he is yet able to walk. The issue seems doubtful, for there is a look of sore conflict in his flushed face as he catches the gleam of the fragrant liquor, though he has just sense enough left to resign himself, and, putting his feet in the homeward direction, submit to be haled off with all the might which his distressed wife and poor little girl can muster. The pathetic and the humorous are here, as in so many other works of Wilkie's, closely intermingled and exquisitely blended. That poor child is evidently not for the first time supporting the steps of a drunken father. There is an expression of precocious care and sorrow about her thin little figure, which tells of a home rendered noisome and squalid by drink. Such scenes are too common around us in their revolting misery; but the art of the painter has robbed this of its coarsest traits, and made it beautifully painful. This group is among the finest of Wilkie's. There is no other of equal merit to bear it out, unless the scene of half-drunken gallantry at the corner of the large window, which in the original painting is sunk in an exquisite grey tone of colour, and put in after the most felicitous manner of Teniers. Other groups and scattered figures keep up the spirit of the scene of revelry, among which may be signalised the negro, whose face literally shines with mirth and drink; and the shy lassie in the balcony, to whom a half-tipsy admirer is offering a glass of something potent, with no good intention doubtless. In the foreground is a drunken figure, which, if it reads a moral lesson, serves withal to impart a somewhat too repulsively bacchanalian character to the whole composition, On the whole, we should not select this from among the finest works of Wilkie, preferring the "sober glee" and dry humour of his own country, to this scene of coarser English revelry. The beauty of the colour, perfection of tone, and touch and finish of the picture are indeed inimitable, and show great study and increasing refinement of style in these respects.

"The Cut Finger" is one of the prettiest of Wilkie's minor domestic pictures, and comes home to our infant days' remembrances. We are evidently here in the cottage of a most notable old dame, where there is a place for everything, and everything is in its place, even to the cat: everything breathes an orderly atmosphere; nor is there a vestige of litter but what is perpetrated by the pet of the house—the little grandson, who has been indulged in the dangerous pastime of cutting out miniature ships in stick, and rigging them with paper, with a handbasin for an arsenal. He has cut his finger—not very seriously, if we judge by the calm looks of the dame and her maid; but, alarmed at the sight of blood, he is ruefully blubbering, with a comical visage, in which fright manifestly predominates over pain; griping hard all the while the instrument which caused the mischief, which he refuses to yield to the neat-handed damsel, who strives to extract it from his grasp. The experienced old dame, who has everything ready, is at work with her lint and rag, which she gravely adjusts to the bleeding finger with calm complacency, as if used to the business; while an elder sister watches the process with looks of interest not unmingled with alarm. Wilkie's journal gives us the progress of this pleasing composition, of which every portion was painted carefully from models. That for the old woman, he tells us, he was lucky enough to find ere he had gone the length of the street, as he sallied forth in search of one.

"The Jew's Harp" is also a charming subject, painted with a raciness and picturesque force, admirably transcribed in our engraving. The story is too well told to need explanation, and it carries us back to the happy period of childhood, easily pleased with any fresh marvel. The little boy is all wonderment at the sounds that his father is evoking from the mysterious instrument—the little lassie all delight: even the tired dog seems not unconscious of the lively influence. No picture of Wilkie's is more felicitous in manner and handling than this: at once vigorous and delicate, it seems painted with a broad, rapid, and masterly pencil. The accessories are admirably composed and put in: in short, it is one of those happy morceaux in which we would not wish a touch more or less, so complete is it in its way.

From long-continued and anxious study, the excitement of town life, and some secret chagrin, perhaps, that the pictures of Edward Bird (a man indeed of no mean talent, but greatly Wilkie's inferior) seemed for the while, in the judgment of certain of his brother

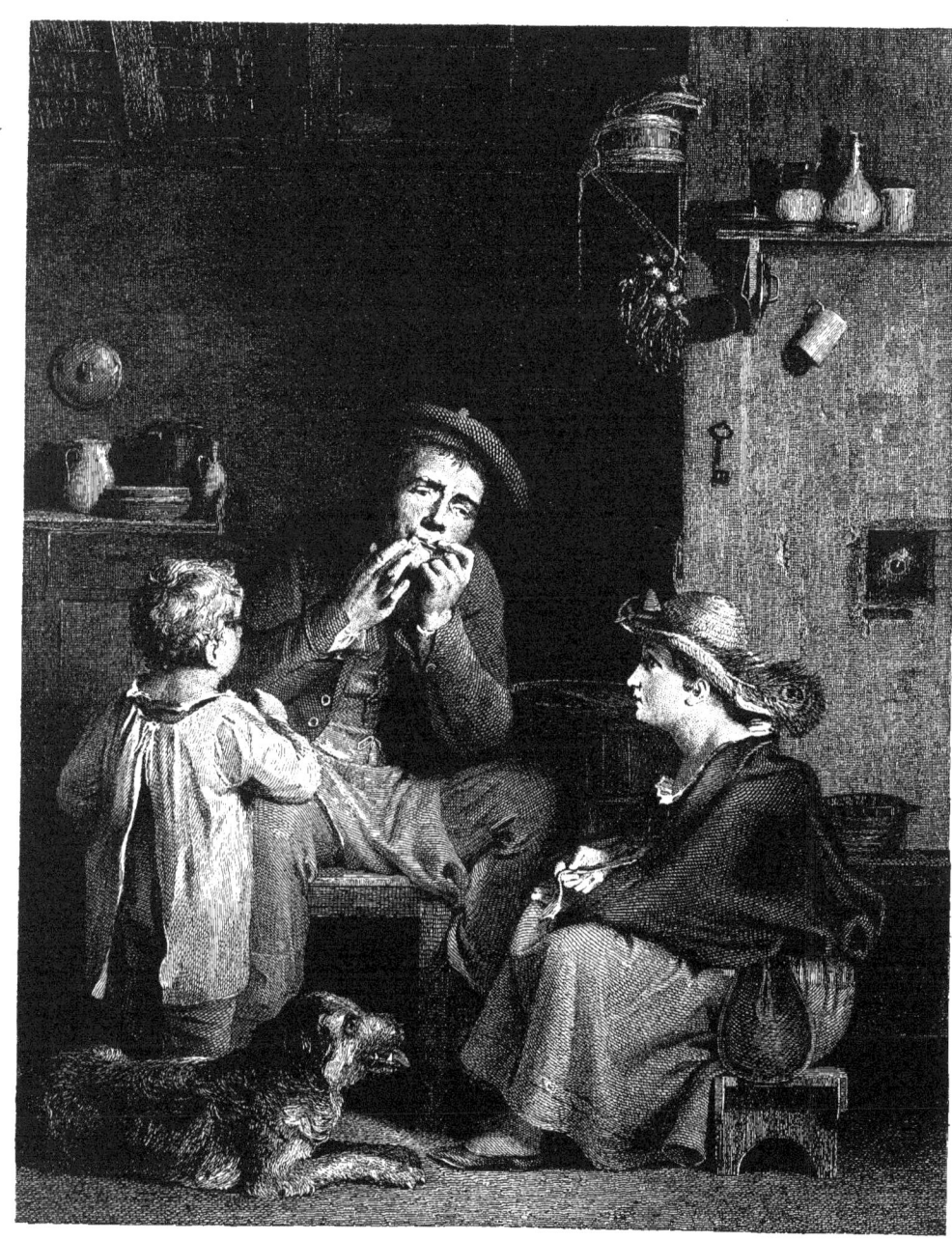

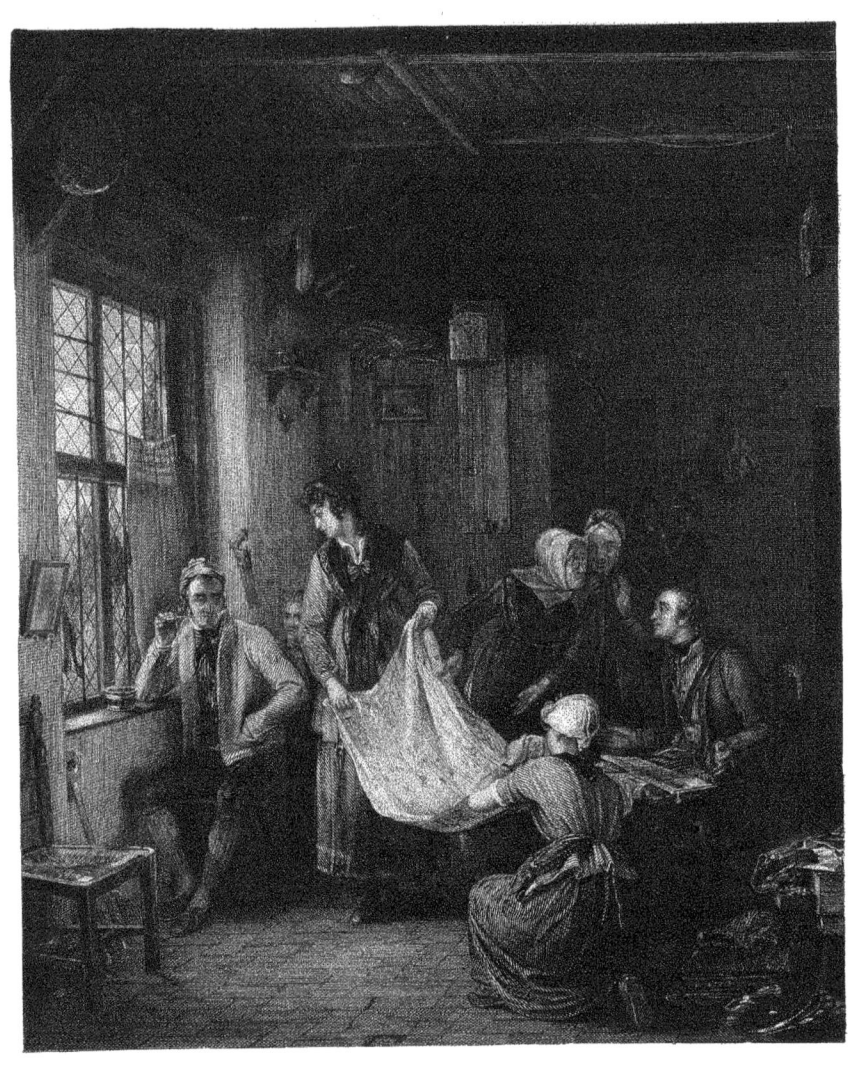

PAINTED BY DAV D WILK E.   G.RATBACH

artists, to threaten an eclipse of his own supremacy, Wilkie now appears to have fallen for the first time into that nervous state which, at a subsequent period, prevented him for months together from using any professional exertions; and he felt compelled to consult his friend, Dr. Baillie. Reports of his illness crept abroad, and alarmed both his family and friends, who, loving the gentle nature of the man, vied with one another in kind offices. Sir George Beaumont had just before, but with delicate consideration for all that affected the feelings of men of genius, privately urged upon Wilkie's acceptance pecuniary assistance, which, however, "with the highest sense of his generosity," the no less generous painter declined to accept. Sir George next pressed him to take a little Coleorton air, or, if it was thought desirable for him to visit Madeira, assures him that he should consider it "most unkind" if he did not inform him of any deficiency of purse which might prevent his carrying out this plan. But Dr. Baillie, aware that the disorder was partly mental, advised him wholly to withdraw for a while from the studies in which he was wrapped up, and to quit the metropolis, for the purer air of its environs; while his sisters, who were meditating a journey into the country, offered to the invalid painter the comforts of their own residence at Hampstead, during the term of their absence. The house which now received Wilkie, and which will derive so lasting an interest from being the abode of Joanna Baillie, is situated in the most breezy part of the village, and within a few minutes' walk of the health-inspiring heath, with its rich variety of home scenery, of broken banks, bright with the yellow furze, of sandy lanes, and blue fading distances; a kind of landscape well suited to the painter's taste, amusing the overwrought mind with its lively variety, while the bracing aromatic air was equally calculated to invigorate his shattered frame. He speaks with grateful thanks indeed of the benefits he had derived from this luxurious seclusion, surrounded with all the attentions of a home, to his distinguished hostess. Sir George Beaumont next attracted him to Dunmow, at that time his residence. Here he began to resume his pencils and palette, with this kind friend as a *moderator*, for whom he dashed in a vigorous sketch or two, which his host insisted on rewarding with a liberality that fairly overpowered the feelings of the convalescent.

It was for his friend Dr. Baillie that he painted "The Pedlar;"—an incident of country life. In the remote village, or still more secluded farm, this personage is of some mark, and his arrival an event;—witness the "Bryce Snailsfoot" of Scott;—for he carries not only his pack, furnished forth like that of his plausible prototype, Autolycus, in the "Winter's Tale," with

" Lawn, as white as driven snow,
Cyprus, black as e'er was crow,
Gloves as sweet, as damask roses,
Masks for faces, and for noses;

. . . .

Pins, and poking-sticks of steel,
What maids lack from head to heel."

but he is also the general newsman and gossip of the district;—he has something for everybody; tidings of weddings and courtings for the young; scandal for the old dame, and politics for the good man—he well knows how to frame his face to all occasions, to tickle every one on the weak side, and turn everything to the main chance. Such an one is here exhibiting the choicest contents of his box, before

> .... "The prettiest low-born lass, that e'er
> Ran on the greensward." ....

A gay-patterned dress, intended, perhaps, for her wedding, has wholly captivated her fancy; and while a sister is carefully examining its texture, she turns with a look of appeal to her father, who, in his perplexity between the value of 'siller' and the desire of indulging his pretty daughter, is drily ejecting from the corner of his mouth a long whiff of tobacco. He is apparently giving way to the pleasing temptation; but in the background, meanwhile, the old dame, (a most marvellous character of Wilkie's,) one who is famous at a bargain, is fighting out a hard battle to save a penny. It is evident that she is well aware that the article is cheap enough, (a female counsellor is holding up her hands, as if to say, you will never have such a chance again,) though she is trying with all her might and main to appear indignant at the Pedlar's extortion: but it is of no use, he is up to the manœuvre, and prepared for the attack, which he knows well how to parry with his blandest smile and most conciliatory manner, resolved all the while not to go a farthing lower:—

> " Like feather bed 'twixt castle wall,
> And heavy brunt of cannon-ball,"

he receives the blow and gives way for the moment; but no impression can be finally made on him, and he carries his point, no doubt, by patiently wearying out his assailant. In point of character, Wilkie never surpassed the expression thrown into this brace of disputants—they are true to nature in general, and to Scotland perhaps in particular—each is the representative of its class, and yet a dramatist with all his resources could hardly stamp upon the mind a more perfect impression of their individuality than is here done within the compass of an inch by the astonishing art of the painter.

Soon after his return to London, the death of Sir Francis Bourgeois left a vacancy in the list of Academicians, and Wilkie, now but in his twenty-sixth year, was duly elected to fill his place; a honour which, though reflected back with equal or greater lustre upon the body of his brethren, he could not but feel proud of, and which, together with the general sympathy for him occasioned by his illness, must have proved a cordial to him in his state of anxiety and weakness.

To the Academy he presented the customary diploma picture—"Boys Digging for Rats." This has always been considered as one of the most remarkable of his minor productions in all artistical qualities. The subject is one, which although it might interest a sportsman,

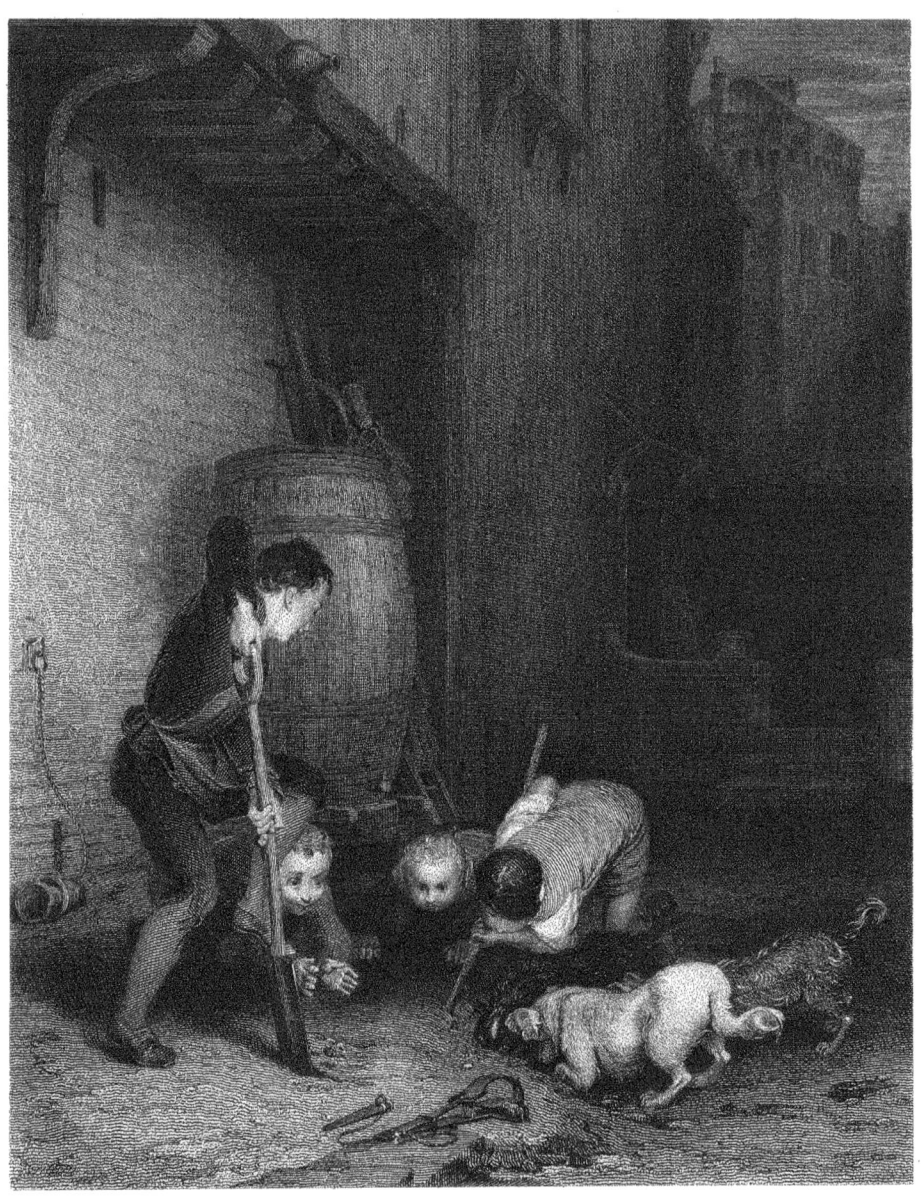

PAINTED BY SIR DAVID   ENGRAVED BY

is wholly indebted to the skilful manner of treatment, for its attraction to the lovers of art. It is hardly necessary to describe it, so well is the story told. A group of boys and dogs are engaged in hunting out the destructive vermin that infest the yard; the game has wholly absorbed them; and the nearer they get to the hidden retreat, the keener they become. The painter has seized the moment of approaching success, and has given to both dog and boy the characteristic expression of eager, high-wrought anticipation, in which the charm of the picture consists, and which redeems, with the magic of art, the insignificance of the subject, which in the hands of an ordinary painter would have been a very common and perhaps unpleasant one. But in the grouping, expression, light and shade, and colour, we see all the qualities that belong to a master hand; and that can throw over the simplest incident an interest and refinement that it is the object of art to create, detecting the beautiful and characteristic, when the ordinary eye would fail to discover it.

But Wilkie was now withdrawn from consideration of himself and his own honours, by the rapidly declining health of his venerable father. The great distance, and consequent loss of time, in days before steam had brought the remotest parts of the kingdom in such close proximity, had prevented the painter from complying with the oft-repeated wish of his family that he should revisit Cults; and their anxieties about his own health, and even his circumstances, as it would appear, were continual. In August 1811, he went down to Scotland, where he found his father in a very weak state, though still in the possession of his vigorous mental faculties. In the interval of his absence, his sister Helen had grown up into a fine accomplished girl; and from this period commences his correspondence with her. He reviewed all the old familiar scenes with a fresh eye; with practised taste selected new materials for future compositions, just dawning upon his fancy—he was impatient at the long hiatus in his studies, which illness had occasioned—and as his brother, Thomas Wilkie, had, during his absence, busied himself in finding for him a new abode and painting-room at Kensington, he returned to town, his health now fairly re-established, for the while, with renovated vigour, and rejoiced as a giant to run a new career of fame.

But though Wilkie had struggled successfully through the difficulties that beset the path of the aspirant, and stood crowned with the highest honours of his profession, anxieties of another kind began henceforth to thicken around him. His prices were indeed higher, but his expenses were increased; and although he had derived some advantages, (not indeed what he ought to have done,) from the success of the masterly engravings, executed by Burnet and Raimbach, after his pictures, yet his means were so low, that the project of forming an exhibition of his works presented itself to his mind, in a tempting, though doubtful light. He consulted his friends, and received the usual variety of opinions, varying from sanguine anticipations of success to prophecies of blank and utter failure. He ventured on the experiment, and was disappointed in the issue: some pecuniary loss probably resulted from the speculation, though his fame was extended by it; and Mr. Cunningham believes, on no doubtful authority, that to an incident connected with the project, we owe the conception of one of his very finest works, "The Distraining for Rent." This, it seems, was the seizure of one of the pictures, not for any debt of his own, but for one due by the party of whom he had rented the room, and which he probably got back again. When, indeed, as Mr. C. remarks, did vexation produce such fruit? Besides this misadventure of his own, he was called upon to attend to his fast sinking parent, who was becoming unable to perform his duties, and for whom an assistant had scarcely been provided, after anxious care, ere the old man, after a deceitful interval of apparent renovation, sank calmly to his final rest, full of years and honours. Wilkie said little of his own feelings in his letters to the desolated family at Cults—though to one of such fine and true nature, and who had lived with his father on terms of almost patriarchal simplicity and affectionate confidence, unchilled by time or distance, his loss must have been most deeply felt. In the affliction of his mother and sister he was no less afflicted; and after ministering such pecuniary aid as lay in his power, he began to turn his thoughts seriously towards bringing them up to London.

His sister was delighted at the prospect of this union of the long-scattered members of the family, and no less so, at her lively age, with the exciting idea of a residence in the great metropolis; but Mrs. Wilkie was almost rooted to the spot, to which all the recollections of her youth attached, where her father and mother and old associates still survived, and where she had brought up a family in honour. Yet her reluctance on these grounds was overcome by the thought of enjoying the protection of her son during her declining years, under his own roof; and she prepared for the formidable removal, with feelings of mingled pain and pleasure. Wilkie's plan was to give up lodgings, and take a house, which was to be fitted up with the furniture from the manse, and he particularly dwells on certain articles of antique fashion, which had perhaps served already to adorn his earlier pictures, and which were useful as studies—" an old Gothic chair and copper-saucepan were favourites, and often sat for their likenesses, and always with effect." His health, now tolerably re-established, required care to maintain, by the enjoyment of fresh air and cheerful walks; and he retreated accordingly from the centre of fashion to Kensington, famous for its salubrity, and then more open and rural than it has since become. He removed from his old friends, the Coppards, with whom he had so long resided, and, August 30th, 1813, took possession of the house, No. 24, Phillimore-place, with his mother and sister.

This was perhaps the proudest and happiest period of his life. His honoured mother, to whose indulgent interference in his behalf he probably owed it that he had been permitted to follow the bent of his inclination to painting, now sat by his fireside, witnessing the success that had attended his efforts, and with the old familiar furniture

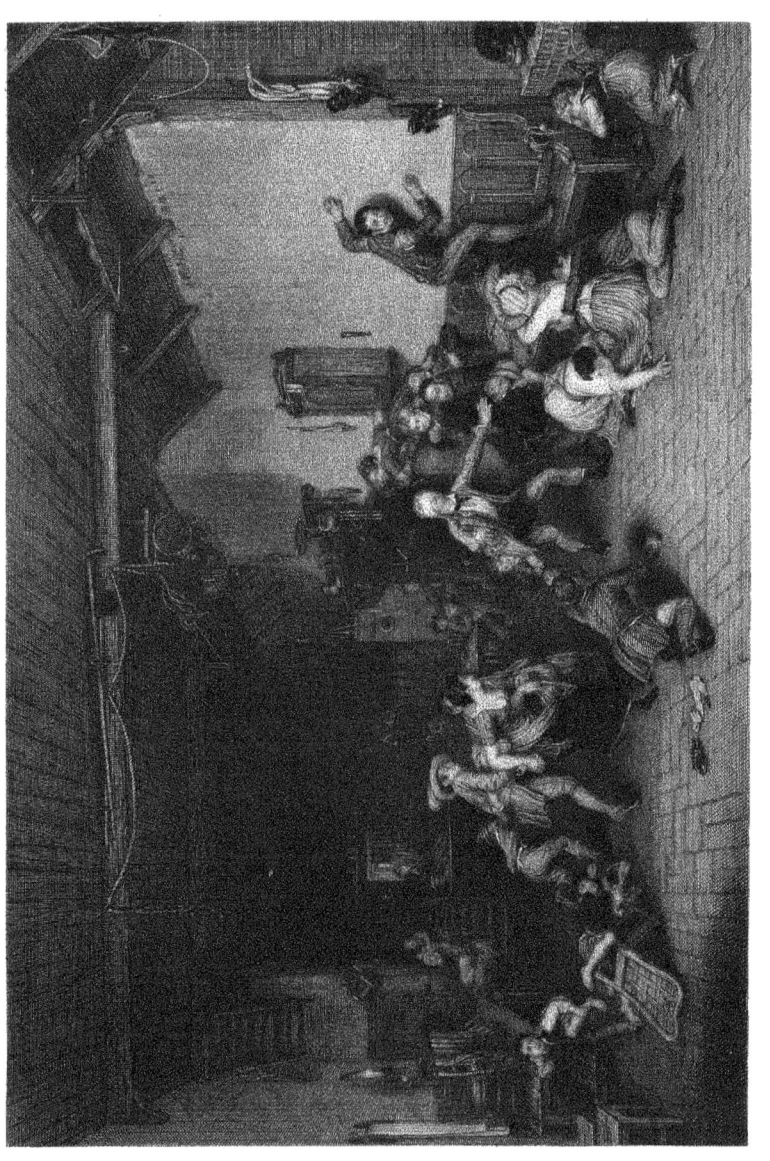

around him, " he could imagine himself in Stratheden again, till he looked out of the window and missed the blue Lomonds."

Wilkie shone in the preceding Academy exhibition. His picture of " Blindman's Buff," painted for the Prince Regent, by the award of his brother Academicians, occupied the post of honour in the centre of the room, and was considered by the public equal to anything he had ever painted.

We have here another of those picturesque interiors that Wilkie loved—the large room of an old-fashioned publichouse, with long benches attached to the wall, and moveable chairs and tables, which have been piled up out of the way, to afford scope for the roystering game. In the background, an old dame, who has charge of an infant, has seated herself out of harm's way, though she follows the doings with an interest that makes her young again. The game has just begun, with a whirl of fun, mischief, and disasters. The young peasant, on whom the lot has fallen, has not yet been tormented out of temper with the tricks and gibes of the rest, and is deliberately feeling his way, with a knowing smile on his countenance. His outspread fingers are within an ace of lighting on the head of a fellow who is crouching down, with an expression of comic alarm that is positively wonderful, even for Wilkie; behind him there is a sudden crush into the corner—an old man, who had sat down as a spectator, finds himself part of the game itself, and is drawing back with outspread arms and placid glee—a lovely fair-haired boy, with his eyes earnestly intent upon the movements of the blindman, and a sturdy buxom lass, are rushing hastily behind him; and the combined movement has almost squeezed the breath out of the body of a little urchin, who is roaring to get free. A little in advance are a couple of romping lassies—one stealthily crawling, cat-like, out of the blindman's way; the other arrested, and, to all appearance, nothing loath, by a brace of sweethearts, who are pulling her in opposite directions, one of whom has her round the neck, and is revelling in her lips, the other lies " perdue," with twinkling eyes, and with his arms wreathed around her waist, waits till the movement shall reach them. Above them, a light-limbed fellow who has taken off his shoes, that his steps may not be heard, is leaping over the bench; and the " composition" on this side " is carried out," to use a technical expression, by the figure of a little girl, with eyes all fun and alarm, who has hidden herself in a safe nook behind the bench. This may, indeed, be called a wonderful group for its exuberant variety of humour; full to the very brim, without any alloy of grossness, and an infusion of beauty of form, that shows the progress of Wilkie in general refinement of style. The left-hand group, though less marvellous, is well contrasted with the first; here all is in merry motion—a kneeling figure strives to draw the blindman into a snare: another rustic, with her hand fast locked in her laddie's, is whirling gaily around, full of gibes and jokes, heedless of a chair they have knocked over, which has come down with crash and overthrow upon the naked shins of two of the younger fry, one of whom is ruefully limping aside, the other prostrate upon a devoted dog, who, buried at the bottom of the *mêlée*, seems setting his teeth to exhale what little breath is left in him. But the game is too good to be interrupted by these trifling disasters, or the little episodes of an amorous kind which are slily going on; such is the general excitement, and so inimitably has the painter contrived to subordinate all his rich variety of incidents to the predominant expression. The background is delicious in its subdued and mellow tone. The crossing-sweeper, with his broom, who has left his avocation to get a distant glimpse of what is going forward, the girl peeping through the lattice, and the old woman and children in the stair-corner, are all exquisite secondary *morceaux*. In tone, colour, and high-wrought finish it surpasses all the previous works of Wilkie.

This picture was the first-fruits of that royal patronage in which Wilkie afterwards largely participated; and we may confidently affirm, too, that it is the best. It is in his true walk, and full of his characteristic excellencies, with all the refinement of experience. The Prince Regent for the first time saw Wilkie in the room of the Academy, and with his usual grace of manner, complimented him on the success of his first picture painted for him; at the same time wishing to have another when the prior commissions of the artist were fulfilled. He appears now to have worked for some time with animation upon several of the happiest of his minor pictures—" The Letter of Introduction," " The Piper," and " Duncan Gray."

" The Letter of Introduction," like that of the " Distraining for Rent," owes its origin most probably to some unpleasant experiences of the painter's own, when, after leaving Scotland with a few letters to persons of small note, but greater pretensions, he first sought to obtain a footing in the great metropolis. He complains, in his journal, of the cold reception of some, the empty promises of others, so feelingly, that we might almost suppose he intended to wreak a pleasant revenge upon them in this picture, in which he turns his early mortifications to so rich an account. There is probably no one, at least in the working ranks of society, who cannot from his own experiences in some degree appreciate the merits of this very characteristic composition. To a young man new from the country, especially, nothing can be more trying than the presenting a letter of introduction. His steps, so firm on his native fields, become timid as he approaches the town mansion. His awkward knock at the door betrays the novice; he quails at the searching, supercilious stare of the footman, and all remaining heart ebbs out at his fingers' ends, as he approaches the dreaded sanctum of the great personage himself. Still he summons courage to present the letter; and here he stands, with all the self-possession he can muster, as Wilkie stood, and as Thomson stood before him. He has donned his best, and is sedulously neat; his shoes are well blacked; his stick, hat, and gloves are all irreproachable; but he has withal an inveterately provincial

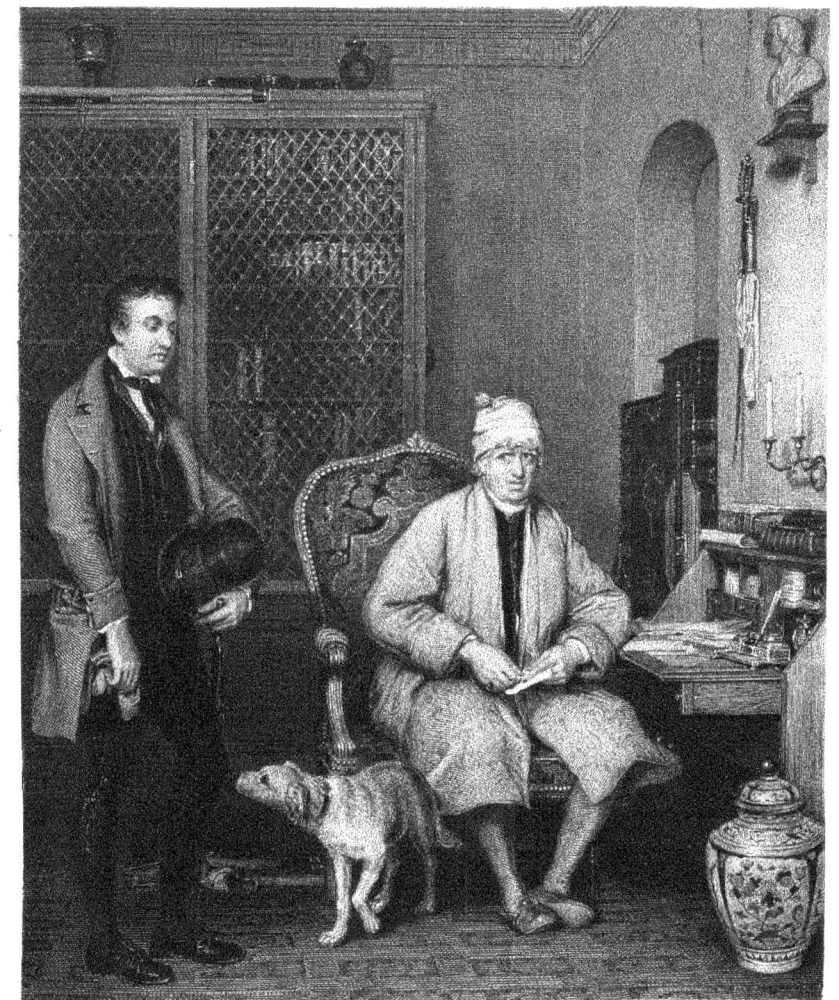

PAINTED BY SIR DAVID WILKIE — ENGRAVED BY W GREAT

look: he may be known at a glance for a recent arrival; the very dog smells country air about him. From his uneasy attitude, his downcast look, and an expression, in which embarrassment and chagrin, at the evident coolness of his reception, struggle with manly pride, it would seem that nothing in the world could be so unpleasant as to be the deliverer of a letter of introduction; unless, indeed, to be the recipient of one. In this latter category is the selfish old man before us, who has evidently a natural horror of everything that may intrude upon his time and ease, or tax his very limited stock of compulsory generosity. From his embroidered chair, his ancient cabinet busts, china jars and Etruscan vases, we conjecture him to be a fastidious, narrow-minded virtuoso; possibly enough, some one whom the painter himself may have known; for such an expression, so bitterly rich as that written on the old man's face, he would not have failed to remember and to treasure up. It is evident that the old man wishes the unfortunate intruder at the devil, and can hardly conceal his chagrin at his appearance sufficiently to be outwardly civil. Vexation is written on his whole figure and face; his mouth is verjuice-lipped; his feet are pettishly drawn together; his hand is about reluctantly and mechanically to break the seal; and as he shrinks to the further side of his easy-chair, he steals a glance of mingled malediction and scrutiny at the offender, ere he measures forth the precise modicum of civility necessary to get decently rid of him. Of all this the young man is painfully conscious: we see him dismissed with cold or formal delusive promises, and plausible smiles; we see his burning cheek, and enter into his sinking of the heart as the door closes behind him, of which he will never again, in all probability, cross the threshold.

The painter has finely contrasted the ruddy, open countenance of simple, trusting youth, with the cold, scrutinizing physiognomy of an experienced, suspicious worldling. This is a picture in which there is more than meets the eye. There is youth full of hope, side by side with age chilled into selfishness. What a gulf appears between! And yet how often does the former end sadly in the latter! how do the experiences of years blunt the fine feelings, till age may well weep, less for what time takes away than for what he leaves behind!

"The history of the painting of 'Duncan Gray' is to be found in Sir David Wilkie's Diary, where he notes with his usual simplicity:—'Began my picture from Duncan Gray, the same size as my Letter of Introduction;' and then again he confesses to having rubbed out a petticoat which had taken him three days to paint. We extract, for the enlightenment of those curious in such matters, his account of how a petticoat should be painted. 'Began it anew,' writes Sir David. 'and tried to paint it much thinner in the half-tints, and only thick in the high-lights, and to keep a little more of the orange in its colour.' But what will interest our readers still more, is the fact, that as far back as the year 1814, Mulready sat for the portrait of the ill-used Duncan. It is impossible not to be struck with this portraiture of one of the most lifesome ballads that even Burns ever wrote; the accessaries are admirable, the making up of the characters perfection: Meg is the embodiment of female wilfulness—hard to woo, hard to win. Time frequently sobers without souring such a temperament as Burns and Wilkie have stamped with immortality. Meg looks a woman whose obstinacy could be conquered by a frolic, a freak, a whim ; but not by reason, nor by the ordinary modes of loving or lovers—in her painted mood.

"Duncan might not only talk of the 'Lover's Leap,' but *take* it, without producing any visible emotion on the thick-set features which bewitched and bewildered the tender-hearted farmer. Meg is evidently a spoiled child ; and the more her father and mother entreat her to consider and ponder before she refuses, the more surely will she pout, and frown, and refuse—yes, until she almost believes herself to be in earnest, which she is not. There is an old rhyme that old ladies used to repeat to their wilful progeny ; and Meg, often as she has heard, has never heeded it—

'She who will not when she may,
When she will, she shall have nay.'

If Duncan would uprouse him, and flout, as he has been flouted, all would be well; she would come round, and declare, like the ' Jenny' of another favourite ballad—

'Indeed I was joking with you all the while.'

"But brave men become timid on such occasions ; their love gains strength by opposition ; they have not courage to change the fashion of their wooing ; while the rest of mankind view their angels as common-place mortals, they think a general league is being formed against their peace, and that every man who casts a glance at the chosen 'one,' is a Lothario in disguise ; this insanity influences high and low, rich and poor ; and as long as this is the case, Megs will be tyrants, and Duncans slaves.

"This is the state of affairs in the court of love before marriage. But women should beware ; the lover who would not suffer any human being to insinuate that his chosen fair one is not the perfection of womankind, changes his opinion in a few months, and the slave becomes the tyrant : the maiden played it, and, it must be confessed, played it to the life ; the husband *is it*; there is no play at all in his tyranny—it is reality—and all she can do, if her love be strong enough, is to endure, the more patiently the better. The quarrels of lovers may be the renewal of love—the quarrels of husband and wife are too frequently its death.

"Wilkie was a keen and yet by no means an unkind observer of human nature. There was more humour than sarcasm in his delineations of character; his benevolence overpowered his sense of the ridiculous; he atoned for any little touch of severity by some repentant illustration of human good ; and thus the man is shown in his works.

"The picture now universally known as 'Duncan Gray,' was for a long time called 'The Refusal:' it was purchased by Dr. Baillie for the sum of 330 guineas ; but the Doctor changed his mind after a time, and prevailed upon the painter to exchange it for 'The Pedlar.' 'The Refusal,' thus becoming the *refused*, was then engaged by Lord Charles

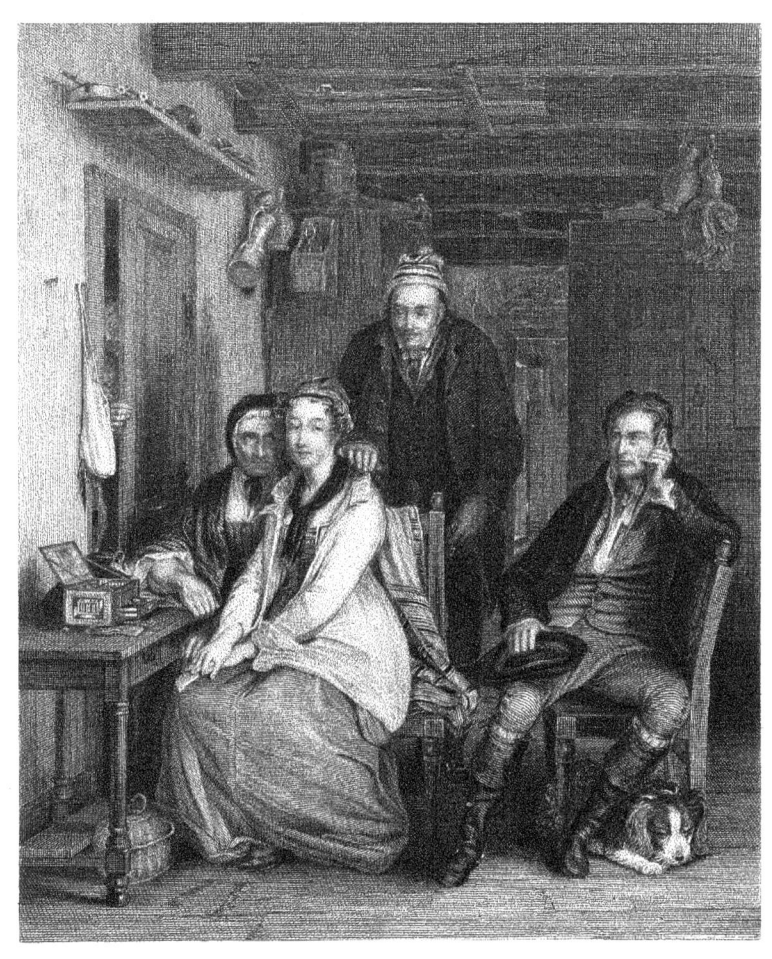

BY SIR DAVID WILKIE R.A — ENGRAVED BY

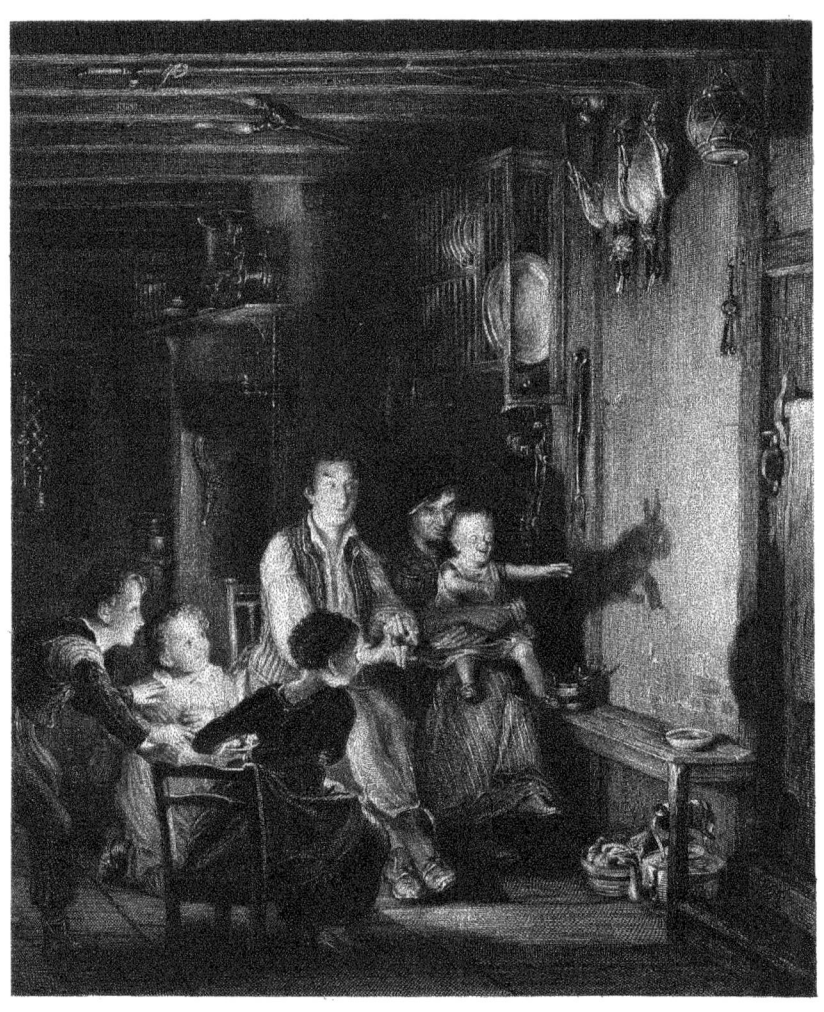

AINTED BY SIR DAVID WILKIE R.A   ENGRAVED BY W GREATBACH

Townsend; but left on the artist's hands, by which it gained much of its minute and admirable finish. It is now one of the many treasures in the most beautiful collection of J. Sheepshanks, Esq., a gentleman of pure taste and sound judgment; a critic, and yet a liberal and extensive patron of British art; one whom it is an honour to know, and a pleasure to write about; for his patronage has urged forward many who never would have achieved 'high art,' but for the confidence with which his praise never fails to inspire the young and stimulate the old."

Wilkie now, with his friend Haydon, paid a visit to Paris, where the classical school of David and his pupils, with which he had little sympathy, was then in vogue. He carried with him some of his prints, but found little encouragement; the journals of this, and his other travels, which is given by Mr. Cunningham at length, will be read with pleasure— they are lively and full of interest; but we must notice them very briefly here. He was struck with the novelty of everything, particularly with the picturesque old city of Rouen, with its quaintly-dressed population and Gothic streets—the magnificence of the capital impressed him, but had little to lay hold of his peculiar taste; and after a careful examination of the galleries, and having seen the "ateliers" of the principal painters, he returned to London in July 1814, little influenced by his insight into French life and art.

At this period were painted "The Rabbit on the Wall" and "The Distraining for Rent."

"The Rabbit on the Wall" has a charm to touch a misanthrope, and win him back to life and happy thoughts; no one can look on it without feeling for the time a wiser and a merrier man. Here, in one of the humblest nooks of the land, is a world of glee, cheaply purchased, but right genuine in the quality: while human nature lasts, such a work as this will come home to it. Wilkie, fastidious, modest, as he was, in his estimate of his own works, thought he had succeeded here better than usual; and, indeed, in artistic qualities the picture is deliciously happy, the composition charming, easy, graceful, and varied, without affectation; the management of the candlelight and shade most subtly skilful, and the handling in the painter's very finest manner. But qualities that would make the success of another painter, are overlooked in Wilkie, in his marvellous truth of expression and natural genuine humour. The happy, merry infant, ready to leap off its mother's knee at the shadowy appearance, to it as real as life; the radiant looks of the children, all delight at the successful imitation; the comic gravity of the father as he performs the trick, will never be surpassed, and will awake a pleasant smile and cheerful feeling, while men have hearts for the enjoyment of domestic happiness and cheap fireside pleasures.

There is a fine moral tone in the works of Wilkie, and their circulation among all classes of the community cannot fail of producing, together with a taste for art, refining and humanizing influences. They deal with the common things of life, and, with subtle penetration, but no unkindly feeling, satirize our common infirmities and foibles, detect and exhibit the humorous and ridiculous, unalloyed by grossness or vulgarity, and throw an interest over the simple and joyous amusements of domestic life. They reflect the painter's own character; his deep insight into human nature; his kindliness, simplicity, purity, and benevolence of heart; and his singular power of perceiving and combining the humorous and pathetic aspects of life. While the admirer of his genius gazes with delight on the results of consummate art and original powers, he is receiving, unconsciously perhaps, but not less surely, a higher influence into his mind than that of passing pleasure. His feelings are drawn out; he sees what he had before never remarked; familiar things assume also a more beautiful aspect, and he becomes, in a measure, more gentle, refined, and charitable in his tastes and feelings.

A journey which afforded more gratification than that to France, and produced more fruit, was one he next made into Holland and Belgium. Here he revelled in the pictures of Ostade and Teniers, so akin to his own style, and strove to penetrate the secret of their colouring: he was struck too, as every one must be, who is acquainted with the works of the Dutch masters, with the unchanged resemblance of everything in the country to their local pictures, though painted so long ago. Here may be seen the sandy shores and gray leaden skies and seas of Vandevelde and Backhuysen, the glassy yellow canals, and rich golden meadows, and peculiar atmosphere of Cuyp; and the subjects of Teniers, Ostade, and others are reproduced in the quaint old costumes, village cabarets, gabled houses, and canals lined with trees and covered with picturesque market-boats or "Schuyts,"—unchanged in every particular. "Nothing," he observes, in a letter to Sir George Beaumont, "seemed new to me in the whole country, for I had been familiar with it all upon canvass; and what one could not help wondering at was, that these old masters should have been able to draw the materials of so beautiful a variety of art from so contracted and monotonous a country."

Desirous of obtaining fresh materials for another subject, commissioned by the Prince Regent, he went down to Scotland in July 1817. His details of this journey are full of interest. He revisited the familiar scenes of Edinburgh, the old High Street, with its stately and picturesque magnificence, nobly terminated by the palace of Holyrood, French rather than English in aspect, its beautiful chapel, tapestried chambers and old historic nooks.

With these scenes, and the old beggar-men, and other characters that he met with, he stored his sketch-book anew. He visited the Highlands, after a route given him by Sir Walter Scott, sketched deer at the princely domain of Blair Athol, and admired the old piper, who, after antique fashion, still "plays regularly an hour before breakfast and dinner, and walks with stately majesty before the house."

The bagpipe is a primitive instrument. In the mountains of Calabria and the Roman Campagna the pifferari, or pipers, are a picturesque race, well known to us by the pictures of Eastlake and others; the wild shepherds of Auvergne are sometimes seen in the streets of London; but Scotland appears to be the paradise of pipers; for there they form part of the

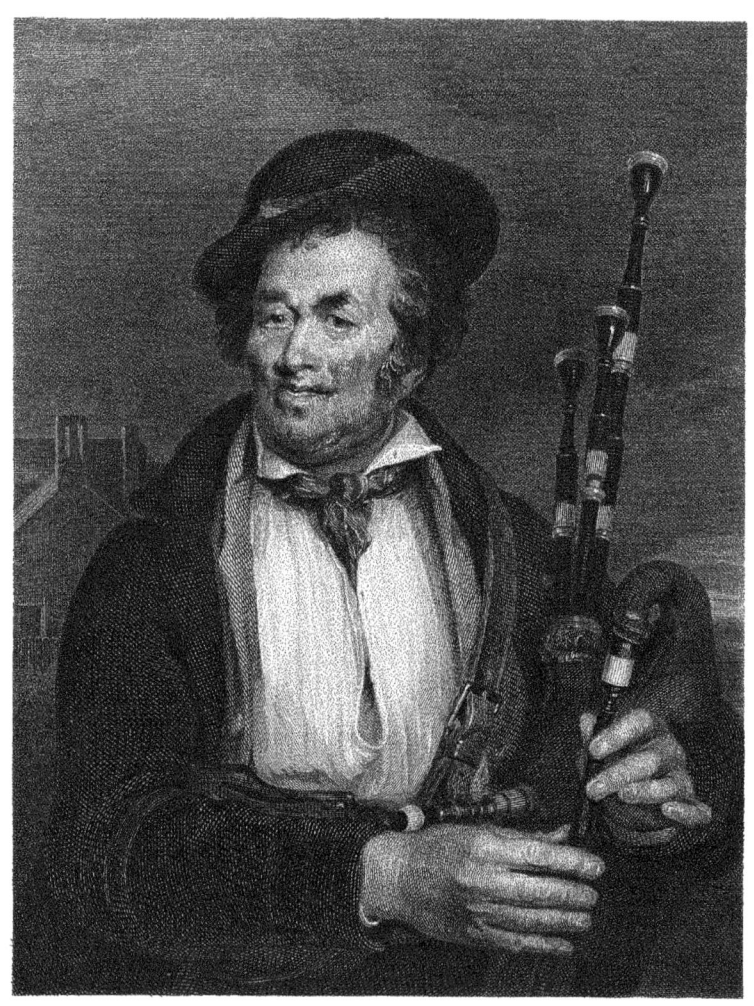

state of the old aristocracy ; their wild and stirring notes are called for in war, to thrill through and inspire the Scottish soldier ; and no less indispensable are they at wake, and fair, and merrymaking. With this we can well understand the sayings, "As proud as a piper," and "As drunk as a piper ;" both one and the other are natural, and to be expected. A more gallant figure than one of the domestic pipers, retained in the old families, whose office it is to play in state before the house on grand occasions, it would be difficult to imagine ; and clad in the tartan of his clan, ornamented with pouch, and dirk, and plumed bonnet, he marches erect, and conscious to the full of his honourable position. Wilkie has given us a right merry and characteristic specimen ; he has touched to the life the rich and racy physiognomy of an undeniably jovial old soul ; a careless wanderer in the open air, over heath and moor ; and one at home in village and solitary farm ; familiar with every strath and nook the country round ; with an eye full of humour, yet capable of kindling with deeper expression ; proud of his ability, with the magic of his rude instrument, to waken sad or merry feelings in the national heart ; an universal favourite, and a good companion, and made free of the oatcake and brose, and the whisky too, which he will drink till he reels again. All this we think we can read in the life-like impersonation before us, which is painted to a touch, *con amore*, by the hand of a perfect master.

To the Scottish people Wilkie must be peculiarly dear, for he may be called their painter of life and manners ; and universally interesting as are his works, they contain a variety of traits so peculiarly national, as only, perhaps, to be fully appreciated in the land which originated them. Allan Cunningham observes, with justice, that he was confessedly less happy in his representations of English character and habits, with which he was not so intimately acquainted, and which, perhaps, in the present day, do not present among the lower classes so much scope for lively and varied exhibitions of art. The racy, truthful picture of " The Piper" is one which will bear out these remarks ; it breathes the very air of Scotia, and must fill with delight her sons, whether at home or afar.

The nobles of the land delighted to show him honour, but it was with his visit to Sir Walter Scott—then in the height of his prosperity, keeping open house at Abbotsford, hunting, and shooting, and planting all the day, and yet pouring forth, as by magic, romance after romance, with astonishing rapidity—that he was most impressed. During his stay, William Laidlaw, immortalized in the Life of Scott, took Wilkie a ramble up the Yarrow, showing him all the scenery by the way, and brought him to Altrive, to introduce him to Hogg. Here they found the Shepherd in his cottage, and while he was preparing for them a cheerful breakfast, Laidlaw pointed out to Wilkie some objects that he thought might interest him. The poet, on this, began to look and listen. "I had not," he says, " introduced Wilkie as an artist ; and it is probable he had taken him, as he did a great poet, for a horse-couper. He however turned round to me, exclaiming, 'Laidlaw! this is not the great Mr. Wilkie ?' 'It is just the great Mr. Wilkie, Hogg,' I replied. 'Mr. Wilkie,' exclaimed the

Shepherd, seizing him by the hand, 'I cannot tell how proud I am to see you in my house, and how glad I am to see you are so young a man.' When I told Scott of Hogg's reception of Wilkie, 'The fellow!' said he; 'it was the finest compliment ever paid to man!'"

Wilkie took the advantage of his stay at Abbotsford to execute a group of Sir Walter and his family, which, although its good taste is questionable, and we might have preferred to see these interesting personages, who belong to history, in their every-day appearance, rather than in so picturesque a travesty, will ever be considered a valuable memorial, as well as a beautiful painting. It is best described by Sir Walter himself to Sir Adam Ferguson, in a letter published to accompany a small engraving of it, in "The Bijou."

"MY DEAR ADAM,—The picture you mention has something in it of rather a domestic character, as the personages are represented in a sort of masquerade, such being the pleasure of the accomplished painter. Nevertheless, if you, the proprietor, incline to have it engraved, I do not see that I am entitled to make any objection.

"But Mr. * * * mentions, besides, a desire to have anecdotes of my private and domestic life; or, as he expresses himself, a portrait of the author in his night-gown and slippers;—and this from you, who, I dare say, could furnish some anecdotes of our younger days which might now seem ludicrous enough. Even as to my night-gown and slippers, I believe the time has been when the articles of my wardrobe were as familiar to your memory as Poins to Prince Henry; but that period has been for some years past, and I cannot think it would be interesting to the public to learn that I had changed my old robe-de-chambre for a handsome douillette, when I was last at Paris.

"The truth is, that a man of ordinary sense cannot be supposed delighted with the species of gossip which, in the dearth of other news, recurs to such a quiet individual as myself; and though, like a well-behaved lion of twenty years standing, I am not inclined to vex myself about what I cannot help, I will not, in any case in which I can prevent it, be accessary to these follies. There is no man known at all in literature who may not have more to tell of his private life than I have: I have surmounted no difficulties either of birth or education, nor have I been favoured by any particular advantages; and my life has been as void of incidents of importance as that of the 'weary knife-grinder.'

'Story! God bless you! I have none to tell, Sir.'

"The follies of youth ought long since to have passed away; and if the prejudices and absurdities of age have come in their place, I will keep them, as Beau Tibbs did his prospect, for the amusement of my domestic friends. A mere enumeration of the persons in the sketch is all which I can possibly permit to be published respecting myself and my family; and, as must be the lot of humanity when we look back seven or eight years, even what follows cannot be drawn up without some very painful recollections.

"The idea which our inimitable Wilkie adopted, was to represent our family group in the garb of south-country peasants, supposed to be concerting a merrymaking, for which some of the preparations are seen. The place is the terrace near Kayside, commanding an extensive view towards the Eildon-hills. 1. The sitting figure, in the dress of a miller, I believe, represents Sir Walter Scott, author of a few scores of volumes, and proprietor of Abbotsford, in the county of Roxburgh. 2. In front, and presenting, we may suppose, a country wag, somewhat addicted to poaching, stands Sir Adam Ferguson, knight, keeper of the regalia of Scotland. 3. In the background is a very handsome old man, upwards of eighty-four years old at the time, painted in his own character of a shepherd. He also belonged to the numerous clan of Scott. He used to claim credit for three things unusual among the southland shepherds: first, that he had never been *fou* in the course of his life; secondly, that he never had struck a man in anger; thirdly, that though entrusted with the management of large sales of stock, he had never lost a penny for his master by a bad debt. He died soon afterwards at Abbotsford. 4, 5, 6. Of the three female figures, the elder is the late regretted mother of the family represented. 5. The young person most forward in the group, is Miss Sophia Charlotte Scott, now Mrs. John Gibson Lockhart; and 6, her younger sister, Miss

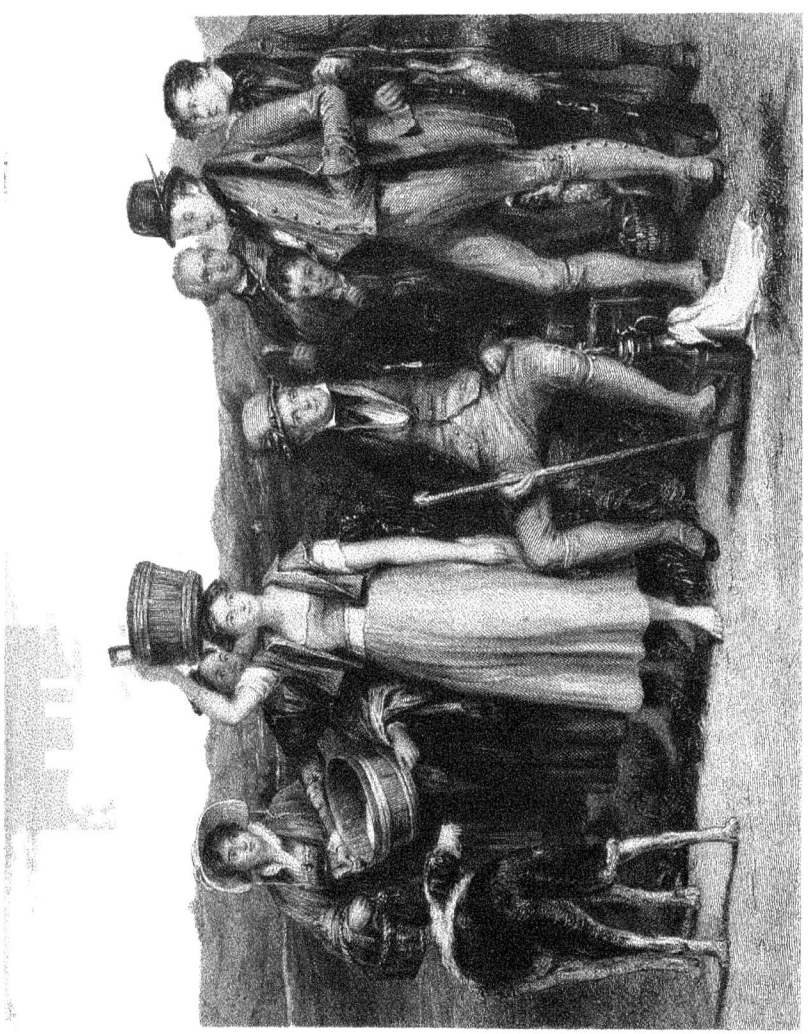

Ann Scott. Both are represented as ewe-milkers, with their *leglins*, or milk-pails. 7. On the left hand of the shepherd, the young man holding a fowling piece is the eldest son of Sir Walter, now captain in the king's hussars. 8. The boy is the youngest of the family, Charles Scott, now of Brazen-Nose College, Oxford. The two dogs were distinguished favourites of the family: the large one was a stag-hound of the old Highland breed, called Maida, and one of the handsomest dogs that could be found; it was a present to me from the chief of Glengary, and was highly valued, both on account of his beauty, his fidelity, and the great rarity of the breed. The other is a little Highland terrier, called *Ourisk*, (goblin,) of a particular kind, bred in Kintail. It was a present from the Honourable Mrs. Stuart Mackenzie, and is a valuable specimen of a race which is now also scarce. Maida, like Bran, Lerath, and other dogs of distinction, slumbers 'beneath his stone,' distinguished by an epitaph, which, to the honour of Scottish scholarship be it spoken, has only *one* false quantity in *two* lines.

'Maidæ marmorea dormis sub imagine Maida
Ad januam domini sit tibi terra levis.'

Ourisk still survives, but, like some other personages in the picture, with talents and temper rather the worse for wear. She has become what Dr. Rutty, the quaker, records himself in his journal as having sometimes been—sinfully dogged and snappish.

"If it should suit Mr. * * *'s purpose to adopt the above illustrations, he is heartily welcome to them; but I make it my especial bargain that nothing more is said upon such a meagre subject.

"It strikes me, however, that there is a story about old Thomas Scott, the shepherd, which is characteristic, and which I will make your friend welcome to. Tom was, both as a trusty servant, and as a rich fellow in his line, a person of considerable importance among his class in the neighbourhood, and used to stickle a good deal to keep his place in public opinion. Now, he suffered, in his own idea at least, from the consequence assumed by a country neighbour, who, though neither so well reputed for wealth or sagacity as Thomas Scott, had yet an advantage over him, from having seen the late king, and used to take precedence upon all occasions when they chanced to meet. Thomas suffered under this superiority. But after this sketch was finished, and exhibited in London, the newspapers made it known that his present majesty had condescended to take some notice of it. Delighted with the circumstance, Thomas Scott set out on a most oppressively hot day, to walk five miles to Bowden, where his rival resided. He had no sooner entered the cottage than he called out in his broad forest dialect—'Andro', man, did ye anes *sey* (see) the king?' 'In troth did I, Tam,' answered Andro'; 'sit down, and I'll tell ye a' about it:—ye *sey*, I was at Lonon, in a place they ca' the Park, that is, no like a hained hog-fence, or like the four-nooked parks in this country—' 'Hout awa,' said Thomas, 'I have heard a' that before: I only came ower the knowe now to tell you, that, if you have seen the king, the king has seen. *mey*' (me). And so he returned with a jocund heart, assuring his friends 'it had done him muckle gude to settle accounts with Andro'.'

"*Jocose hæc*, as the old laird of Restalrig writes to the earl of Gowrie, farewell, my old, tried, and dear friend of forty long years. Our enjoyments must now be of a character less vivid than those we have shared together;

'But still at our lot it were vain to repine;
Youth cannot return, or the days of Lang Syne.'

"Yours affectionately,

"WALTER SCOTT."

"*Abbotsford*, 2*nd August*, 1827."

Besides this he painted one of the best portraits of the great novelist, though the distinctive traits are perhaps a little too much idealized.

On his return to town Wilkie began the studies for his celebrated picture of "The Chelsea Pensioners," in the progress of which the Duke of Wellington took great interest. In the meanwhile the King of Bavaria, whose revival of German art will cause his name to be handed down with immortal honour, a patron too of so catholic a taste as to admire the finest productions of every class, desired to possess a specimen of so eminent and original a member of our English school as Wilkie, and commissioned Lord Burghersh, then at Munich, to order him to paint him one. This was justly regarded as a great honour by the painter, and he wrought with the feeling of one who is aware that his work is to be placed amidst a collection of chef-d'œuvres. After some discussion with the Bavarian envoy as to the subject, he decided on "The Will," originally suggested, as before observed, by the comedian Bannister. Previous to its being sent to its destination it was exhibited in the Royal Academy, and was considered equal to the finest class of Wilkie's efforts. Out of this arose a circumstance at once embarrassing and honourable to the painter. The Prince Regent, through Sir Thomas Lawrence, intimated his wish to possess the picture, and that a duplicate should be sent to the King of Bavaria. To this Wilkie replied, that though his first desire was to comply with the request of his royal highness, he was bound by his previous promise; and on his consulting the Bavarian envoy, that functionary considered that the picture certainly belonged to his royal master, and could only be ceded by him on an application from the Prince Regent, which, strange as it may seem, was really confided to the English ambassador at Munich, though, from the absence of the King of Bavaria, he had no opportunity of making known the "delicate" and not very agreeable commission. In fact, before he could do so, the Bavarian monarch had written to urge the matter afresh; and, on this being made known to the Prince, he desired that the application might be entirely renounced.

The picture which was the object of such high contention well sustained the reputation of Wilkie, and was deemed by the cognoscenti, as well as the public at large, as one of his most genuine pictures of life. The King of Bavaria was highly delighted with it; and he added 100 guineas to the original price; at a subsequent sale of his pictures it fetched nearly £1,200, or thrice what it was painted for, a circumstance most gratifying to Wilkie, and indeed to all lovers of British art.

"The Reading of the Will" is a truthful and somewhat humiliating portraiture of human nature. Upon the wall of a comfortable apartment, in the mansion whose master has just been carried to the dark and narrow house, hangs indeed his likeness; but he seems to be already forgotten, and all his kindred are gathered in eager expectation, or curiosity, to learn the disposal of his substance. There is a world of mean, and envious, and selfish feeling, in that assembled group; nor is the exhibition of these evil qualities less stamped upon the visages of those who, in the course of nature, must the soonest follow the departed. It is a harsh and painful exhibition; but the painter, by the alchemy of his consummate art, has known how to render it even pleasing. The old attorney has just come to the decisive passage, placid and unmoved himself, with his calm business air; while all around him is the excitement of satisfaction or angry disappointment. The young widow, who has contrived

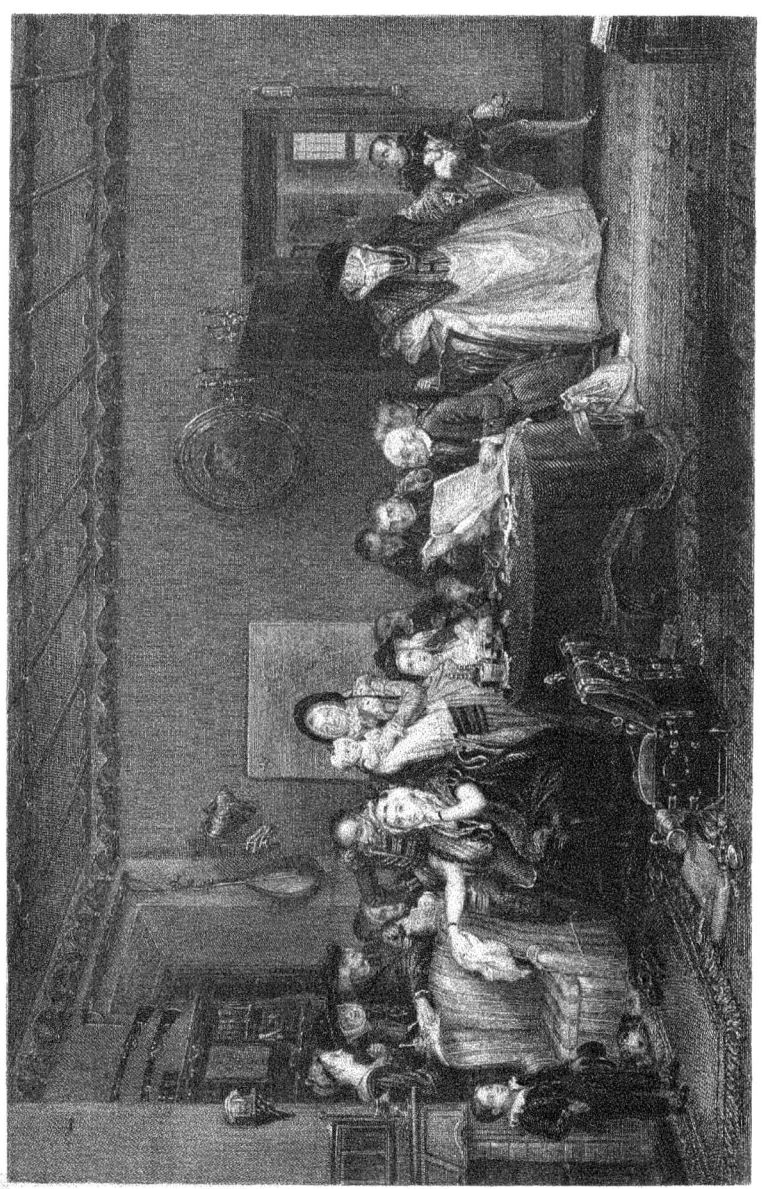

READING THE WILL.

PAINTED BY R. DAV. WILKIE R.A.

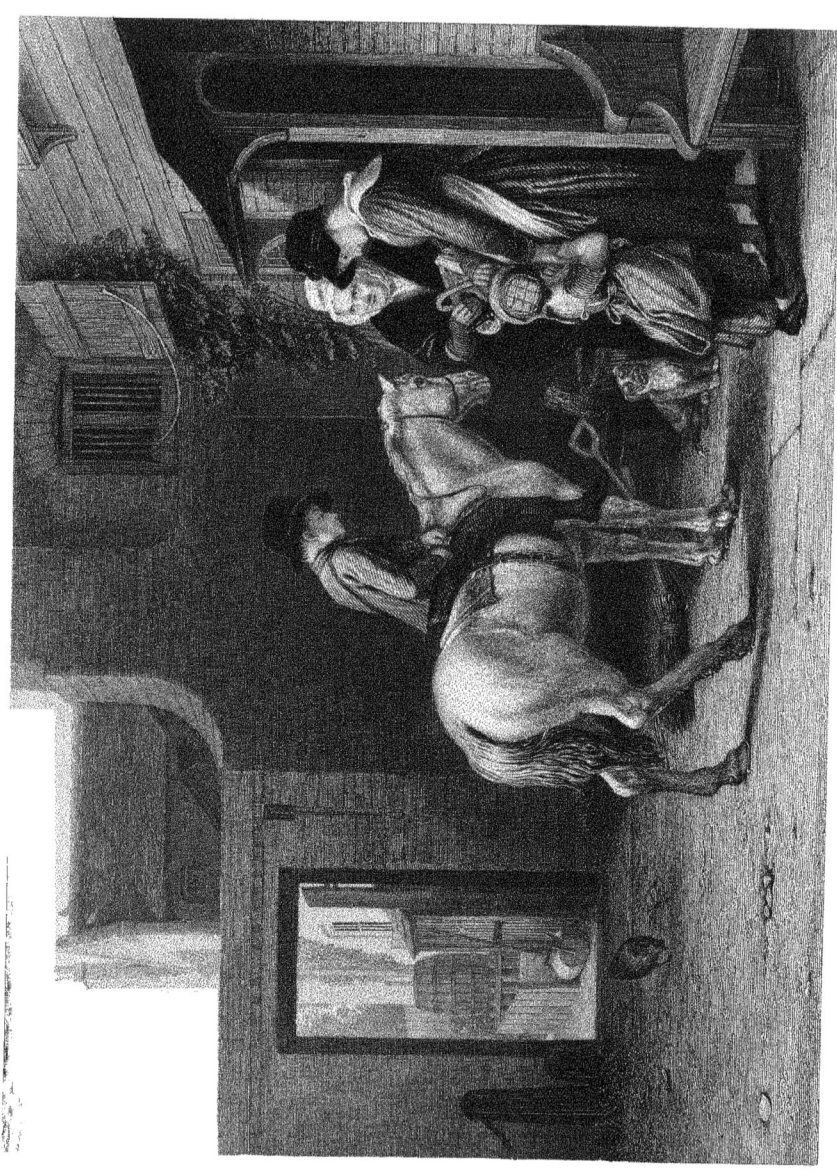

to set off her lovely person with the very trappings of woe, has apparently just learned, what she probably was half assured of before, that her husband's wealth is hers; she listens with tranquil complacency; her back is averted from the door, and she turns in the direction of a young officer, who hangs about her; his head is inclined, and he drinks in this important piece of information with the deepest satisfaction. The prim old grandmamma, who stands nursing a lovely babe, smiles with an air of triumph. The very acme of the opposite feeling, together with undissembled rage, agitate the withered figure and keen face of an old lady of large expectations and mighty pride, who has repaired to the meeting in her most elaborate and antiquated toilette: a mulatto footman bears her gold-headed cane, pattens, and pet poodle: he is looking up with wonder at his old mistress, who appears to have been provoked into some unwonted derogation of dignity, as, with keen, selfish eyes, she flashes annihilation at the averted group, and rustles, with all her silks, indignantly from the apartment. This figure is wonderfully painted. These are the principal personages of the scene, and they are well contrasted; but the feeling is well sustained by the other subordinate personages: curiosity and interest the most intent appear in the old man with the ear-trumpet, and the youth behind him;—trembling hope; dejection, and disappointment, on the pale faces of some poor female relatives;—curious surprise in the old clergyman;—vexation and irritation in the old dame leaning on the chair; while the apathy of the boy, too young to feel his loss, and the smiling unconsciousness of infancy—the dog who has missed his master, and, scared by the assemblage, crouches under the well-known chair, are traits exquisitely introduced to relieve the harshness of the predominant action. A tone, rich, subdued and grave, finely befits the nature of the subject.

In 1822, Wilkie completed, after much labour, the well-known work of "The Chelsea Pensioners." The Duke of Wellington, for whom it was painted, had repeatedly seen it in progress, and noticed with great satisfaction the portraits of different well-known characters who had served under him. This picture made a great sensation; so much so, that the painter was obliged to obtain the consent of his brother Academicians to have a railing put up before it to protect it against injury from the crowd. This is one of his finest works; but unable as we are to offer an engraving from it to our readers, it would be useless to dwell upon it.

A less ambitious subject, but one displaying a very happy treatment, is the smaller subject of the "Errand Boy." There is a beautiful subdued cool tone about this picture; the high lights sparingly touched in, and the management of the reflections admirably skilful. We have here a group at a farm-door, of which the prominent personage is a small boy on a large farm-pony, rough and incult, equipped with saddle and bridle of the most primitive simplicity. The lad is a spare and limber slip, but not "within the roll of common boys," for there is.an air of precocious responsibility diffused over his little thin face and figure and dangling legs, as well there may be, for is it not too much "for one small head to carry all that his must do"—to chronicle in the duodecimo volume of his youthful brain all the wants of all the old women of the parish, besides commissions of a softer kind from the younger? And when we consider, moreover, the little distractions occasioned by wayside recreations, games at chuck-farthing and marbles, to which he is addicted, "like most of the untaught striplings of his age," while his vagrant pony is left to graze the while quietly in the hedge, it is no wonder if there is now and then a confusion of parcels and of billets-doux—if the old woman misses her snuff, or Jennie finds, to her consternation, that her tender confessions have gone to the wrong man, and receives in return the protestations destined for another. This little marplot appears to be in difficulty; an old woman, with an eye like an awl—an awful eye for seventy—is receiving her parcels, and something he has forgotten, or taken to the wrong place, evidently, from his confused look, as he dives ineffectually into the recesses of his pocket for the missing article. There is a ludicrous distress in the downcast face of the culprit, afraid to look up and encounter that terrible eye of the old woman, who has him in the manner, and is about to administer some very caustic reproof. Keen as is that old dame, something appears to be going on of which she wots not, if we may judge from the conscious looks of the pretty maiden, into whose hand a young child, with her eye on the old dame all the while, is slily slipping a love-letter; the horse, with sidelong look, seeming as if he too were in the secret. This is one of those things that gains on one the more it is looked at. The old woman's face is one of the richest and most comic things Wilkie ever hit upon, the downcast maiden exquisite, and the lad a perfect type of the genus to which he belongs; while each figure, horse and all, has about it a perfect stamp of individual portraiture.

We must not forget to notice here two subjects from Allan Ramsay's "Gentle Shepherd," in illustration of which it was once his intention to paint an entire series; indeed some of his first sketches at the Scottish Academy at Edinburgh were compositions from this poem, illustrative of its different scenes. In interiors he always shone, and had stored up in his sketch-book and memory every nook and corner and domestic utensil of the lowland cottage, of which he has made such excellent use in his various pictures. For picturesque effect, and light and shade, he certainly never excelled the composition before us, "Glaud, Jenny, and Peggy." The two lasses, Jenny and Peggy, are making their toilette at a more natural hour than is customary with city belles: washing utensils, the small looking-glass, and the box full of rustic finery, are spread around.

> "While Peggy laces up her bosom fair,
> Wi' a blue snood, Jenny binds up her hair;
> Glaud, by his morning ingle, taks a beck,
> *The rising sun shines motty through the reck;*
> A pipe his mouth, the lasses please his een
> An' now an' then his joke maun interveen."

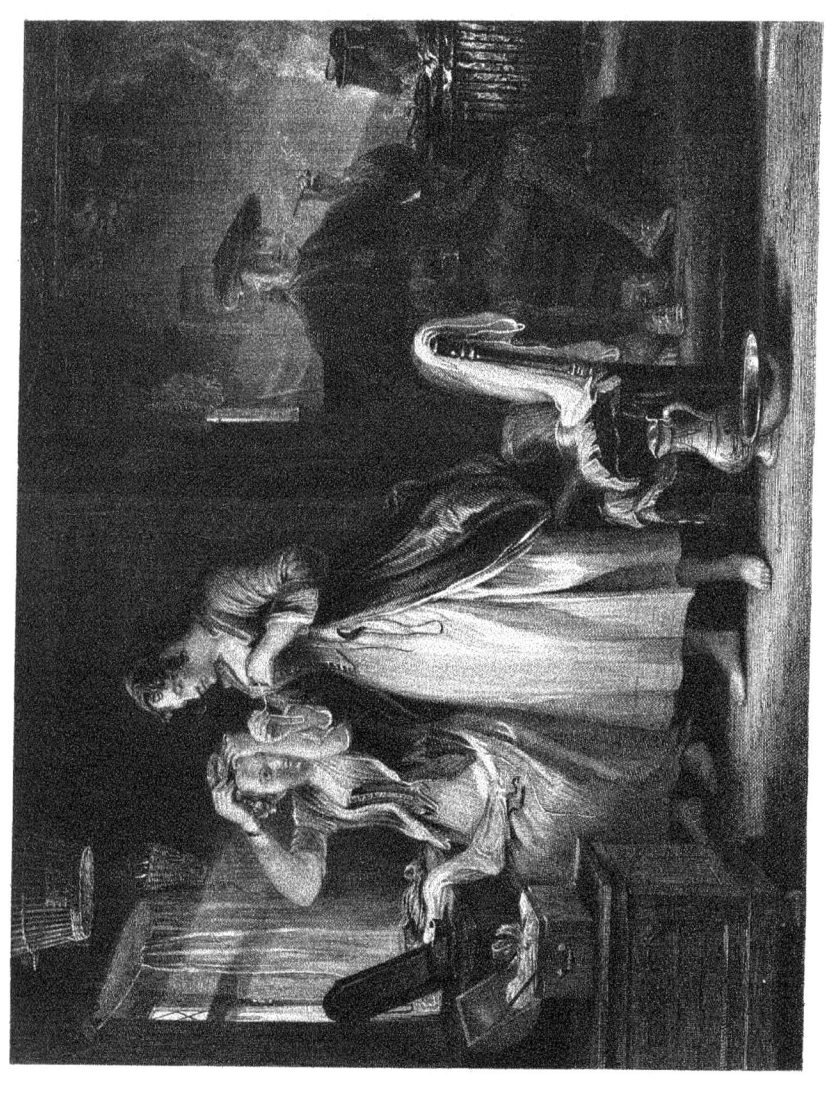

Fatie, the Gentle Shepherd, has just proved to be the son of Sir William Worthy. At this discovery, Peggy, the object of his vows, while both were in a humble station, is alarmed for his constancy; but he has just renewed his promise of unchanging fidelity. Glaud, however, not aware of this recent contract, thinks well to warn his reputed niece against giving encouragement to the addresses of the new-made gentle :—

> " GLAUD.—I wish, my bairns, it may keep fair till night,
> Ye dinna use sae soon to see the light.
> Nae doubt, now, ye intend to mix the thrang,
> To tak your leave o' Patrick or he gang:
> But do ye think that now, when he 's a laird,
> That he poor landwart lasses will regard?

> " JENNY.—Tho' he 's young master now, I 'm very sure,
> He has mair sense than slight auld friends, tho' poor.
> But yesterday, he gie us mony a tug,
> An' kiss'd my cousin there frae lug to lug."

This proof of his unaltered regard is not, however, so satisfactory to the old man as to his simple nieces :—

> " Ay, ay, nae doubt o' t, an he 'll do 't again;
> But be advised, his company refrain.
> Before, he, as a Shepherd, sought a wife,
> Wi' her to live a chaste an' frugal life;
> But now grown gentle, soon he will forsake
> Sic godly thoughts, an' brag o' being a rake."

Peggy is here quite at a loss :—

> " A rake! what's that? Sure, if it means aught ill,
> He 'll never be 't, else I hae tint my skill."

And so the dialogue proceeds. Wilkie never did anything more charming than the figure of the girl binding up her hair. It is exquisitely graceful, without being, as is so often the case, tinged with affectation; and the effect of the sunbeams gleaming through the casement, and producing a glow of hazy light upon the head and bust, cannot be surpassed. The other figure is less happy, but still very pleasing; and both are perfectly natural. Wilkie's peasants are such indeed—there is a freshness and reality about them. The background of the picture is remarkably fine, as a piece of effect; the old man in shadow, with a few gleams of subdued light on his cheek and hair; the sunbeams catching on the smoke, which rises from the hearth, are perfectly given. As a study of an interior, as well as a scene of national character, this is certainly a very delightful picture.

"Roger slighted by Jennie," is another incident from Wilkie's favourite poem; and it is full of the air of nature and of the manners of the Scottish peasantry. The composition is the simplest possible; yet there is a charm about that very simplicity. Roger has long loved the daughter of old Glaud; nor is she at all ignorant of his passion; but as he is slow in speech, and nowise dexterous in courtship, she affects to despise him, and plays off upon him not a little coquettish raillery, both from the love of mischief, and, perhaps, from a wish to drive the slow-spoken shepherd to declare himself more plainly. Of this hard treatment Roger bitterly complains to his more fortunate friend Fatie :—

> " In ilka place she jeers me air an' late,
> An' gars me look bombaz'd, and unco blate.
> But yesterday I met her yont a knowe,
> She fled, as frae a shelly-coated cow:
> She Bauldy looes, Bauldy that drives the car,
> But geeks at me, an' says I smell o' tar."

But, sorer still, he adds :—

> " When I begin to tune my stock an' horn,
> Wi' a' her face she shaws a cauldrife scorn.
> Last night I played, (ye never heard sic spite,)
> Oe'r Bogie was the spring, an' her delyte;
> Yet, tauntingly, she at her cousin speer'd,
> Gif she cou'd tell what tune I play'd, an' sneer'd.
> Flocks, wander where ye like, I dinna care,
> I'll break my reed, and never whistle mair."

Patie, upon this, ironically advises him to make his quietus :—

> " Yonder's a craig, sin' ye hae tint a' houp,
> Gae till't your wa's, an' tak the lover's loup."

Roger, however, demurs; and, as his only remaining chance, Patie counsels him to return her scorn for scorn, and thus bring her to her senses :—

> " Seem to forsake her, soon she'll change her mood;
> Gae woo anither, and she'll gang clean wud."

The " cauldrife scorn" is not badly expressed, but perhaps the most beautiful part of the picture is the figure of the shepherd with his dog and staff, in half-shadow, relieved from the background of distant grey moors, with one or two high-lights judiciously touched in. It is a perfect study, suggestive of a whole world of associations of pastoral life.

The Prince Regent (now George IV.) had expressed a wish for a second picture by Wilkie; and the painter, who at this time formed the idea of his " Knox Preaching," submitted the sketch to His Majesty; but the subject did not please him. He desired a picture of a humourous cast, or at least less severe than this novel vein of Wilkie's. The prince was about to visit Edinburgh, and his reception there might be expected to

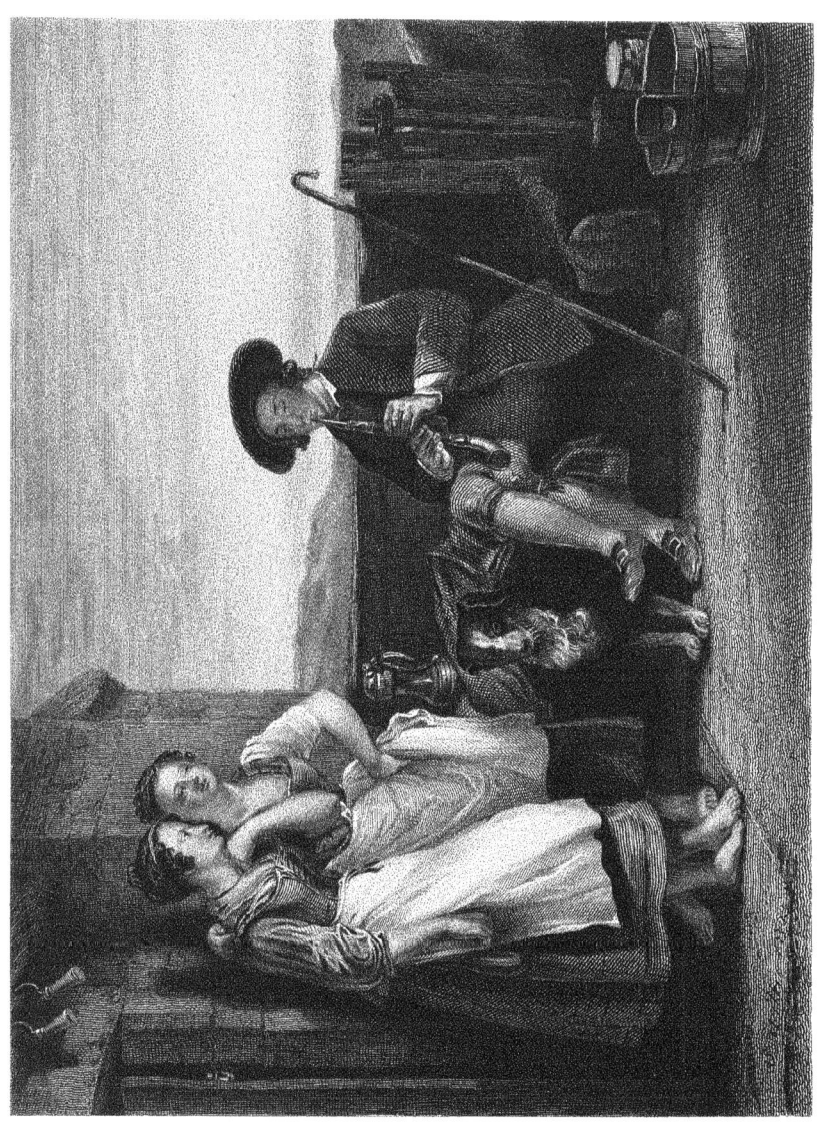

offer some subject which, while it presented an opportunity of picturesque composition, would also be gratifying to His Majesty ; and with this view Wilkie revisited the Scottish capital, and collected sketches of the different incidents connected with the royal progress, as well as local materials for his contemplated picture of "Knox." While in Edinburgh, he was introduced to that distinguished patron of art, Sir Robert Peel, who also wished to possess a picture by him, when able to undertake it. Shortly after died Sir Henry Raeburn, who held the appointment of limner to the king in Scotland, when, by Sir Robert's recommendation, the vacant office was bestowed on Wilkie.

About this time he finished and exhibited the picture of "The Parish Beadle; one rather serious than humorous: some such exhibition of petty tyranny might have prompted the lines of Shakspeare:—

> "O, but man, proud man!
> Drest in a little brief authority,
> Plays such fantastic tricks before high heaven,
> As make the angels weep; who, with our spleens,
> Would all themselves laugh mortal."

It is fair-day in some country village, for the flag is flaunting from the old tower, and we may almost hear the merry peal of the bells ; the booths and tents glance lively in the sun, and we see the throng moving to and fro in the market-place. On such occasions that important functionary, the Beadle, appears in the full-blown dignity of scarlet plush, gold lace, and cocked hat, with staff of office, to assert at once the dignity of the parish and his own to boot: something he must do, to quiet his sense of responsibility and show his authority; and as, with such worthies, discretion is the better part of valour, he has wisely turned aside from the more turbulent of the crowd, to pounce upon an easier class of victims—a poor family of wanderers from the sunny south, gaining their painful bread by the combined attractions of a dancing bear and dog, a monkey, tambourine, hurdygurdy, and Savoyard song; and who, attracted by the festival, ply their vocation between the "Scylla and Charybdis" of the insolence of office and the brutality of the rabble. These unfortunates the Beadle is haling off to the house of correction, of which one of his myrmidons is unlocking the heavy guarded portal. Well has the painter given to his portly person and full-fed face its characteristic air of vulgar importance, and mean, triumphant authoritativeness over the defenceless —the exhibition of a cruel, harsh nature is subtly dashed with a comic expression of the mock-heroic: we scarce know whether to weep or laugh, as the sturdy tyrant of the charity-children marshals the way to prison with his official staff, sternly grasping the youngest of the party, a gentle sunny-faced lad, whose features of classic regularity proclaim the clime from which he sprung: he looks out of the picture with half surprise and alarm in his soft eyes; his monkey, with a physiognomy not less expressive, his antic mood all gone, crouches against his shoulder, and the dancing dog, "a very sad dog" indeed, tricked out in his comic finery, with subdued, appealing looks, and his tail curled under him with awe, steals reluctantly forward to the place of durance. The mother of the lad, a fine dark-eyed brunette, is vainly endeavouring with broken words, eked out with signs and offers, to appeal against a proceeding, the meaning of which she evidently cannot comprehend, as does the father, who with rueful and astonished looks is offering to handle his tambourine gratis; but nothing can mollify the wrathful functionary. In the back-ground we have the filling up of this melancholy picture—here some young blackguards, whose faces one might almost swear to, so entirely are they typical of their class, are cruelly taunting and harassing the captured vagrants in the rear; while poor goaded Bruin and his leader seem half disposed to resent the ill treatment of the rabble with their claws and staff. In this picture there is "more than meets the eye; "we sympathize with that poor, harmless, isolated knot of wanderers, amid none but hostile faces, with none to befriend them; we follow them in idea into the noisome cage; the mean and cruel tyranny of the beadle fills us with indignation, as the low moral tone of the unfeeling rabble with sorrow and disgust; and when we reflect that such things should be common in the midst of us, we are constrained to exclaim, "Alas, poor human nature!" and invoke for the masses a more humanizing education.

The picture is very rich and deep in effect and colour, and in point of character it is inimitable.

At this time commenced a series of family trials, which, in connexion with the constant anxieties connected with his professional engagements, (for Wilkie was one who threw his whole soul into whatever he was engaged in, and some of his subjects were exceedingly difficult, and such as he could hardly have painted *con-amore*,) appear to have induced a state of nervousness which for a long time interrupted his labours, and sent him abroad in search of relaxation, and, if it might be, health. The family who had once occupied the manse of Cults was now fast breaking up; the mother of Wilkie was gradually sinking, and her infirmities were increased by the arrival of her son James, from Canada, hopelessly ruined in health, and with involved affairs. David had become surety for him to a large amount, which he would have to make good, and to assist his brother's widow and orphan children. The oppressive sense of these melancholy circumstances was for a while somewhat diverted (to return with increased force) by the honours he received during another professional visit to Scotland, where he received attentions such as went to his heart: he dined at the Presbytery dinner with the old friends of his father; and he was invited by the authorities of Cupar, his native borough, so to call it, to a public dinner, where "they did not fail, after mentioning the fame he had earned for himself, to allude to the lustre which his reputation reflected back on the bounds of Fife, and on all who foretold or aided in his rise." Alarmed by the rapid sinking of Mrs. Wilkie, he hastened homeward ere his engagements had terminated, but before he could reach London his mother was no more. But a few weeks after this irreparable loss, he received the account of the death of his elder brother in India; while

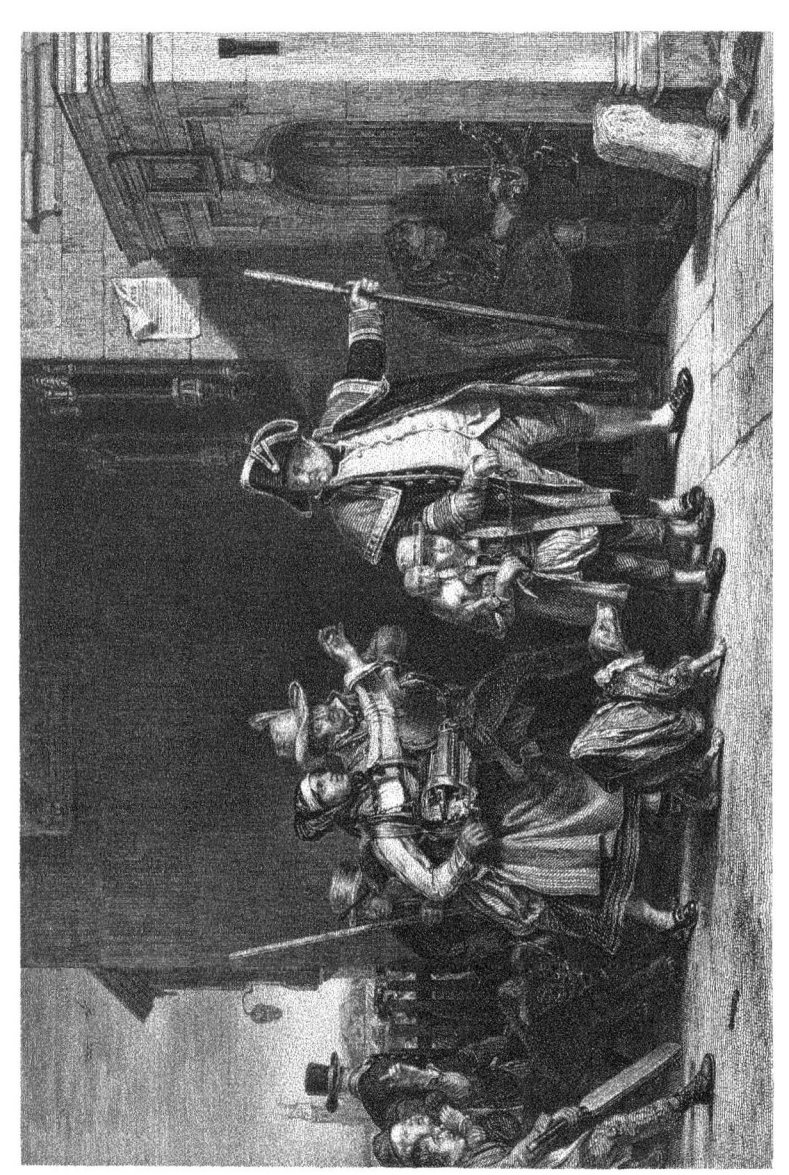

his sister, in addition to their common bereavement, was fated to lose her affianced husband under most sudden and painful circumstances.

These things were too much for him; he was obliged to consult physicians; and after a short visit to Cheltenham, from which he derived no advantage, he returned to London. Hitherto, though suffering, he had continued to work at intervals; but now he found that, after a short application, he was seized with a giddiness of head, and confusion of ideas, which wholly prevented him from continuous application. This distressing state reached the ears of his fast friend, Sir George Beaumont, who sent him a hundred pounds, delicately alleging the increased worth of the pictures he had painted for him; this proof of the continued regard of his early and generous patron, whom he was never to see again, affected deeply the feelings of the suffering painter.

With the hope of re-establishing his shattered system, Wilkie, in the middle of July, 1825, set out on what proved to be a long absence from England; during which he visited France, Germany, Switzerland, Italy, and Spain: his health and fortune were doomed to constant and severe fluctuations, and his ideas on art and style in painting greatly modified, or rather entirely changed. His journals and letters, as given by Mr. Cunningham, now assume a more important character, personal and general; and his sketches of travel, observations on art, and records of the society he mixed with, and the honours he received, will be perused in his volumes with deep interest. In this memoir, we can give but a very brief abstract of this period of his life, and of that too short re-establishment in health and fame in England which succeeded it, ere he set out on his last and fatal expedition to Palestine. And as this collection includes but few engravings of his later works, which, with all their novel merit, we will venture to say, will never be so popular as his earlier ones, it would be fruitless to dwell upon them here at any length.

Wilkie started for Paris in company with that kindred genius, Newton, whose career was brief as his own, and more unhappy. There the doctors, as usual, differed touching his complaint, some advising travel, while others considered him unequal to it. In this dilemma he resolved to follow his own inclination, and proceeded to Geneva by easy stages. To his sister he gives all the details of his journey; he dwells on the magnificence of that grand burst of the Alps, as first seen from the Juras, in terms of enthusiasm: "This morning, before six, we got out to see the view. This is the finest in the world; the lake lay like a great sea spread out before us. We saw the mountains of Savoy beyond, touching the clouds, and at the east end of the lake—what I had not seen before—the sun rising in all his glory above the Swiss Alps. As we moved on, we looked earnestly, to distinguish Mont Blanc; and, to our surprise, as our eyes got to that part of the range, we found its white top soaring majestically above the strata of clouds, into which the highest part only of the others had been able to immerse their heads." His health improved somewhat under the influence of fresh scenes and change of air, and he pursued his way, through Milan and

Genoa, to Florence. Here he began to study the Italian school, beginning with the works of Giotto and the precursors of Raffaelle, and his criticisms on the different works of art are highly valuable to the student. On these subjects his chief correspondents were Phillips and Collins. At Rome he was greatly struck with the ceiling of the Sistine chapel, by Michael Angelo, of which he speaks in terms of enthusiasm, attributing to this great master a merit rarely conceded to him, or rather, overlooked in the blaze of higher qualities, viz.— great appropriateness and beauty of colouring. Besides enjoying the world of ancient art contained in Rome, he was delighted with the picturesque spectacles constantly exhibited in the streets: he speaks of the pilgrims,—"the common dress of the country, surmounted by a broad cape over the shoulders, to which, on the left breast, is fixed a crucifix, and in the hand a long staff tipped by a cross, makes the common appearance of such sojourners; to which, in some cases, is added various wooden bottles, or barrels, for cigars, by their side, and sometimes a heavy bundle of luggage on the back, giving them the perfect appearance of the Pilgrim with the bundle of sins upon his back, which John Bunyan has so aptly described, 'on his way to the gates of heaven.'" In such characters Wilkie must have revelled, and not less in the singular and imposing ceremonials of the Catholic church—among others, the washing of the pilgrims' feet, of which he afterwards painted an exquisite picture.

He speaks too with delight of the balmy clime of Italy. "Though in mid-winter," he says, "we light a fire only at nights, and go out in the day without greatcoats. We see oranges growing on the trees, and many a flower, seen with you only in the hothouse, here growing wild in the fields. The sky is of the clearest blue; the atmosphere so thin, that distant objects are seen most distinctly; the sun's light is brighter, and its shadows are darker, and all colours are stronger and more vivid than in the misty air of England." He mixed much too in the gay world, arranged *tableaux vivans;* surprised the assemblage at Torlonia's, by the good taste and splendour of his masquerade dress; and entered into all the humours of the Carnival, when the sober city of Rome goes mad for a few days in the year. Notwithstanding the "slow and wasting fever of admiration," which lay hold of him amid such scenes, he might have recovered his health, but for the shocks of new misfortunes. Unable as usual to draw a revenue from his pencil, and with the debt incurred to the government as his brother s surety still hanging over him like a cloud, he now received the news of the failure of Hurst and Robinson, the printsellers, on whose debt to him he was mainly depending for support during his prolonged absence. This was a sad and crowning mischance indeed, though he still entertained a lingering hope of their righting themselves. Yet in a letter to his brother he says, "In all these difficulties I feel no want of resource in my own mind. With anything like returning health, I can contest the whole of them, inch by inch." But this inestimable boon was slow in revisiting the shattered frame of Wilkie, and after fresh consultations with Sir James Clarke, and various palliatives, he left Rome, with his malady untouched, and still incapable of any but the most desultory exertions. He had, however, stored his sketch-book with a few studies from the Italian masters, as well as of local character and costume. After a visit to Naples, he returned to Rome, where the last hope of Hurst and Robinson's renewing business was taken away by the accounts he received. In the storm which thus burst over the professors of literature and art in England, a greater than Wilkie was a sufferer, even Sir Walter Scott, deprived at one stroke of the fruits of his labours, by the failure of Constable's house. Wilkie speaks of a letter he had seen, from the immortal novelist, in which he states his surprise that he could bear his loss with so much philosophy, that "having his dog, his gun, and his book left, few of his comforts could be diminished, and he was only now annoyed by the sympathies of his friends." But, however firmly these great men might meet the misfortunes that threatened to overwhelm them, they must secretly have exercised a wasting influence on their health. In a feeble state Wilkie now turned his face to the north of Italy; he had well appreciated the great masters of expression at Rome and Florence, and he now proceeded to study the perfection of harmony, chiaro-scuro, and colour at Parma and Venice. He longed to penetrate the mystery of Titian's colouring, and scrutinized all his great works, particularly the well-known "Assumption," and "Peter Martyr," with incessant attention. Here he received a last letter from his attached friend Sir George Beaumont, full of his usual kind advice. "I intreat you, my dear Wilkie," he says, "to keep your mind tranquil. Remember that nothing will retard your recovery so much as anxiety, deep thought, and over-exertion. To govern the imagination, I know, is an arduous task; but think of the positive necessity of disciplining the mind. You are, I know, happily for yourself, possessed of the only resources which give sound tranquillity to the mind—a true sense of the importance of religion, and a firm reliance on that Providence who is constantly watching over us, and who, I humbly hope and believe, will make you ample amends for all you have suffered." This was the last letter he received from his earliest and kindest friend and patron.

Leaving Venice, Wilkie, ever pursued by unquiet thoughts, and nothing re-established in health, resolved to try the German baths. He remained some time at Munich; the old king of Bavaria, for whom he painted "The Reading of the Will," was dead, and his pictures were to be sold. They were sealed up, but he obtained the indulgence of a visit to the king's private apartment, in which the picture was hung, and was gratified by finding it stand its ground well, though surrounded by the works of Teniers, Wouvermans, and other Dutch masters, and looking, he says, "as, if sold with them, it would bear as good a price;" a prediction fulfilled but shortly after, beyond his expectation. Thence to Dresden and its gallery, Toplitz, Carlsbad, picturesque Prague, and gay Vienna, where he had the honour of dining " *en famille*" with Prince Metternich, and of receiving attentions which induced him to write to his brother:—" In no place have I received such unwearied and disinterested kindness." In four months he had made the tour of the chief cities of

Germany, and remarks, that, for both manners and events, he had found it remarkable and felt satisfied that "if he had done nothing else, he had at least seen the world." Like all English travellers among the Germans, he says, "if they are Goths in one thing more than another, I think it is in the construction of their beds." He now returned to Rome, where signal honours awaited him. The Scotch artists and gentlemen in that city had prepared for him the compliment of a national dinner. The Duke of Hamilton took the chair, Wilkie was placed on his right hand, and his old friend Sir Robert Liston on the left, and besides the Scotch and English artists, Thorwaldsen, Camuccini, the Roman painter, and Benvenuti of Florence, were invited. This mark of distinction from his countrymen must have been highly flattering to the suffering painter, yet he says that "no one need envy him; it is the afflicted state they found him in that had called it forth." In the meantime his picture at Munich had been sold, and fetched three times its original price; a circumstance in which he felt pride, as honourable to British art, as well as favourable to the increasing value of his works, when he should be able to resume his labours. He had, in fact, began to paint again, though with caution, having in the course of the winter executed two small pictures, in a less finished style, but in which he aimed at unusual richness and depth of colouring. These may be cited indeed as the first of his *new style*. His returning powers somewhat restored his spirits, while the fruits of his labours enabled him to bear up against the pressure of pecuniary embarrassment.

Before he left Rome he received information of the death of his friend Sir George Beaumont: the shock was great, for no one had so influenced his fortunes or his mind as this generous and accomplished gentleman. "In the time of sickness," he remarks, in a letter of condolement to Lady Beaumont, "as well as in health, how kind, how unwearied have been his attentions! And in the time of adverse fortune, which he has tried to alleviate, as well as in the prosperity to which he has so much contributed, how sympathizing, and how generous has he been in his conduct toward me! I may indeed boast of other advantages—the society and contact with a mind so endowed for the elevation of one's views, and for giving a favourable bias to one's character, has influenced, and I hope improved, my conduct and pursuits in life;" and, in noticing the bequest of £100 to him as a mark of regard by his deceased patron, he consoles himself with the reflection that, "if he is surviving his own powers, and his friends are falling around him, he has at least neither survived nor lost their honour and esteem."

Having examined at leisure the riches that Italy offers to an enthusiastic painter—of which the notices in his journals and letters are highly instructive—Wilkie proceeded to Geneva, where he remained some time, and where he painted some pictures to send to England.

He had been much struck, as before said, with the ceremonies of the Easter week, and with nothing more so than with the washing of the feet of the pilgrims, both male and

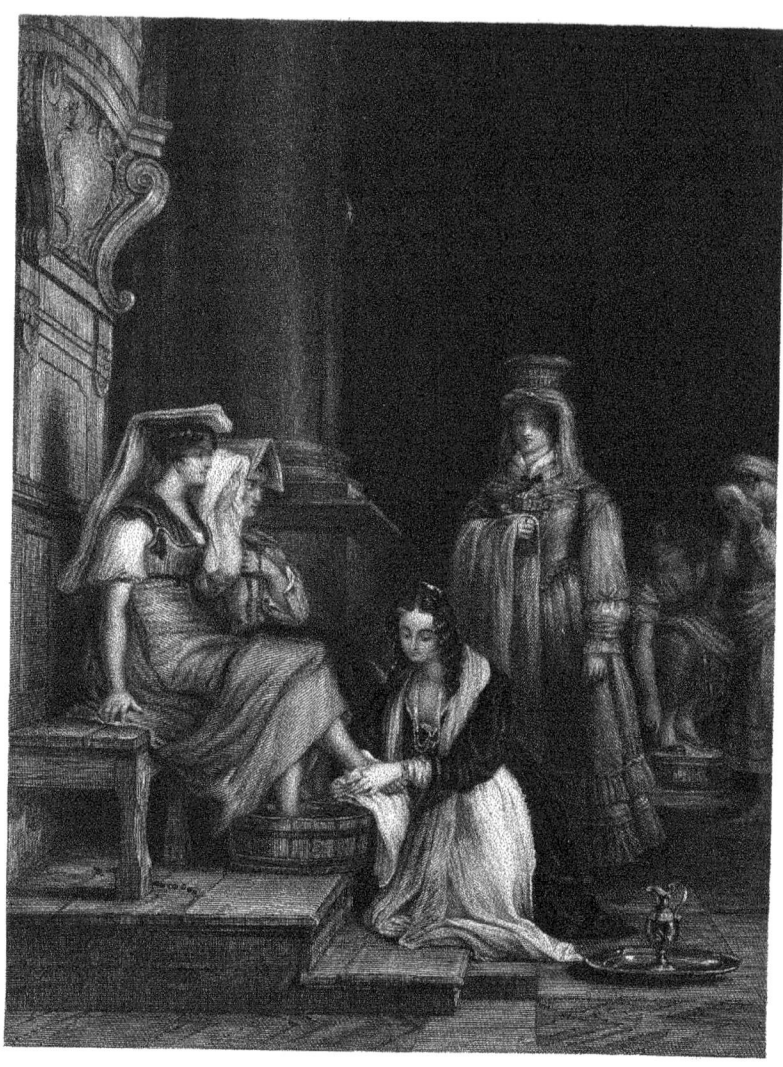

PAINTED BY WILKIE, R.A. — ENGRAVED BY W. GREATBACH

female, in which this somewhat ostentatious humility is often taxed to the utmost of endurance, " for the look and savour of these lowly guests," as he observes in his journal, " were anything but seemly for religious service. As they took off their sandals and stockings, much as washing seemed needful, it yet seemed so severe a task, that from their noble serviteurs the mere willingness to perform would, one would think, have been accepted in lieu of the duty itself. But quite otherwise was the fact." And he proceeds to remark, " that the female pilgrims, who are washed and entertained in separate apartments by themselves, have this kindly office rendered unto them by a sisterhood composed of the first ladies of rank and princesses of the place."

From his observation of these singular scenes, and sketches of character and costume, with which he had, though suffering in health, enriched his portfolio during his stay in the Eternal City, he availed himself of the first return of health to compose the picture before us. It excited great attention from the new style in which, for the first time, the painter, now accomplished in all that a study of Italian art could suggest to him, substituted for that by which he had already wrought out his great masterpieces of character. He observes, in a letter to his brother:—" Before leaving Geneva I completed another picture, making the *fourth*, to send to England. The subject appears to interest: it is that of a handsome young lady, humbling herself, even to the washing of the feet of a poor pilgrim. What is fortunate—the lady is the favourite figure: its progress has made a considerable sensation. A young lady I saw by accident, that resembled the Princess Doria, (the person intended,) struck me as a perfect model. Interest was made to get her to sit; jewels and plate were borrowed, and every assistance procured for me that I could possibly want. Artists have been interested in its progress, and in my manner of painting. For some days after its completion, the house of M. Andioud had been kept in confusion by the numbers of people who have called to see it."

The subdued mellow tone, large amount of reflected lights and half-shadows, richness of surface and texture, and unctuous body of colour, the bolder and broader execution, and the absence of over-minute detail, and of that somewhat metallic hardness that is visible in his first style, distinguished this novel production, which is also full of beauties of a higher character. The principal group is full of feeling. Over the graceful bending figure of the princess, perhaps the most beautiful Wilkie ever painted, is thrown an air of profound humility; and not less admirable is the expression of the Contadina, abashed, and, as with a sense of unworthiness, shrinking from the touch of that white and jewelled hand, and affected to tears by this display of the condescension of the high-bred and the beautiful.

He was now half-way back to England; but, long as had been his absence, he could not settle down in his studio at Kensington before he had explored the treasures of art in Spain, hitherto almost sealed up from the knowledge and research of his countrymen. The works of Murillo and Velasquez, as well as of the other great Spanish masters, were less diffused abroad than at the present day : England possessed but few specimens, and the superb Spanish Gallery at Paris had not as yet been formed and arranged. There was an exciting interest therefore about this breaking of new ground in the fields of art, with which mingled the expectation of meeting with much that was racy and original in the character and manners of the people, from which to draw the materials of subjects in the new style of art upon which the painter had already entered. In all respects his expectations were more than realized. Accordingly, he committed himself to the chances and delays of the slow-going vetturino, a mode of travel which is suitable enough to the painter by the leisure it gives him to see whatever is interesting in his road, and by the variety of life and character to which it introduces him. With the sketch-book ever ready, Wilkie noted down all these, as he also records in his journal the memorabilia of his wayfarings. In passing across the frontiers of France to Spain, by Toulouse and Bayonne, he was in the midst of scenes rendered memorable by the recent victories of his countrymen; and on every hand also were memorials of the chivalrous wars of the middle ages. The Spanish border was in an unsettled state, parties of soldiers patrolled the roads, and at his nocturnal halt in the picturesque Posada, or village caravanserai, so well described in the pages of Borrow, Wilkie had ample opportunity of studying the unquiet spirits of the district then abroad, as well as the permanent national characteristics. It was with a feeling of novelty bordering on surprise that he found himself in the midst of Madrid, where he met with few or none of the travellers that crowd the German and Italian cities, and where the population is almost exclusively Spanish. There, however, he was fortunate enough to meet with Washington Irving, a congenial spirit : in so remote a place two such men must have found a welcome resource in each other's society; but, besides this advantage, Wilkie derived many others, in a place where his name was very little known, and where the aristocracy were shy of strangers, from the good offices of this most amiable as well as accomplished of the Americans. Together they visited the vast conventual palace of the Escurial, where for the first time he revelled to the full in the pictures that he had come to see—an unrivalled collection of the national masters, as well as of Titian and other great Italian painters. At Madrid he set up his easel, and from the novel materials he had collected, and with the inspiration derived from Velasquez and Murillo, rapidly dashed off a series of pictures illustrative of the recent patriotic struggle of all ranks against their French invaders. Of these the most conspicuous and the best known to the English public is "The Defence of Saragossa," an heroic resistance, which deserved to be immortalized by the pencil of Wilkie, as it has been by the author of "Childe Harold." Augustina, the maid of Saragossa, stepping over the body of her lover, takes his place at the gun, and Don Palafox, (whose portrait he was enabled to obtain,) and other personages, figure in this striking and animated composition. A more characteristic picture, with many of Wilkie's native excellencies, is a "Council of War held by a Junta of Priests and

Patriots, in a Village Posada," with some sly traits of national manners in the background. Another is the "Departure of a Guerilla Chieftain to his Post." The progress of these works was watched with great interest by the artists and grandees of Madrid, who, wholly uninfluenced by the "prestige" of Wilkie's name and works, which they had neither seen nor heard of before his arrival among them, warmly applauded his labours.

He next visited Seville, crossing in his way the waste plains of La Mancha, and the ranges of the stern Sierra Morena, memorable for the adventures of Don Quixote and his humorous Squire, the scene of the different incidents and stories in the immortal work of Cervantes, of which, had the Scotch painter been a Spanish contemporary, and familiar from infancy with the humours of the land, he might have left a scarcely less immortal series of illustrative pictures. At Seville he was joined by Irving, who had just performed that journey to Granada, of which he has given so lively an account in his preface to "Stories of the Alhambra." They were much in each other's society; both amiable men and gentle, genial humourists, and who suffered nothing characteristic in the land to escape their observation; well fitted to understand and appreciate each other's talents, and they must have parted with no small regret. But Wilkie was now anxious to return home: he had fully studied, in the schools of Italy, Germany, and Spain, the works of the mighty masters of art; he had matured his taste, deliberately formed his opinions, and adopted a new style of painting, the effect of which upon his professional brethren and the world at large he was now impatient to ascertain.

Three years had elapsed during which the public had ceased to be familiar with the works of their favourite painter on the walls of the Academy, when, in May 1829, he exhibited no less than six pictures, all, save one, Spanish and Italian subjects, those already alluded to as painted at Madrid, as well as "The Confessional," "Pifferari," and two of the ceremony of washing the pilgrims at Rome during the Easter festival. In these works there was little of that sly humour and nice observation of well-known domestic incident, in embodying which Wilkie had gained his reputation; his subjects were more ambitious, and the style of his painting wholly changed likewise. The cool grey and somewhat metallic tone of his early works, his careful and delicate touch, and minute finish, were abandoned for a richer and more unctuous style of colour, bold and broad handling, and depth of effect, redolent, perhaps too palpably so, of Correggio, Rembrandt, Velasquez, and Murillo. A style founded on that of others is, of course, wanting in originality: criticism, as might be expected, was not idle, and different opinions were formed as to the propriety of this change of Wilkie's manner of painting. No doubt it had both its beauties and its faults, and if often grandiose, was sometimes obscure, defective in simplicity and clearness; and. with all the greatness of the painter's talents, he could not transfer to canvass traits of foreign manners and appearances, which he had studied but for a while, with the same inimitable success that attended his personation of the Scottish national character. Without presuming to pass any judgment, we may venture at least to express the opinion, that great and varied as were the powers of Wilkie, and though he has *sometimes* touched successfully on a loftier vein than in his earlier works, it is still by these that he will be remembered by posterity; for while others may have equalled or even excelled him in his more serious style of composition, he stands here confessedly without a rival, and comes home to the universal heart. Be this as it may, the public welcomed with delight these new pictures; the king was so much pleased, that he became a purchaser of several; and Wilkie, now somewhat re-established in health, and in good spirits at the warmth of his reception, *malgré* the unsparing criticism poured out upon him, saw, in the comparative rapidity and effective facility of his new style, the means of extrication from all his difficulties, the prospect of better times, and of even a more exalted reputation. Commissions poured in upon him; he went to work accordingly with spirit. His Majesty now commanded him to proceed with the subject of his "Entrance to Holyrood," for which, as the reader will remember, he had made sketches at Edinburgh, before his journey to the continent.

Early in the following year his accomplished friend, Sir Thomas Lawrence, with whom, while in Spain, he had much interesting correspondence on art, died somewhat suddenly, leaving behind him, with the vacant office of President of the Academy, a reputation for suavity, kindness, and polished manners, only exceeded by his genius. It became a matter of speculation, whether Wilkie would not be chosen to fill the vacant chair: such was probably the wish of the monarch, who had paved the way by conferring on him the office, held jointly with that of President by the late Sir Thomas, of Principal Painter in Ordinary to his Majesty; but the choice of the Academy fell upon Sir Martin Archer Shee—a selection nowise invidious to Wilkie, since the new President, though of respectable talents, could not claim to be placed in the first rank of those over whom he was wisely called upon, for various reasons of policy, to preside.

The picture of "The Entrance of George the Fourth into Edinburgh," which had proved toilsome work, and added nothing to his reputation, was scarcely finished ere that Sovereign died; but Wilkie still continued to hold the office of Principal Painter in Ordinary to his successor, William the Fourth, which brought with it the usual amount of royal and noble portraiture. But he was now fast advancing on a work more to his mind, and which had cost him much research; in which all his powers were taxed to the uttermost; and in which he meant to establish the triumph of his new style of painting over all opposition. This was the well-known picture of "Knox Preaching before the Congregation," originally declined by George the Fourth, but ordered by a far more discerning patron, Sir Robert Peel. With this statesman Wilkie had not become personally acquainted till he had attained the meridian of his fame; but lately he had been much in correspondence with him on subjects of art, and had been indebted to him for many courtesies: from this time forth Sir Robert was one of his warmest friends and patrons.

Much of Wilkie's time was now taken up in court portraiture, such as he could not decline to undertake, and which was besides more profitable, unfortunately, than were the legitimate productions of his genius. Among his sitters were the Queen Adelaide and the Duke of Wellington. The portrait of the duke, with the charger on which he rode at Waterloo, was commissioned for the Merchant Taylors' Hall, by Sir Claudius Stephen Hunter, and executed at the duke's seat at Strathfieldsaye, in a manner which gratified its illustrious subject, as well as the honourable company. Wilkie says in his journal:—
" The whole of this is to me a most interesting visit, and a most interesting labour." For the head he had no less than ten sittings; and he remained two days more to paint in the horse. " The duke," he observes, " was very gracious, and did everything to assist me. There was only himself and Lord Charles; *but the solitude was more exciting and interesting than any society that could be imagined.*" From hence he went to Brighton to paint the portrait of Queen Adelaide, the progress of which picture was interrupted by an attack of illness. " The king," he says in a letter to his sister, " invited me to the grand evening party last Friday—but this private." But the honours and gaieties of Brighton, however they might have flattered the man, had few charms for *the painter*. He observes in a letter to his brother Academician Collins, that " there is nothing connected with art, and few to talk to, particularly for one whose occupations do not admit of mixing with society." Another, and one of the very best of his portraits, was that of the Duke of Sussex, as Earl of Inverness, in the costume of a Highland chief. Wilkie shone in the exhibition of 1834; for, besides his portraits of the Queen and the Duke of Wellington, and two others, he had a beautiful subject, " The Spanish Mother and Child," and one in his humorous style, " The Not at Home." The private view at the Academy was brilliant:—" The king and queen came. The queen appeared kind; thought the duke extremely like; talked of her own picture, which I find rather a favourite, and spoke with much satisfaction of ' The Spanish Lady.' The king called me to him when he came before it, and spoke quite loud as approving of the expression of the child. When the company came afterward, I found all, particularly ladies, approving of this picture." He now made a tour to Oxford; dined in Christ Church College Hall, and was witness to the enthusiastic reception of the Duke of Wellington in the Theatre at Oxford; and heard him on this occasion read his Latin speech, of which he acquitted himself remarkably well. At Blenheim he was delighted beyond measure with the magnificent collection of the works of Titian. He seems indeed at this time to have lived in one round of honours and festivities, and to have mingled, like Rubens or Vandyke, something of the courtier with the painter. " Ten days ago," he tells his sister, " I was present at a very grand party. Lady Holland sent a note to me to come and drink tea about ten o'clock. I accordingly went, sure to meet some great people. The party was very great indeed, and were then joining us from the dinner-table in the library. So high indeed was the party, that I will not say that it was not even graced by

majesty! As it was, I felt myself a very inconsiderable person. Her ladyship, however, contrived in the kindest manner to get me spoken to by the great star; and the others, who were scarcely less than ministers of state, were very obliging and civil." Earl Grey, and Lords Brougham and Mulgrave were among the visitors, and Wilkie complimented the former upon what had been doing for the arts during his administration—the building of the New Academy and the purchase of the Corregios for the National Gallery. Such is the life of a painter whom the great ones of the world delight to honour; and yet we may doubt whether this period was either the most profitable or happy of the career of Wilkie.

He next went down to Scotland to make arrangements for the execution of an important commission, " Sir David Baird discovering the body of Tippoo Saib," which cost him much time and research. On the way he had the melancholy satisfaction of paying a last visit to his old and attached friend Sir Robert Liston, who had been the occasion of the dinner given to him at Rome, and was truly distressed to find his noble mind so deeply impaired that he could scarcely conclude a single sentence. " To all I said," says the painter, " he showed the most acute intelligence—where I had come from, where I was staying, where I was going, and when I was to be back—trying repeatedly to ask me whether I could not remain with him as I had done before; made the more affecting by his saying, 'I am a poor—not able—but I am better—and would be glad to see you.'"

On his return to town he painted one of the best of his Spanish pictures, " Columbus submitting the Chart of his Voyage of the Discovery of the New World to the Spanish Authorities," founded on a fact related in the life of that great man, that, when travelling one day on foot accompanied by his son, he stopped at the gate of a Franciscan convent to ask for refreshment, and one of the friars happening to pass, being struck with his appearance, entered into conversation with him, when a conference took place which opened a somewhat brighter prospect for the hitherto baffled and disappointed discoverer. This was considered with justice one of the finest of his later productions. Among the portraits which he executed was one of a man not a little famous in his day, and whom many of our readers will no doubt vividly remember,—the Rev. Edward Irving, the friend of Coleridge, and who could win the admiration of Lamb,—" long," as Mr. Cunningham informs us, " the intimate friend of Wilkie, and the favourite of all who loved original vigour of mind and grave persuasive eloquence." He adds, what will surprise those who knew him only in the pulpit, that " he had humour too of the rarest kind, and such wit and social glee as made him welcome to all Scottish firesides: the first time I was acquainted with him was at Wilkie's. Sir Peter Laurie and William Collins, the painter, were there: Scottish humour and Scottish stories abounded."

He now turned his attention to Ireland, hitherto little explored by the painter, though offering a mine of the richest materials for his art, and, since the death of Wilkie, worked with eminent success by Maclise, Goodall, Topham, and others. He enjoyed the racy humorous character of Dublin; he sketched street-scenes and jaunting-cars; the Catholic usages and local superstitions, the holy-wells and pilgrimages, also invited his recording pencil. But it was with the west of Ireland, the wild mountains and wilder peasantry of Connemara, and the quaint old Spanish town of Galway that he was most delighted. While the tribe of beggars in the capital of Wicklow were grotesquely arrayed in the cast-off dress-coats and old hats of their betters, in the west the costume was almost Spanish; broad and noble in form, and rich in colour, affording a perfect model. And while he admits that the spectacles that met his eye were painful to the feelings of the patriot, to the painter they furnished all the richest elements of the picturesque.

Several sketches he made, some few of which he afterwards worked up into pictures, in which he embodied these characteristics, and the wildness, poverty, and unsettled habits of the peasantry. These were hastily, if finely done, and could not of course come up to his Scotch subjects in inimitable national fidelity. "The Peep-o'day Boy" was considered the best of them.

His notices of this journey are most characteristic. "On landing in the Bay of Dublin the scene that presents itself—so repugnant to the philanthropist—is to the painter most highly interesting. Velasquez, Murillo, and Salvator Rosa would have found here fit objects for their study. · *The misery did not strike me: it was apparently not felt by themselves.* Dublin, with its splendid squares and public buildings, is essentially English, still the mass of the population has an *Italian and Spanish look*, and one is only surprised that, with their appearance, *their habits, and their faith, they should yet be our own people, and speak our own language!* We then proceeded southward through the wild mountainous district of Connemara to Galway, a region of which the inhabitants are said to be descended from a colony of Spaniards, to whom they still bear a marked resemblance. Here the impression, the aspect of these people, and their cabins made is not to be described. In a state of primeval simplicity, honest, *polite*, and virtuous, with so few wants that even the children run about the cabins unclad, realizing to a fervid imagination an age of poetry, yet which the poetry of our own time has not described, and to painting is entirely new." Every one who has penetrated to this very singular part of Ireland, who has remarked its peculiarities of architecture, totally dissimilar to anything else in the British islands—its houses resembling those of Seville or Cadiz, its traces of the *Moorish arch*—can hardly realize the feeling that he is at home, and among fellow-subjects. And wild indeed are still the "boys" of Galway :—a party of painters, whose pursuits were regarded with a suspicious eye, were mobbed as government agents, and might have been roughly handled, but for the interposition and explanations of the priest; and when at length their real object was understood, and it was known that they were paying liberally for sitters, they were in hardly less danger from the uproar.

Q

ious competition for employment that ensued. A well-known author of "Life in London" celebrity, assures us that when he was lessee of the theatre here, he was forced to arm himself with sword and pistol, to enforce the necessity of payment, a ceremony which the turbulent Galwagians of the lower sort did not seem to comprehend, or relish. Of the costume, he says, ".In. Connaught and Connemara, the clothes, particularly of the women, are the work of their own hands, and the colour they are most fond of is a red they dye with madder. A petticoat, jacket, and mantle brighten up the cabin or landscape like a Titian or Giorgione. Indeed, the whole economy of the people furnishes the elements of the picturesque. They build their own cabins, fabricate their own clothes, dig their own turf, catch their own salmon, and plough their own fields, bringing into their confined dwellings a confused variety of implements not to be described." The scenery of the Lakes of Killarney, he declares that for beauty and grandeur he had never seen surpassed. A singular proof of Wilkie's general popularity is the fact, that though he was quite the court painter, he received an application to paint the portrait of the great leader of Irish agitation. His account of this incident is curious. "The clergyman who ordered it," he says, "wished *me* to do it; for although there was a prejudice against the person at present, he was a great man, and he thought a subject for a fine picture: it was Mr. Daniel O'Connell." This application Wilkie seems to have been in some degree embarrassed with, as appears from a letter on the subject, to his friend Sir William Knighton; and the view he takes of it is singular. "The question of Catholic and Protestant I have considered a theme for art. May not this come within these classes, if an historic portrait can be made of it?" The commission was accepted; the painting was a really noble work; there was a surprising breadth and air of grandeur about it, and it may well claim to be regarded as an "historical portrait," and classed with similar productions of Titian and Vandyke.

In 1835, Wilkie and his friend Raimbach were elected corresponding members of the Institute of France; a distinction of which the painter was justly proud, not only for himself, but for the admirable engraver through whose skill his works had been made known to those who could never have seen the originals. "I was exceedingly gratified," he remarks, in his letter to Raimbach, "to find that *you*r name and my own were included. This is a distinction to which my art could never have arrived, confined in its nature to one place, were it not that it has been fortunately combined with yours, the excellence and beauty of which are wafted forth on a thousand wings, and speak simultaneously to all countries and in all languages."

But higher honours were in store for him at home. The "London Gazette" recorded that on the 15th of June, 1836, "The king was pleased to confer upon David Wilkie, Esq., Royal Academician, principal Painter to his Majesty, the honour of knighthood," which mark of flattering, though well-merited distinction, was communicated through his friend Lord John Russell. It wrought but little change upon the retiring and unassuming painter; "how meekly he bore his honours all who knew him," says Mr. Cunningham, "can bear witness;" his parents, for whose sakes he might have been most proud to wear them, were in the tomb; his early friends and patrons were fast falling around him, Sir George Beaumont was no more, Lawrence was gone, and Scott—whose journal, published in "Lockhart's Life," he might well consider the most interesting book he ever read, and peruse with the deepest sympathy for losses and troubles in which he himself had shared. To this list of the departed was soon after added his kind and valued friend Sir William Knighton, to whom, as he loved to say, "he owed such a debt of gratitude and obligation." It must have been with a feeling of melancholy that Wilkie reflected, as he advanced in years and honours, how many were gone for whose sakes he might have chiefly valued them, and in intercourse with whom he would have desired to wear away his own declining age. He was much gratified shortly after with a proof of the wide popularity of his greatest departed friend, on occasion of a visit paid at Greenwich to Sir Thomas Hardy; "Nelson's Hardy," as he may be called—he "happened to go through several of the wards of the hospital, and into the men's library, where they observe, that the only books the old sailors can be brought to read are the novels of Sir Walter Scott." "This" he says, "is genius."

Wilkie now removed to a larger house at Kensington, with "size and space for anything," as he describes it—and the last he ever occupied. The small size and minute finish of his earlier productions, were exchanged for a larger canvass, and a bolder brush, and he seems to have rejoiced in the acquisition of a large and comfortable painting-room. His subjects were now very exceedingly varied; portraits in different styles; historical subjects; such as "Mary Queen of Scots, escaping from Lochleven;" "The Empress Josephine and the Fortuneteller;" and last, and still the best, "The Cotter's Saturday Night," a beautiful realization of the truly national verses of his fellow-countryman Burns. This picture was painted for Mr. Moon, the publisher, to whose liberal spirit of enterprise the public are indebted for the production of the best engravings of modern times, which will hand down to posterity, even should the originals themselves be destroyed, the works of Landseer. Eastlake, and other of our first painters, as well as the later ones of our immortal Wilkie.

The world rolled on in its shifting course, and there was change in the high places of the land, as well as among the friends and connexions of the painter. William the Fourth died, and a queen succeeded, "one young and lovely, in whose looks was the promise of a long reign, and in her firmness of mind the promise of a prosperous one." Sir David received again the renewal of his appointment of Painter in Ordinary; and with it the immediate patronage of Her Majesty, who was pleased to command him to execute a picture of her "First Council," a work of no small importance, but accompanied with great difficulties, both professional and politic:—the adjustment of precedence is more awkward to the painter, perplexed with the justling claims of personal vanity and pictorial composition, than to the lord chamberlain himself:—some whom Wilkie would have desired in profile, were anxious to be exhibited in full face; " some, who were in the rear desired to be in the van;" and others whose fine looks, rather than fine intellect, pushed them into favour, were solicitous about their complexions, and, heedless of tone and sentiment, called out, like the expiring lady in Pope, for a little more red." Such are the vexations and perplexities of the fashionable painter. Wilkie surmounted them as well as he was able; and has handed down to posterity many of the great names of our stirring age, which history will record and judge—a Wellington, a Peel, a Russell, a Grey, a Palmerston, and others of minor mark. Of our beloved Queen he gives in one of his letters a verbal portraiture so happy as to equal that of his pencil—an estimate, it must be remembered, of a youthful sovereign, untried as yet by the perilous possession of power, but whose early promise time has so nobly confirmed. His words are beautiful:—" The regal power in so lovely a form is perfectly new to us; it seems sent to charm the disaffected by presenting a settled government under the most engaging aspect. Her majesty is an elegant person; seems to lose nothing of her authority, either by her youth or delicacy; is approached with the same awe and obeyed with the same promptitude, as the most commanding of her predecessors. *She has all the buoyancy and singleness of heart of youth*, with *a wisdom and decision far beyond her years*." With his own reception he was delighted, observing that " Her Majesty has been most gracious, appearing to recognize me as an early friend."

In 1838, he made another tour into Scotland, to see the hall where John Knox first administered the sacrament; of which incident he was preparing materials for a picture. He embraced this opportunity of paying a visit to the "land of Burns"—saw the "Twa brigs" of Ayr; drank whisky with the old man who keeps the cottage where the poet died; went to Kirk Allowa', the deserted church, with the old bridge over the dark sullen Doon, with its wildly wooded and romantic braes, the famed localities of Tam o'Shanter. How much is it to be regretted, after all, that Wilkie, instead of having his talents drawn aside into a more showy and lucrative walk of art, had not been enabled by a more judicious patronage to throw all his great powers into a class of works, principally Scottish—illustrative of her national peculiarities, of the works of her poets, and of some of the more suitable scenes from her history. Here we must not omit to notice two of the latter. The first of these is his " John Knox preaching in St. Andrews;" embodying one of the most stirring scenes that brought on the Reformation of religion in Scotland. This powerful picture, a commission from Sir Robert Peel, is well known to the public by the masterly engraving of it by Doo, published by Mr. Moon. The painter has introduced among the assembled congregation most of the leading characters of the time, both Catholics and Reformers: the former, galled by the furious invectives of the impassioned preacher, seem ready to burst forth into open violence; but are restrained by the latter, who welcome the ardent and fearless exposure of the abuses of the church, which, urged by the eloquence of Knox, they were incited to remedy, by carrying out the suppression of the monasteries, by the destruction of images, saints, pictures, and other and more sweeping measures of reform. The vehemence of the preacher, and the suppressed passions of his audience, are finely conceived and executed, and of that depth and power of tone, and rich impasted colouring, so different from the comparatively thin and metallic style of his earlier productions, it may be regarded as, perhaps, his best specimen; indeed, the original picture would bear its place, and lose nothing as regards effect, in the midst of a collection of the works of Correggio and Rembrandt.

The picture of "Knox administering the Sacrament at Calder House," of which we here present an engraving, was projected by the painter as at once a companion, contrast, and sequel to the "Preaching" of the great reformer, of which the engraving promised to be highly popular; and, as in the case of this latter work, great local research was employed, in order to bring together the prominent personages of the time, so as to give it a positive historical value. His letters contain numerous queries proposed to parties who could best assist him in his object; yet he appears to have been able to obtain but very scanty information respecting Calder House—the ancient mansion where Knox was a visitor,—or the members of the family, though he suggested the ransacking of the "old chest" for something which would throw light on the contemporary history of the first Lord Torphichen. He asked the Dowager Lady Torphichen whether Sir James Sandilands, Knight of St. John, &c., and the first lord, could ever have been married; and if so, who was his lady and her family. "Any light on this," he says, "would help me in the visitors present—*gentle and simple* —as stated, and in the personages who would be chief partners in the holy commemoration." To those who are apt to regard a picture as a work of pure fancy, these circumstances may serve to show the time and difficulty required to arrange and group the multifarious and often discordant details collected by antiquarian diligence. As an instance, he says, "The hall I am obliged to restore to what will recall an ancient hall of that period; the chimney I ornament, and must try to renew the carved screen which you say divided the room in old times from the entrance. I also put in the Lord and Lady Lorn, the Regent Murray; perhaps, also, Morton and the aged Earl of Argyle. I also wish to introduce in a prominent place the knight of St. John, (Sir James Sandilands,) and, whether right or wrong, *in armou*r." A large wine-cooler is also made prominent; and, as suggested by Dr. Sommers's account of the parish, a Calder witch is to be placed conspicuous. "This," he observes, "is a mixture, but it is of that kind of compound that goes to the formation of what we call a picture." So far as its very imperfect state will allow us to judge, this composition would even have surpassed the "Knox Preaching." There is grandeur and unity of expression, a solemn and reverential feeling, about the central group, relieving in a fine dusky tone from the broad white sacramental cloth, which is extremely fine. The grave and somewhat stern figure of Knox is exquisitely relieved by the grace of the female who hands him the consecrated wine; and the intermingling of armour, the corslet of Sir James Sandilands, and the morion reverentially doffed by the noble figure on the left of Knox, besides being picturesque variations of the costume, call up the associations of an age when men were called upon to *fight* for their creed, and something of the harshness of the feudal warrior yet lingered among the professors of a purified and humbling faith—traits subtly mingled by the skill of the painter. The figure of the mother and child is among the most beautiful of Wilkie's creations; and it must be admitted by those who in general prefer his earlier productions, that he has here fully equalled them in a more serious walk. The figure of the aged nobleman supported on cushions, whose head is a fine study, and the children, who appear full of the premature seriousness of an all-pervading religious excitement, as well as the other foreground groups, are broadly and nobly done. Wilkie proposed to make one of the "Calder witches" conspicuous; but, unless the sinister face to the left of Knox be intended to represent one of these singular beings, we cannot make out any one. This unfinished picture was acquired, after Wilkie's death, at the public auction of his works, by the Royal Scottish Academy, for one hundred and eighty-nine pounds; and perhaps, as Mr. Cunningham observes, "no portion of their funds was ever better spent in the purchase of a work of art."

The exhibition of 1839 was distinguished by the fine picture of "Sir David Baird discovering the body of Sultaun Tippoo Saib after storming Seringapatam." "The scene of this Eastern drama," says Mr. Cunningham, "is laid in the gateway of the inner fort of Seringapatam: the principal persons are Tippoo Saib, the chiefs of his army, his son, and his household, and his conqueror, Sir David Baird, with the soldiers whom he led to the assault.

The last journey of Wilkie to his native land was in the August of 1839. He went through the lakes of Cumberland, visited Wordsworth and his family, and called on Southey. After crossing the border, and following the sweet sylvan streams of the Ettrick and the Tweed, so full of the memories of pleasant holidays passed there with Hogg and his departed friend Sir Walter Scott, whose deserted mansion and favourite plantations of Abbotsford awakened many painful recollections, he reached Edinburgh, the scene of his first anxious labours and successful attempts. His contemporaries gathered around him: his friend Allan brought together at a large party a congenial circle of his friends and admirers. For the last time he revisited his birth-place, where not one of his family remained. New comers had occupied the old manse: they received him warmly. In a letter to his brother, he observes, "I saw our father's monument; it is very well lighted, and seems to fit and greatly adorn the place." How little could he have anticipated that his own career was so near its close, or that the burial-place he would himself have chosen was to be exchanged for the lonely ocean!

For we now approach the closing scenes of the life of Wilkie. Somewhat suddenly in 1840 he left London, in company with Mr. Woodburn, to perform a pilgrimage to the Holy Land. Various rumours were afloat as to the causes of this expedition, but the principal inducements to undertake so long and perilous a journey appear to have been the indulgence of a pious wish, and the confident hope of originating a new style of art. The early impressions gathered in the serious household of Cults had not been obliterated by long intercourse with the world: the current of religious feeling run deep, though often concealed; the enthusiasm of art had but refined and elevated it. Wilkie was well aware that Christianity had inspired the greatest masters of art in Italy and Spain, and that their most wonderful works are those which embody its histories and traditions. Without ever visiting the sacred soil of Palestine, unacquainted with its local scenery, or the races that tenant it, with their costume and manner of life, Raffaele, Michael Angelo, and the Italian masters had drawn the materials of their compositions from what lay around them in the land where they laboured; and more modern painters had been compelled to invent conventional and fanciful attributes and costumes for the different characters of sacred history. The idea of Wilkie, therefore, was a happy one, of seeking among the very scenes of the Bible for local traits and characteristics that would impart to ideal compositions a truth and value over and above their other merits as works of art, of reproducing, from the actual character, costume, and scenery, less varied in the lapse of two thousand years than elsewhere upon the world's surface, the very personages of sacred writ, as well as the scenes in which they lived and moved. Should he succeed in his attempt, he would lead the way, with a great increase of personal reputation, in establishing a new and important school of art. The same idea appears to have occurred to the eminent French painter, Horace Vernet, who also visited the Holy Land, though he has confined the adaptation of his materials entirely, we believe, to scenes of the patriarchal time, in which he has introduced with admirable truth and effect, the Arab manners and costumes, which have probably remained unchanged since that remote era.

Wilkie took a deep interest in everything relating to Palestine. At that time was exhibiting the admirable panorama of Jerusalem, by Mr. Catherwood; and that gentleman has assured the writer that Wilkie was often in the habit of coming there for the purpose of seeking information on a subject to which he seemed enthusiastically devoted.

His route was through the Netherlands, where he again visited all the principal collections. His impressions are thus summed up:—"One feels wearied with the perfections of the minor Dutch paintings, and finds relief in contemplating even the imperfect sketches and incomplete thoughts of those great Italians. My friend Woodburn used to say when we were in Italy, that collectors begin with the Dutch pictures, but *end* with Italian." At Amsterdam the house of "the uncouth, but mighty Rembrandt," as he finely terms him, and of whom he was so ardent an admirer, disappointed his expectations and wounded his professional pride. "It seems," he observes, "a most unsuitable residence for this great master, leaving still the mystery unravelled of how he was esteemed and rewarded, and in what station he lived. His house will in its appearance and dimensions bear no comparison with the house of Titian in Venice, the Casa Buonarotti in Florence, or the mansion of Rubens at Antwerp." And in another letter he consoles himself with the conclusion, "that, like the shell which encloses the caterpillar, it was only a temporary abode for the winged genius to whom art owes so much of its brilliancy." Of Cuyp he was reminded by the sight of Nymegen, and all the circumstances of trees, houses, and cattle of the surrounding country.

But nature as well as art conspired to the enjoyment of his journey. He next pursued his way through the "glorious Gothic scenes" of the "castellated Rhine," as Byron calls them. "Here," as he observes, "the wood in raft and the steam-boat meet, the earliest and the latest invention in seamanship. We have met with several: the logs of wood seem curiously attached to make a body of great length, as well as sufficient width; about six or eight people are maintained in the service of conducting it, with a small boat in attendance, and a sort of hut of deals for their occasional dwelling. At the stern is a paddle, or rudder, and at the head another paddle, which all the hands we saw were working to direct the raft in the proper channel." He passed through the fine old Gothic city of Nuremburg, abounding with specimens of German art, and made a pilgrimage to the house of Albert Durer, with some of whose works he was greatly struck, and even reminded of the high excellencies of Fra Bartolomeo.

At the capital of Bavaria, which he had visited some fourteen years before, he was astonished at the great revival in art wrought by the energy of the King of Bavaria. New streets and palaces had sprung up, in the architecture of Rome and Florence; churches, decorated with magnificent frescos, statues, and stained glass, to execute which had called forth a host of talented artists, who laboured with a successful energy and enthusiasm proportioned to the munificence and taste of their patron. With all this Wilkie was delighted, though he could not go so far as the German artists in their devotion to the simplicity of the early Italian school. In a letter to Sir Robert Peel, he expresses his doubts whether such a style would suit the taste of the English public, and rejoices in the hope that his own experiment might prove more successful.

In another letter he gives a judicious estimate of the modern German school:—" In your visit to Italy you will ·be frequently struck, as you will be in every quarter reminded of it, by the works of the period of the early growth of the art. These, with the greatness afterwards attained, have somewhat the connexion of cause and effect. The German students, with the labours of one of whom you have interested me, have founded their process of study upon this—*that by the study of the same materials as Raphael they might arrive at the same excellence.* This, though in their hands carried to excess, with a kind of heraldic minuteness and detail, bordering too much upon Albert Durer, is yet a more reasonable system than that of Mengs and David, who, with an aim the converse of Bernini in reducing marble to the picturesque, have imposed upon painting the feeling and restraints of ancient sculpture. Still, in the works of these Germans, which I admire extremely, there is too much left out and dispensed with for qualities long left behind in the march of invention. *The world that has once seen the grandeur of Michael Angelo and the breadth of Rembrandt*, is incapable of being excited by early simplicity; it is only as a *part of a study, and not as a whole*, that it is valuable; and could their system serve us, which I think it may, as the Border minstrelsy did Sir Walter Scott, it would be to any student a most admirable groundwork for a new style of art."

By way of the Danube he proceeded to Constantinople, profoundly struck, as is every one to whom the spectacle is presented for the first time, with the marvellous novelty of everything oriental. Some of his notes of the voyage are exceedingly interesting.

"Till we left Vienna," he observes, "works of art were our chief pursuit, and a most luxurious treat we had of the wonders of former times in the German capitals: here we neither see nor hear of pictures; but, in exchange, we at every turn contemplate the sort of life and nature which has scarcely yet been the subject of art. The dresses we see are still European, but verging strongly on the Turkish or Asiatic; the jacket becomes short, the trowsers more ample, and hat more turban-like." . . . . . .

"The Turks on board are civil and silent; the character and dresses are the most splendid to be imagined. This, of course, is felt as *new ground*—as *new life*—and as a subject-matter every hour of the day for the pen and pencil. The first night we anchored at the Turkish town of Widdin; and, when sitting at tea and coffee in our cabin, were told to listen to the voice of a man on the minaret of a mosque hard by, who was busy in calling the faithful to prayers. It was a sort of chant, sometimes fine, but not very musical; it was continued—then ceased; and, in the interval, we heard a more discordant voice on a further minaret, repeating the same religious call to the surrounding Moslems. As the night was dark, the weather fine and still, and the mosque lighted, it was a novel and impressive scene. . . . .

"I can remember my first impression when, landing at Dieppe, I first saw France; and when, in passing the Bidassoa, first saw Spain; but at Rustchuk, where we landed on the first of October, the wonder of the *first sight* of the first town, city, or village I have seen of the *Moslem* empire has far exceeded either."

The Byzantine capital fairly carried him away with its picturesque singularity. "So uncouth, unexpected, and strange," he says, "was every object, in the first week of our arrival, that I could not help exclaiming to my English companions, what Dandie Dinmont said on his first view of Pleydel in the chair of High Jinks, 'Deil the like o' this I ever saw before.'" Among such bewildering novelties, neither the pencil nor the pen of Wilkie were idle: he filled his sketchbook with a great number of scenes, incidents, and portraits, many of which have been since lithographed and published, and his letters to his friends are more than usually lively and amusing. It was a time of stirring excitement at the Turkish capital, the decree of expulsion from Syria had gone forth against the old lion of Egypt, and the combined English fleet had sailed for the coast and the famous stronghold of St. John of Acre, the key of the country, and which the Pacha had fortified at a vast expense, was reduced in a few hours by the thundering broadsides from our wooden walls. Constantinople was rejoicing, the English were in a state of exultation, and Wilkie and Woodburn gave a feast on the occasion to all their hospitable friends.

The moment was well chosen to obtain sittings of the Sultan, who was in the highest degree excited with the favourable turn given to his affairs by the aid of England, and desirous that his portrait should be presented to the queen of his victorious allies. Wilkie accomplished this work to the great satisfaction of all parties, and forwarded the picture for her Majesty's gracious acceptance. At the last sitting the Sultan presented him with a splendid snuff-box of gold. Soon after, he left Constantinople for Smyrna, taking leave of the ambassador, Lord Ponsonby, who had honoured him with great attentions, of the consul, Mr. Cartwright, of well-known hospitality, and other friends who had contributed to render his stay agreeable in a city not famed for the cordiality of its society. Shortly before his departure, Wilkie remembered that he was entering his fifty-sixth year, and rejoiced with thankfulness that his health was yet so good; he knew not how deeply it was undermined, and how the indulgence of his wish to visit the scenes of sacred story was to become the cause of its rapid and fatal decline. He soon reached the gay and hospitable city of Smyrna—still more Asiatic than Constantinople—admired for the first time the poetic and picturesque appearance of the trains of camels, recalling the weary journey over the arid hill and sandy wilderness; fell in with a venerable company of Israelitish pilgrims, which awakened all his artistic enthusiasm, and of which he gives a very graphic verbal picture; and, at the same time, points out the difficulty that here seems first to have struck him, of adapting existing circumstances and habits to representations of Scriptural events.

"I observed about the Bazaar a number of persons of remarkable appearance. These were grave and elderly individuals in robes and long beards, belonging to the scattered remnant of Israel, who came from the distant parts of Germany and Poland on their way to the land of their forefathers, and who, we were told, were to be our fellow-passengers: they return from the land of strangers to their ancient home, and, like their ancestors, from bondage and captivity, and to the same Land of Promise which in happier times was the possession and portion of the chosen race; and we cannot help being struck with the feeling of attachment which, under many circumstances of privation, makes so distant a country, and a glory departed, so eager an object of contemplation. The question then is, whether an interest, both with Jew and Gentile, so deep-rooted and so universal, may not be helped by the faculties of art being pressed into the service, and try, from localities now existing, to revive indeed the impression of those events that have in so lively a manner been handed down to us from former ages. . . . Many of the localities disappoint, and there are multitudes of habits and appearances which these Asiatic countries afford, that with the same taste and discretion must be subdued. It would require a good deal of reasoning to *reconcile this sort of contradiction*. . . . It is not the actual custom that we see that will help us; but a change must be made, not only to suit our previous ideas, *but to remove a sacred and historical subject to a former time*; and it is by contrasting the present appearance, to consider what *will* serve, and what will *not* serve, that this journey has been undertaken." Such was the constant aim of Wilkie during this journey; and it is evident that the excitement of scenes and incidents so novel, and to adapt which to his purpose he viewed moreover with an intensity of study far greater than that required by the mere copyist, must have told seriously upon his system, especially in a climate which is not favourable for such constant and unremitting exertion, at least to natives of the colder north.

Leaving Smyrna, of which he gives the same record as does almost every traveller, however undistinguished, that "he had been most kindly and hospitably entertained," he went on board the steamer, on the deck of which was a most promiscuous assemblage—men, women, and children; many from the north, yet of strong Hebrew caste; many again Asiatic, perhaps also pilgrims, and if so, on the way to Mecca. The course he was now following was one of the highest historical and Biblical interest. As the vessel tracked the intricacies of the Greek Islands, "where Phœbus rose, and Delos sprung"—he recalled to memory the names of ancient heroes, philosophers, or poets—he noticed "the lonely island or rock of Patmos, where St. John in exile wrote the Revelations;" while on the left were Samos, and Miletus, where, in idea, he saw Paul taking leave of the elders of the church. He was on the very course of the great Apostle of the Gentiles, as described with such fidelity in the "Acts." Like him, passing the Straits of Cos, he reached Rhodes, where he had the opportunity of spending a few hours in the examination of its chivalrous remains; "greatly struck with the triple walls and fosses, built with more than European strength; streets clean, and well paved; strong stone-built houses, with many knights' coats of arms on the walls, the whole bearing a strong contrast to any city we have seen since we entered the confines of Turkey.. He was shown a small harbour, at the entrance of which, tradition says, close to a fort, was placed the famous Colossus upon pedestals approaching one another; it has every appearance of being its station, where, each foot being fixed upon opposite sides of the harbour, several of the small ships would sail in and out between the separated legs of the figure. This remarkable statue, so renowned among the ancients, has been so long destroyed, that there is no tradition of any vestige being preserved within the range of modern times."

He was now drawing nigh to the cherished object of so much professional and pious anticipation. At half-past six, on the 8th of February, he was awoke by the cry of

Land!" The sun was just rising behind the long snowy range of Lebanon, with its feet in the blue waters of the Mediterranean, and sustaining on its breast innumerable villages and convents. His sensations were indescribable. On deck all was stir and preparation: the various aged persons of the chosen people were decorating themselves with the sacerdotal robes of the sacred office, and, though tranquil, were yet apparently deeply moved. Some with the Bible in hand, with a black strap twisted round their naked left arm, and with a small ark or tabernacle tied round the brow, were, with an oscillating movement of the head, repeating some appropriate prayer or thanksgiving upon the near accomplishment of the object of the voyage. Their appearance, though they were meanly dressed, was imposing in the extreme. He observed that they looked not exactly in the direction of Lebanon, to which the head and course of the ship was pointed, but their faces were turned far along the coast of Sidon and Tyre to the right, leaving little doubt, that, in memory of the consecration of Solomon upon the building of the Temple, they were, upon the present, as upon so many other occasions, bending their hopes and desires upon the holy hill of Zion.

The impression of strangeness and novelty that took such hold of Wilkie at Constantinople, was still more powerful as he set foot on the quay of Beyrout. Here for the first time he came in contact with the Arab races, and felt himself on Biblical ground; and the characteristics of the people and the land fell in at once with his preconceived ideas of what should constitute the element of a school of authentic Christian art. Here were the very materials he wished for, the very faces and costumes he had long dreamed of; and he set himself to work in earnest to fill his portfolios with sketches that he ere long hoped to turn to important account.

At Beyrout he was detained twelve days, waiting for an opportunity to Jaffa; at length he obtained a passage in a small brig. At this most ancient of seaports, he was on the threshold of Judea, and on the road to Jerusalem. He now revelled in the picturesque, such as his soul loved; his wandering caravan with its Arab escort, toiling across the arid plain, or threading the lonely defiles; his noonday halt at the well amid trains of camels and flocks of sheep, brought up before him at every step images of that unchanged ancient life he had come to study. Through the rocky hill region he continued to ascend, till he reached the high wild country, where stands in its loneliness and decay the awful capital of Judea. Of the first view of Jerusalem travellers have given very different descriptions, varying according to the mood, more or less enthusiastic, in which they have drawn nigh to her gates. The view on this side is not so remarkable as on others; yet Wilkie was struck beyond everything with the enduring look of the walls and towers, and his first impression of the Holy City was powerful and abiding.

And when he came to enter those sacred walls, he found his anticipations more than realized. In the aspect of the streets, the style of the buildings, the ground, irregular with the heaped ruins and wrecks of ages, the hoary vestiges of Jewish or Roman date, he saw everywhere the rich and appropriate material for the backgrounds, while the antique simplicity of Arab costume, and the more primitive usages of the people, gave him a new idea of what should be the style of scriptural compositions. True, everything was not exactly identical with the Jewish period; much there was that in the revolutions of ages had changed in character and costume; yet withal sufficient remained to afford scope for authentic and appropriate materials. But these changes had principally affected the city itself; and when the enthusiastic and pious painter, who could not refrain from internally repeating a Psalm as he stood over the tomb of David on Mount Zion, went forth with his only hand-book—the Bible—to the eternal hills and valleys around, unaltered in features, though saddened and more touching in aspect than in the time of Jerusalem's glory, he found the whole scene of the evangelic history unrolled before him in vivid distinctness, and the impression was, to use his own expression, "beyond what can be again felt in any other place in the world;" for here he beheld "the *originals*, in conjunction with the great events that have there occurred. "Here," he remarks, "from the arrival of Jesus Christ by the very path where he beheld the city and wept over it, to the time of the Passover, the Crucifixion, and the Resurrection, every turn and resting-place can be traced by the pilgrim." Wilkie delighted above all things to wander about the Mount of Olives, and look down from its mysterious summit on the outspread city: he regrets that Roberts did not do more, and with a more scriptural feeling; and longs for Turner to invest the scene with the poetic glory that he casts over his compositions; he loved, too, the little sequestered nook of Bethany, which recalled to him "Tivoli and Aricia," hung on the sterile mountain's side among its patch of groves.

Wilkie visited repeatedly the Holy Sepulchre, about the identity of which he was not troubled with any scruples, though disgusted with the palpable absurdity of many monkish inventions, and little edified, picturesque as might be the mingled assortment of monks, "white, black, and grey, with all their trumpery," with their fierce disputes and squabbles for precedency in the holy places. The wailing of the Jews beneath the walls of the ancient Temple profoundly impressed him. He went forth too into the environs, to Bethlehem and the Dead Sea; gives a graphic account of the extraordinary site of the Convent of Santa Saba; made some barometrical experiments on the waters of the accursed lake; and picturesquely describes his nocturnal bivouac at the Fountain of Elisha, near Jericho. Of the old and well-known Sheik who was his guide on this occasion he has left one of his most capital sketches, inimitable for its truth of portraiture and striking Arab character. To his sister Helen, and his friends Sir Robert Peel, Professor Buckland, and brother Academicians, Collins and Philips, his letters are most interesting, and express great enthusiasm about the new walk of art of which he hoped to prove the founder.

Some most interesting notices of the closing scenes of Wilkie's life are brought before us in the following paper, obligingly furnished by W. T. Young, Esq., at that time Consul in the Holy City, to whose kind attentions and hospitality so many have been indebted.

"12th *June*, 1847.

"DEAR SIR,

"As you have asked me to give you any recollections I may have retained of the late Sir David Wilkie's visit to Jerusalem, I have referred to my notes and letters written at that period, which have refreshed my memory, and carried me back to many of the incidents and subjects of our intercourse together, which at the time, made a lively impression on me.

"In a letter which I wrote from Beirout on the 6th February, 1841, I find I mention Sir David's arrival in Syria by the steam-packet from Smyrna, but I had not then had the pleasure of meeting him. The country was at that time in a very unsettled state, and the effects of the war were only very gradually subsiding—indeed, Palestine was actually in a state of disruption, from the vicinity of Ibrahim Pacha's retreating armies.

"By a letter which I wrote to England on the 10th February, I notice Sir David and his friend Mr. W.——— having done us the honour to call upon us at our humble lodgings in gardens near to Beirout:—I say, 'Sir David Wilkie came down by the last Austrian steamer from Smyrna. I shall have great pleasure in doing all in my power to facilitate his object, which he stated to be, to study the habits and customs of the people, and to compare them, and also the features of the country, with the descriptions given in Scripture. He talks of making some little stay at Jerusalem. He tells us that he had the honour of painting the picture of the Sultan, who presented him with a valuable snuff-box, set in diamonds.'

"Sir David and his friend asked us a great many questions as to what preparations were requisite for the journey. We regretted our inability to wait a few days that we might have the pleasure of their company through the country, and of introducing them to the adventures of Syrian travel. I felt that such a 'compagnon de voyage' as Sir David Wilkie would give a new colour and fresh interest to many of the localities we should pass through or rest at for the night. I discovered from his conversation that he was full of enthusiasm; and though he complained of not having been very well, yet his heart was with him in his work, and evidently overflowing with the pleasing visions of what was before him.

"He spoke as a true pilgrim longing for a realization of the dreams of his youth. It was delightful to witness the joy of his anticipations, which I felt would be more than realized. He told me that a journey to the Holy Land had been with him through life an object which he never abandoned the idea of being at one time or another able to accomplish;

and well I remember the expression of his countenance, when, on taking leave of us after his first visit, he suddenly seemed to feel that he was actually standing as it were on the very threshold of his long-hoped-for wishes.

"We reached Jerusalem on the 24th February; but I believe it was not until a few days later, that Sir David and his friend arrived. Here our acquaintance was renewed; and I had the gratification of having it in my power to place at their disposal a small house in the south-west corner of the city, which we had formerly ourselves inhabited, containing, for Jerusalem, two very tolerable rooms, and where I was sure Sir David might feel himself at home and quite at his ease, in case he should wish to be visited by any of the people of the country.

"We had the advantage of seeing a good deal of our amiable and distinguished countryman; and I was continually struck with the lively gratification which he derived in studying his art amid so many objects on which his mind had evidently long been dwelling 'at a distance,' as he himself expressed it.

"It might be supposed, judging from the style of painting by which he had mainly become a favourite in England, that Sir David Wilkie had no mind for the higher, and I may say the highest, field of labour in the art, viz: that of Sacred Historical Painting. It was far otherwise, for I believe his heart was already full of grand feelings, and his mind seemed only to have wanted the opportunity to lay hold of the living spark which early Scripture reading had let drop into his soul, to conceive representations worthy of the best times of the art. A new world in his vocation seemed to be opened before him, and he would exclaim, 'Ah, if the Italian masters had but visited Palestine, what treasures of scene and attitude and costume might not have been added by them to the noble legacies they have left us in drawing and colour!'

"It is difficult for me to find language in which to convey to you the absorbed feelings with which he seemed to be penetrated, when talking over of an evening some of the views and combinations he had fallen in with during the day. He was most indefatigable and laborious in pursuing his object; but it appeared to me—excuse me for presuming to give an opinion on a subject on which I am, of course, so little acquainted—as though there was a struggle going on within him to dislodge something of his old style, in order to give place to those new materials which were now crowding for admittance.

"I placed a Janissary at his disposal, and begged of him not to venture out sketching without taking him with him; for the country was as yet not very settled under its new government, and I feared lest he should meet with any obstruction or unpleasant occurrence to neutralize his zeal and pleasure.

"He was much occupied in studying his Bible, to the reading of which I believe it was his custom to devote the chief portion of his evenings. While walking out with him, Scripture subjects were ever before him, and he would speak with delight when we came across any view or group of people that presented to his mind a picture from Holy Writ. I had frequently the pleasure of this intercourse with him; and sometimes I would miss him from my side, when, on looking back, I found he had come to a sudden stop before some object of new effect that had fallen under his inquiring eye.

"I remember this occurring one day when we were passing the street of the corn-market together, where there are fine remains of the substructions of the Hospital of St. John: he had spied out beneath one of these mysterious and artificial caverns, a motley group of Fellahs, together with their camels and asses, half of them brilliantly illuminated with a sunbeam, and the other half shrouded in the obscurity of an almost nightlike shadow, which was neither light nor darkness.

"As I returned to him, he pointed beneath the arch, and putting his hand above his eyes to throw off the vertical light, exclaimed, 'Wonderful! the patriarchs and their sacks of corn!' We were on our way to the Jews' Place of Wailing. With this sight, peopled as it was with aged Jews bowing down in prayer and sorrow over their fallen glory, he was also much struck, and at once proposed to himself a grand picture in 'Thy children think upon her stones, and it pityeth them to see her in the dust.'

"Thence we proceeded to visit several of the Jewish families at the opening of their sabbath, when their quarter of the city, as well as their dwellings, are seen to the best advantage. I obtained permission from 'Useph Zamiro,' my Hebrew dragoman, who was a remarkably fine specimen of a Rembrandt study, for Sir David to visit him at any time, and draw from the groups which are always to be seen both within and without the crowded courts of the Jewish quarter.

"We also visited together the synagogues and the houses of the chief rabbies. The polite and hospitable reception which we met with from these venerable fathers of their people pleased Sir David amazingly, who was himself always so amiable that it was a pleasure to be his ciceroni.

"I was also enabled to induce Abdrachman, the celebrated Sheik of Hebron, to sit to him, as well as some portions of the families of two of our own servants. As these people are in too savage a condition to appreciate the meaning of painting, they are generally too ignorant and suspicious to be induced to allow themselves to be pourtrayed on paper or canvass.

"I well remember how exceedingly he was struck with the first view he had of the 'Ecce Homo' arch. We had been paying a visit to the governor, and had been enjoying the view of the city and Temple area from the top of his house, when, as we descended the steps of the Seraglio, and were about to return home by the 'Via Dolorosa,' he suddenly stopped just as we caught sight of the arch; and when I told him what it was, he retraced his steps, and took up a position at the corner of the street, opposite Pilate's Palace, from which we had just emerged, and commenced dilating upon the

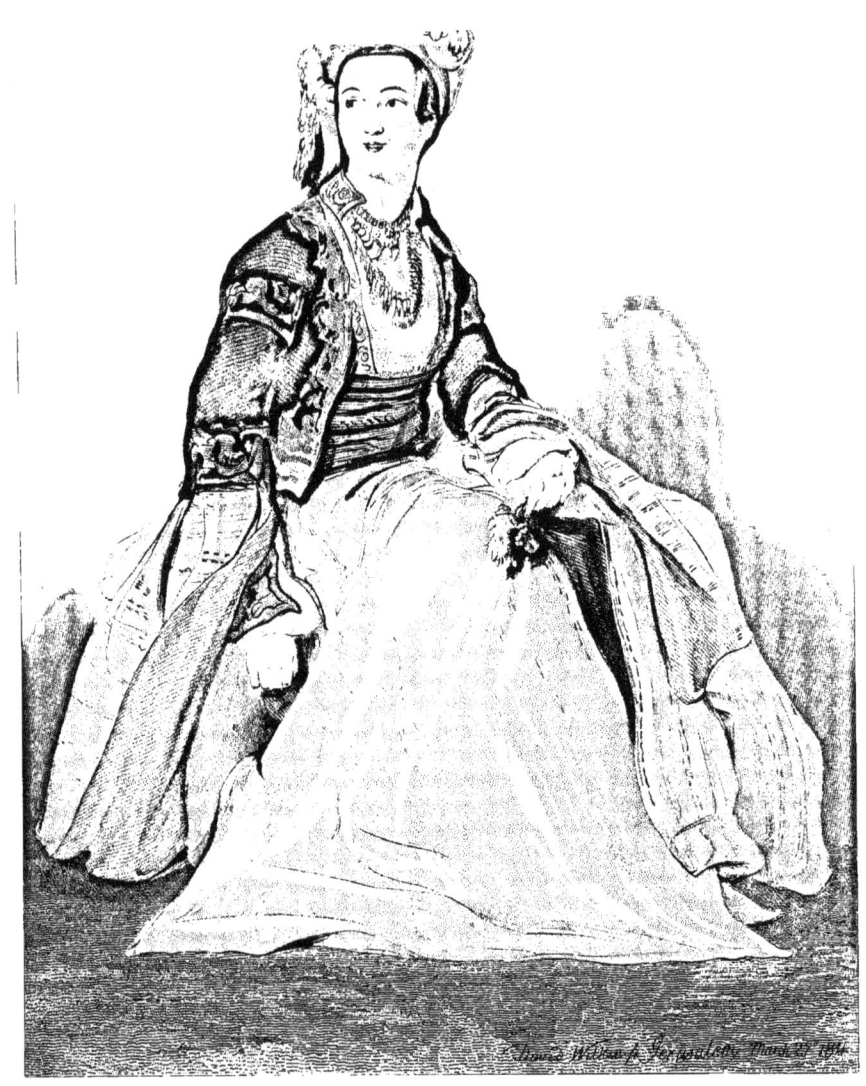

extraordinary impression which the locality, and the effect of a portion of the city seen through the arch, made upon him. He scattered around us the material for a grand picture, and, in a few words, laid out the subject of 'Christ before the Judgment of Pilate.'

"As we ascended the 'Via Dolorosa,' his mind was full of the solemn incidents which this holy ground naturally calls to one's recollection; and his conversation showed how deeply he was impressed with the view which he confessed a painter ought to take of the opportunities afforded him of illustrating scenes of such sacred interest as now everywhere surrounded him. He spoke of the advantage it would be to the young Academician if, in addition to his study of the old masters, he could pass some months in this country. On this subject, as connected with the Royal Academy, I recollect Sir David's having mentioned to me his intention to address a letter to Sir Robert Peel, and to Lord John Russell.

"The pictorial decorations of the new houses of parliament was a subject on which I also heard him speak. He was of opinion that there were many Scripture subjects which would be most appropriate, as serving to record God's dealings with nations, and to remind our legislators of him by whom princes rule and senators are taught wisdom.

"Sir David's sojourn in Jerusalem gave both Mrs. Young and myself the greatest pleasure; and if we were by any means enabled to contribute to his comfort there, we were only doing what it was our duty to do by our country, and what we were more than repaid for doing by the gratification derived from our intercourse with so excellent and amiable a man, whose death, we felt, must not only have proved a personal affliction to all who had the privilege of his acquaintance, but a shock to his profession, and a real national calamity; for it seemed to me from his conversation that he had gathered during his journey through the Holy Land, a mass of most useful materials for future study, which he destined to be devoted to the improvement and welfare of the British School of Scripture Painting.

"Besides the remembrance we shall long retain of Sir David Wilkie's visit to Jerusalem, from the pleasure and improvement we derived from his society, he presented me with a drawing of Mrs. Young, which he suggested should be taken in the native costume of the better class of the Christian inhabitants, that it might not only be a pleasing recollection to himself, of his own visit to the Holy City, but that it might provide a future token of our identity with a country so full of sacred interest.

"With this drawing of Mrs. Young, I may say, closed, as far as Palestine is concerned, the labours of this eminent artist; for an incident occurred which seemed to induce him to hasten his departure, otherwise, had he had but his own inclination to follow, and no duties requiring his presence in England, his disposition was to linger on many days longer, amid scenes which evidently roused within him dreams which had slumbered from the days of his earliest devotion to the arts.

U

"In my letter of the 3rd of April, I say, 'Sir David Wilkie is still here: he talks of leaving in a day or two * * An artist sent here by the Emperor of Austria to paint a picture of Acre, &c., called on me last week. When I went to return his call, I found him breathing his last; he was in perfect health last week, and was going to bring his drawings to show me, as I had been at the siege of Acre: but, poor fellow! the next time I saw him, only three days after, he was stretched out, lying dressed in his uniform ready for burial, with four wax tapers burning by his side. It is said he over-exerted himself the day he left my house, in visiting the various spots of interest, and took cold from exposure to the evening air when very warm. He had an Englishman in his company, and himself spoke English perfectly well. His drawings were beautiful.

"'This sad death, as there is some idea it might be the plague, has rather alarmed Sir David, who is not very well, so he at once began to pack up and prepare for an early departure.'

"On taking leave of us he expressed great regret that his stay in Jerusalem could not have been prolonged, for he quitted it, he said, with feelings of deep regret, at having been obliged to crowd into only hours of study, that which demanded months and even years properly to digest; but he said he found that each day he remained only added to the accumulation of matter which he could do no more than arrange in a very hurried and crude form, but which he hoped would prove most useful to him, when he renewed his studies at home.

"If you think what I have written of the recollections I have of Sir David's visit to Jerusalem will be of interest to the public, pray make such use of them as you may think fit.

"Believe me, dear Sir,

"Yours truly,

"WM. T. YOUNG,

"*Late H. M. Consul in Palestine.*"

The ardent anticipations of the great painter were never destined to be realized, the sands of life were quickly though insensibly running out, his days were almost numbered. The intense heat, of which he sometimes complains, his irregular manner of living, and that unusual mental excitement, often fatal to Eastern travellers, even when robust in health, were secretly undermining his little remaining strength. After leaving the Holy City, he embarked at Jaffa in a small vessel bound for Damietta: a stormy passage, and much tedious delay in this uncomfortable vessel, appear to have considerably hastened the catastrophe. In Egypt, however, he seems to have been in good spirits; and at Damietta was delighted with the first view of the Patriarch of rivers. On reaching Alexandria he was much revived by the comparative comforts and quiet of the hotel; and, at the instance of the Pasha, commenced a portrait of that remarkable man, with whose appearance he was much struck, considering him the finest subject for a picture he had met with in the East.—He writes to his sister in good spirits; tells her of a dinner which he had got up for Waghorn; and directs that his home should be prepared for his reception. In anticipation of a speedy arrival, he embarked on board the Oriental Steamer. The weather was beautiful, and he appears from his last letter to his sister, dated from on board, off Malta, to have enjoyed his passage, and his closing words are, in allusion to his friends, "How glad I shall be to see them all again!" This was on the 26th of May. The conclusion is of startling suddenness. On the 1st of June, as the vessel reached Gibraltar, he was seized with a fatal attack, his mind wandered, he became gradually insensible, and about eleven o'clock expired without a struggle. The commander of the Oriental immediately put back to Gibraltar to ask permission to land the body, but owing to the quarantine regulations, this could not be permitted; and shortly after, and at noon, the vessel was beyond the Straits. The carpenter had prepared a coffin; at half-past eight, in the open Atlantic, the engines were stopped, and the ship paused awhile upon her course, that the funeral rites might be performed. The Rev. James Vaughan, rector of Wroxall, near Bath, read the burial service, and the body of Wilkie was committed to the deep.

When the intelligence of this sudden death reached England, it produced a profound sensation. Wilkie was, beyond any other, the public favourite; his works were felt by all ranks of the people, uncultivated or refined; and among his friends the simplicity and genuineness of his character had rendered him universally beloved. The Royal Academy sent an address of condolence to his brother, Thomas Wilkie, and his sister Helen, signed by 225 artists. A public meeting was called with a view to devise means of showing honour to his memory. It was a time of much political excitement: the Whigs, with their leader, had just been overthrown; Sir Robert Peel was reinstated as head of a Tory administration, and on the very day of his triumph presided at the meeting. And, with a truly generous feeling, which was warmly responded to by the assembly, his defeated rival, Lord John Russell, also attended. On that occasion Sir Robert delivered one of the most graceful and feeling of his speeches:—"I feel it a great honour," said the right honourable Baronet, as it is a great satisfaction to my private feelings, to have been requested to preside at this meeting. I feel, too, altogether relieved from the necessity of pronouncing any studied or elaborate eulogium upon the merits of the late Sir David Wilkie—his loss has been so recent, his name stands so permanently high, the productions of his genius are so familiar, not only to his own countrymen, but to Europe in general—but I am justified in saying to the whole world, that I think it would be out of harmony with his character, unbecoming the simplicity of that character, were I to attempt to pronounce any studied or elaborate eulogium upon it. Gentlemen, I had the honour of accounting Sir David Wilkie as one of my private and intimate friends. I am addressing many here who stood in the same relation to him; who were not only admirers of his genius, but were admitted to the intercourse of his private friendship; and those who stood in that relation to him can sympathize with my feelings of deep regret for the loss which we have sustained. There was something in the simplicity of Sir David Wilkie's character, in the generosity which he showed to every competitor in art, that must have, and that has, endeared him to all who were admitted to familiar intercourse with him."

These feelings were warmly responded to by other speakers. Lord John Russell observed, " I believe there is not one who knew the late Sir David Wilkie, but who is ready and eager to testify to his worth as a man. (Cheers.) Among his near relations he inspired the strongest affections, among his friends he was universally received with the warmest regard and the most profound esteem. (Cheers.) To brother artists of all descriptions he was a friend, a protector, and an assistant. There was nothing in his nature of ill-will, envy, or bitterness to any, be they whom they might." Lord Mahon, in an eloquent speech, in which he touches on his journey with Wilkie in Spain, dwelt upon, " that mild and fine temper, that kind and feeling heart, so meek, and so fearful of offending, yet kindling to warmth whenever it could promote the interests of art, or advance the prospects of a brother painter. Wilkie was not only an extraordinary artist, but a good, a truly good man." No panegyric can surpass this. His love of art and truth was greater than his love of self. Among artists of eminent talent this is but rarely the case, though generally true of the very highest order of mind, both in ancient and in modern times; and among such spirits, Wilkie may worthily take his place and go down to posterity as being endowed with a soul as true and fine as that which shines through his humanizing and immortal productions.

When we take into consideration the different classes of subjects that occupied the genius of Wilkie, in which, though his success might be unequal, he displayed great powers, while in some he was confessedly inimitable, we can hardly refuse the meed of praise bestowed upon him by his friend and biographer Allan Cunningham, that he was "the most original, and vigorous, and varied, of our British painters; the darling artist of the people, learned or illiterate, for he spoke to all degrees of knowledge, and to all varieties of taste."

As the "child is father to the man," so the early impressions and training of the painter were stamped upon his works, and gave to them their distinctive character. Brought up in a pious and regular household, and enjoying the advantages of a liberal education, his humour was chastened by a feeling of reverence for sacred things; a sense of moral propriety and a profound intelligence and insight into human character is to be traced through all his productions. His works have the noble distinction, like the writings of Scott, of being pre-eminently moral, humane, and improving. His subjects are mostly from humble life, like those of Ostade and Teniers; but how widely different in all other respects! In general, we look in vain among the Dutch masters for any pervading moral sentiment, or intelligent

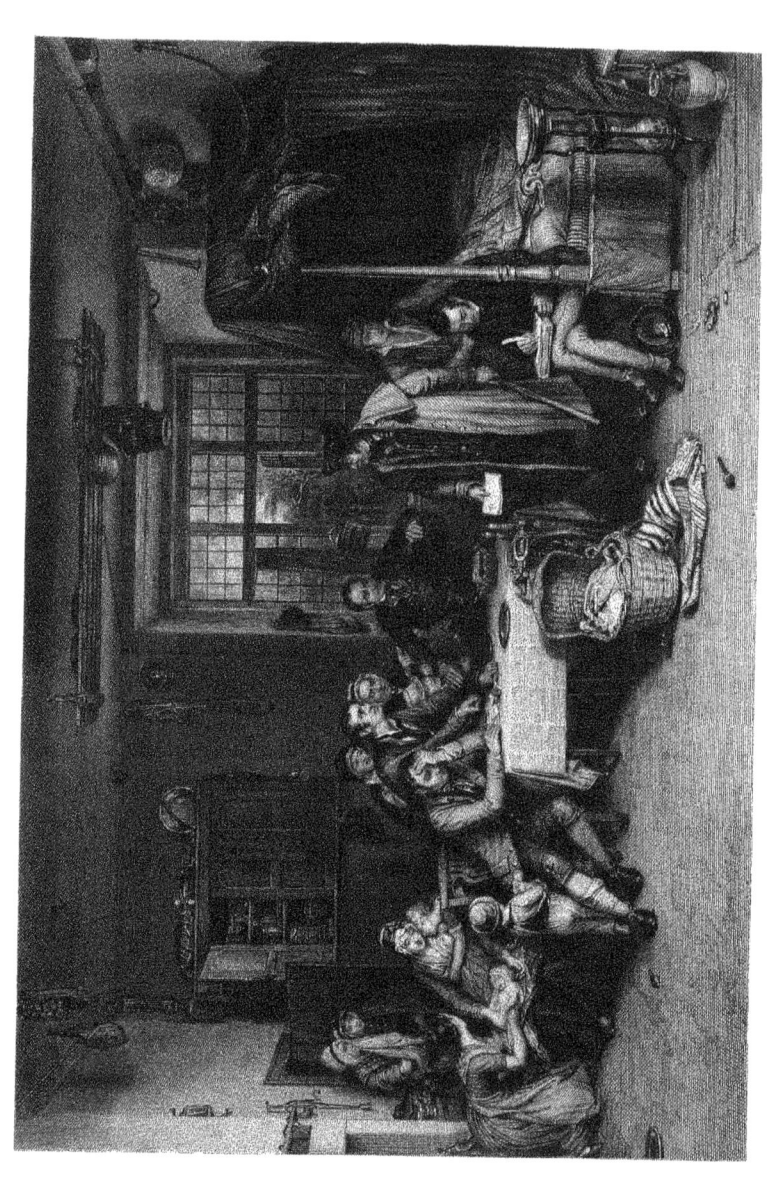

and good-humoured satire; coarse amusements, drinking, and often drunken scenes, abounding with disgusting violations of propriety, are the staple of their school; and the exquisite beauty of tone and execution too often disguises the paucity of invention and the absence of refinement. As suggested in the commencement of this memoir, the characteristics of Wilkie's productions are national; their traits, those of the Scottish peasantry, perhaps at once the most intelligent and thrifty in the world, humorous and serious alike, as Burns, and Scott, and Wilkie have depicted them.

As a specimen of the more pathetic class of his productions, let us take the "Distraining for Rent." This production may be said to have originated in a misadventure of the painter's, when his picture of "The Village Holiday," now in the National Gallery, and which formed a part of the exhibition of his works, was seized for a debt due by some prior tenant of the premises in Pall Mall. This might, indeed, have suggested the subject, but nothing more; the character and expression were the results of long and profound study. "The House," says Mr. Cunningham, "is not without warnings of what is coming: the idle jack, the burnt-out fire, the empty bee-hive, are so many intimations of mismanagement or slackness of industry." Perhaps we may be justified in thinking that distress, rather than want of thrift or economy, has produced the catastrophe; that the poor man before us, sunk in listless moody misery, upon whom falls the desolation of wife and bairns, is the victim of unavailing struggle with misfortune; such, at least, we cannot help thinking that the painter intended to represent him. His fallen countenance and neglected dress denote the stupor of an o'erfraught heart; he is apparently unmoved by the proceedings around, and shrinks from the endearments of his pet child, whom it is now agony to look upon. Meanwhile the work of spoliation proceeds. The lawyer is no less absorbed than the victim, but in a different way: he is quietly and carefully taking his inventory of the forfeited furniture; he has no concern with consequences or with tears, with the homeless or the heart-broken; beyond what it will fetch in hard money, there is no value to his mind in the humble furniture of the cottage, of which, perhaps, every article now about to be wrested from them has to the tenants its little history and associations. He is a purely professional figure, and the painter has known how to contrast his total absence of emotion with the deep and varied feelings that agitate the groups around him. The neighbours and gossips have assembled to cheer and console the afflicted family;—one, busied with the poor mother, offers to take from her lap the smiling infant she seems scarce to have strength to retain, yet is unwilling to part with; a little girl mingles her tears with those of her mother: in the corner is a servant weeping. In the centre of the picture is a group full of indignation at the proceedings:—a man, almost beyond himself, his eyes flashing, his frame swelling with anger, points with clenched fist to the deficient notes on the table, and, carried away with the injustice and cruelty of the affair is apparently threatening violence to the bailiff; a tiny boy also is armed with a stick; while two old matrons are pointing to the odious minister of injustice, and assailing him with their outcries. The bailiff, strong in the law, presents his warrant, and with a stout cudgel seems ready to repel force with force. The excitement is at its height, and the fray ready to begin, but for the mediation of the village cobbler, whose feelings are tempered by prudence, and who, aware of the consequences of opposing the myrmidons of power, is restraining his indignant neighbours from an outbreak which can only aggravate the mischief. The half-rifled bed—the open cupboards—the air of disorder and discomfort cast over the whole, inspire a feeling of desolation, speak of the loss of home, and of the darkening prospects of the ruined family.

Such is the sad story told by the painter with such truth upon his immortal canvass, that as long as sympathy inhabits the human breast, it will never fail to excite the same emotions as those with which it was regarded on the first day of its exhibition. As remarked in the case of " The Blind Fiddler," the sense of *nature* is so exquisite that it hides for a while the consummate *art* by which it is produced; we stand suspended in our feelings, as in a moving drama, and forget that we are looking on a cunning production of the pencil. The silent stupor of despair; the lighter grief that is relieved by tears; infantine simplicity and unconsciousness; righteous indignation at wrong, stirring the frame of the strong man, and agitating even the old and peaceful; the wariness and cautiousness of prudence; the callous insolence of office; and the cold and calculating abstraction of interest—are blended together in this drama of domestic life. Such was Wilkie's true walk in art; and in his powerful exhibition of which he might boast, like Wordsworth,

> " The common growth of mother earth
> Sufficeth me—her tears—her mirth—
> Her humblest mirth and tears.
>
> " These given—what more need I desire ?
> To stir, to soothe, to elevate—
> What nobler marvels than the mind
> May, in life's daily progress, find—
> May find—or there create ?"

In short, this is one of that happy class of productions which arrests the most indifferent, and satisfies the most critical.

The humour of Wilkie—the pervading characteristic of all his best works, is not broad unconstrained, and gross: as Mr. Cunningham observes, " He never committed folly or coarseness in colours;" *discretion* was his controlling duty in all things: He never over-does in his canvass any act he has to perform; all is done with ease and grace; *his laugh is not loud, but the whole man laughs inwardly;* and the same spirit of *subdued* enjoyment runs through all his compositions." In short, it is the "dry humour and sedate glee" of his country. "He could distinguish by a touch of his pencil between the humour which pertained to a heart naturally kind, and that which flowed from a nature sarcastic and

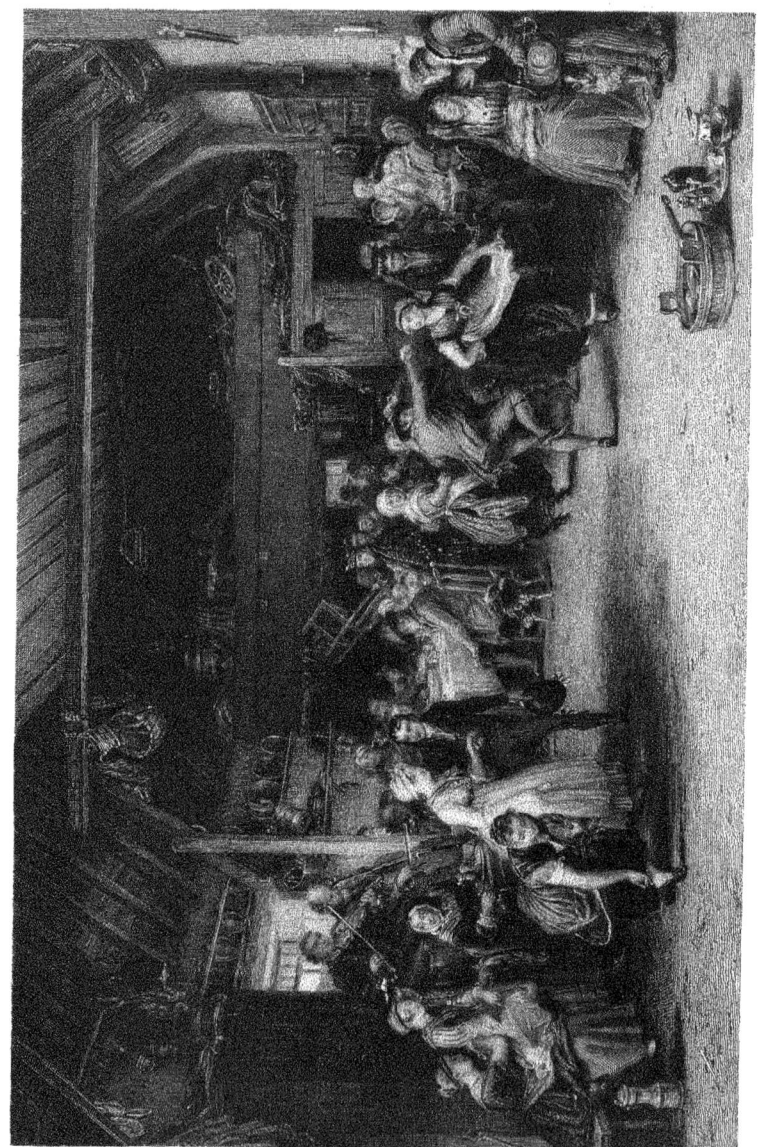

PAINTED BY E. V. W. K. ENG^D BY W. GREATBACH

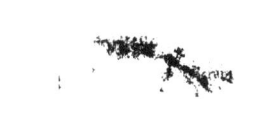

biting. The advice-giving look of the north has found its way into most of his pictures in which manners mingle." If we seek for a subject in which he could thus be "merry and wise" at once, informing his canvass with a depth of hearty rustic enjoyment, with traits of sly humour, but without overflowing into indelicacy, where shall we find one more to the purpose than "The Penny Wedding?"

In Scotland, as in the East, the custom is, that all the guests at a wedding should make their offering—and hence the title of this picture. Among Allan Ramsay's Collection of Songs is a description of the humours of such a scene.

> " Fy, let us a' to the bridal,
> For there will be lilting there,
> For Jock's to be married to Maggy,
> The lass wi' the gowden hair.
> And there will be lang kail and pottage,
> And bannocks of barleymeal,
> And there will be good sawt herring
> To relish a cog of good ale.
> Fy, let us a' to the bridal, &c.
>
> " And there will be lappered milk kebucks,
> And sowens, and farles, and baps,
> With swats and well-scraped paunches,
> And brandy in stoups and in cups:
> And there will be meal-kail and castocks,
> With skink to sup till ye rive,
> And roasts to roast on a brauder
> Of flewks that were taken alive.
>
> " Scrapt haddocks, wilks, dulse, and tangle,
> And a mill of good snishing to prie,
> When, weary with eating and drinking,
> We'll rise up and dance till we die.
> Then fy, let us a' to the bridal,
> For there will be lilting there,
> For Jock's to be married to Maggie,
> The lass wi' the gowden hair."

The table, spread with these, to a Southron, unintelligible delicacies, is surrounded with a number of the guests, many and motley as those in the song; brandy, and other stimulants, in "stoups and in cups," circulating freely, "put life and mettle in their heels;" and under its influence, and that of the indefatigable fiddlers, the dance is beginning to wax full of fun and spirit. The prominent couple is composed of a sort of " Willie of the wanton leg," who is flourishing and snapping his fingers with great energy, and a braw and lovely lassie, who carries it off with a graceful wave of her apron; another and yet merrier couple is behind. The bride, more modest, is being led out by her bridegroom, and other couples are preparing to follow, as the mirth grows infectious. There are two charming side groups: on the left, a lass of sweet sixteen is listening, with a downcast and demure look, to the solicitations of her lover to join in the dance; and, if we mistake not, the prim old lady mother, with her hands folded, is lending an ear, with a smile of satisfaction, to a similar proposal on the part of a gallant old gentleman, who is, perhaps, recalling to her memory the feats of their younger days. In this picture there is less broad fun than in the "Blindman's Buff," but it abounds in beauties of a subtle kind; each group is a separate study, each character almost a portrait, and the picture of Scottish manners and maidens complete, though not quite so "high-kilted," it is said, as was desired by George the Fourth, for whom the picture was painted.

In a broader style, approaching Hogarth, is the rich morceau of "The Clubbists," painted for his friend Leigh Hunt.

This represents a Village Club, at the height of its conviviality, when men drank deeper than is at present fashionable. "There were giants in those days," of whose amazing powers and perseverance, in what Thomson calls "serious drinking," remain many amusing if not edifying stories. The hand of the clock points to one in the morning, yet the principal topers are evidently but just warmed, without being as yet in the least subdued by their potations. The Baillie, in cocked hat and wig, and chairman of the club, is in the heat of a dispute with apparently the laird; the punch, which has served to inflame, if it did not originate, the controversy, is exhausted, and he is handing the vacant bowl to the landlord for replenishment. The latter, roused from the chair in which he has been dozing, reluctantly prepares to execute the commission. The prudent doctor, who has had just enough, is taking out his watch and about to depart while he is yet able. The weaker heads of the company are already overcome; one, armed with a plate and bottle, is about to crash them together; another toothless toper is encouraging the combatants, with the clatter of his stick on the table.

> "Thus, as they swim in mutual swill, the talk,
> Vociferous at once from twenty tongues,
> Reels fast from theme to theme; from horses, hounds,
> To church or mistress, politics or ghost,
> In endless mazes, intricate, perplexed.
> Meantime with sudden interruption, loud,
> Th' impatient catch bursts from the joyous heart;
> That moment touched is every kindred soul;
> And, opening in a full-mouth'd cry of joy,
> The laugh, the slap, the jocund curse go round.
> * * * * *
> As when the tempest, that has vexed the deep
> The dark night long, with fainter murmurs falls,
> So gradual sinks their mirth. Their feeble tongues

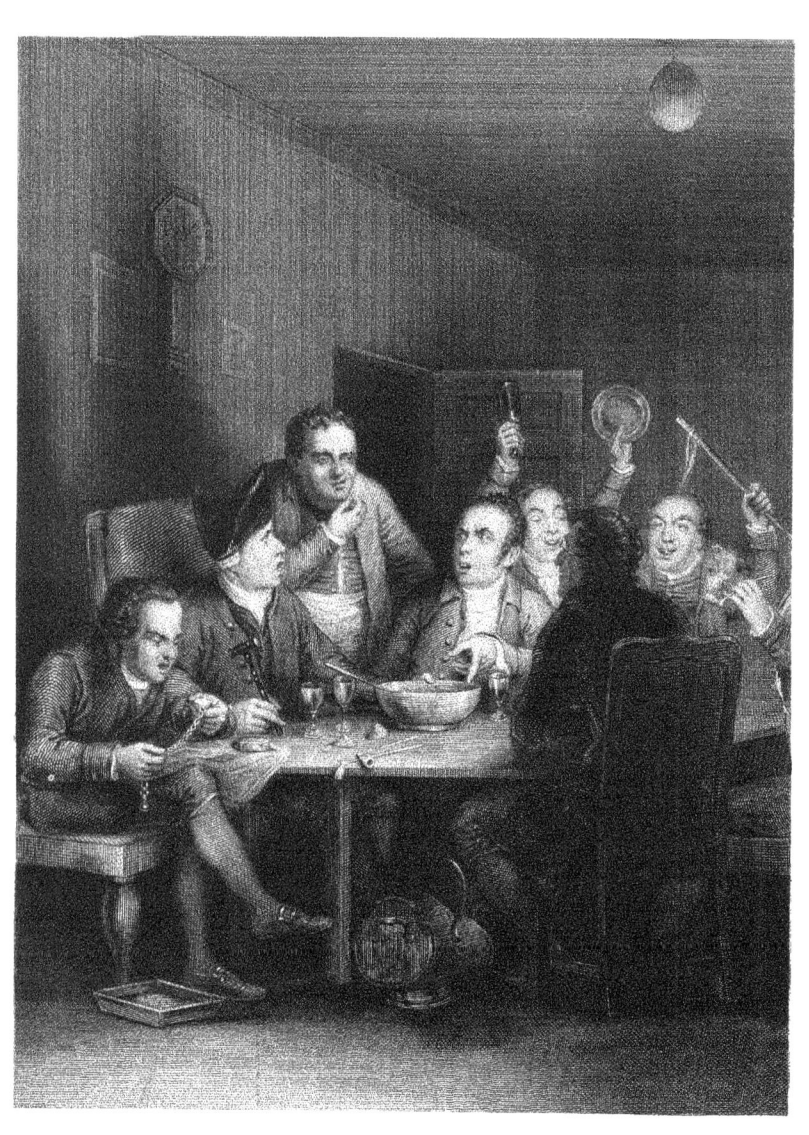

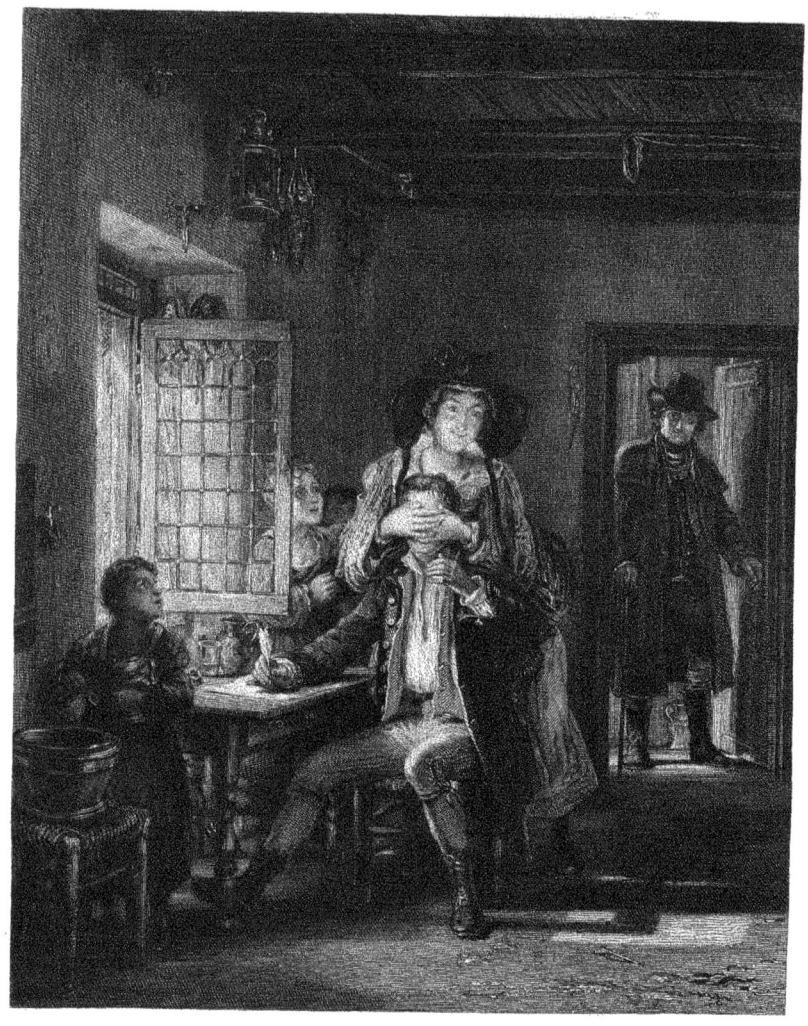

SIR DAVID WILKIE   ENGRAVED BY W. GREATBACH

> Unable to take up the cumbrous word,
> Lie quite dissolv'd. Before their maudlin eyes
> Seen dim and blue, the double tapers dance;
> Like the sun wading through the misty sky,
> Then, sliding soft, they drop. Confus'd above,
> Glasses and bottles, pipes and gazetteers,
> As if the table even itself was drunk,
> Lie a wet broken scene."

The different heads in this picture, from their individuality, have all the semblance of portraits. For richness of humour, we must certainly give the palm to the Baillie. He seems a perfect Boanerges, stentorian in lungs, Johnsonian in arrogance, though not in learning; and we fancy that he, like the toping doctor, with whom Thomson concludes his drunken description:—

> "—— of tremendous paunch,
> * * * * *
> Awful and deep, a black abyss of drink,
> Outlives them all; and from his bury'd flock
> Retiring, full of rumination sad,
> Laments the weakness of these latter times."

Poor Boniface is also most comic—dying to go to bed, but unable to get rid of his uproarious guests.

From this racy production—which recalls the novels of Fielding and Smollett—let us turn to one light as light, and free as air itself, and joyous as the open sunshine, which the painter has diffused over it with an effect of positive magic. This is the little picture of "Guess my Name," "embodying very happily the rustic feat of a girl gliding unseen behind her lover's seat, clasping her open palms over his eyes, and exclaiming in a feigned voice, 'Guess my name.' The heroine of this picture, as the painter himself informed Mr. Cunningham, had the mortification to hear the man whom she loved pronounce another name than her own; and, retiring in confusion of face, resolved, he added, to think no more of one who thought not of her." Yet from the almost laughing countenance, eager with curiosity, but full of security, it is evident that the painful eclaircissement has not taken place which is to substitute "the pangs of despised love," for the trusting confidence of requited tenderness—the wrong, the fatal word has not been spoken, though it trembles on the lips of the delighted lover; who, in the act of inditing a declaration to the object of his affection, and full of her alone, fancies, as he feels the pressure of a soft hand upon his eyelids, that his passion has already been discovered and returned.

In the management of the reflected lights in the girl's face, one would think that Wilkie had been looking at the celebrated "Chapeau de Paille" of Rubens; but, indeed, the disposition of the light throughout, especially that behind the very characteristic figure of the old man, in the background, whose gravity contrasts with and heightens the excitement of the foreground, is very masterly.

This picture was painted in 1821, and is a specimen of the transition between his earlier and later styles; as respects tone, colour, and handling, there is about it what is technically termed, a *fatness* of pencilling, a solid and rich body of colour, and an absence of the somewhat metallic look of his first pictures; he seems already to have come to the conclusion he elsewhere records, "that white is not light, nor detail finish."

The materials of Wilkie's best pictures, Mr. Cunningham informs us, were familiar to him from infancy. "When he painted any of his leading pictures, he thought over his stock of characters, went out to hunt for more among his acquaintance, and then he supplied others from his imagination. He seemed to have a relay of remarkable faces for every occasion; with Highland and Lowland both he was familiar. The proud visage which matched the tartan, and the serious look which suited the maud, he had both at command. With all the pipers and deer-stalkers in Athol he seemed to be acquainted, and dearly did they love to get acquainted with him. A touch or two of his pencil, and they were immortal; from a chief with his tail to the gilly who would be hanged to please the plaid, he knew, and he limned all; nor had the bosom of snow which modestly swells below the tartan escaped; how could it at a glance which noted all, yet nothing seemed to note?"

His picture of "The Highland Family," albeit in its *canine* portion inferior to the glorious works of Landseer, is a proof of this. Wilkie was indignant at the snuff-shop Highlandmen of English artists, "a man with gloomy brows and high cheek-bones, with a conventional kilt, bonnet, and claymore, dressed in an imaginary tartan which never existed, and rejected by Highland and Lowland both." But the true Highlander, as Mr. Cunningham describes him, in one of his happiest passages, " is much of a gentleman, silent and reserved among strangers; one who lives in a world of his own, which he has peopled with the memories of his ancestors; and out of the creations of a poetic imagination, chooses his companions, for perhaps no human being lives so much in the past. With him every stream of his native hills has a voice, and every breeze which sweeps his wild mountains a tongue which speaks of the past." This picture, a commission from the Earl of Essex, was painted when Wilkie was suffering from illness; and is designated rather as a portrait of what he had seen in the North, than a work of the fancy. It is more than a mere picture of costume, however; a domestic interest is thrown over it: the Highlander has returned from war; his wife presents him with a bonny bairn; on the floor are preparations for making the favourite oat-cake, and a flask of Glenlivet is at hand. The picturesque old bothy is homely, and even rude; but its tenant is a noble fellow, "a martial shepherd, ready to fancy an affront, and prompt to resent it; but in his highest rank, he is a high-souled prince, affable, generous, and as true to his word as the heather is to his mountains, with nothing mean or sordid in his nature:" and thus Wilkie has depicted him. We

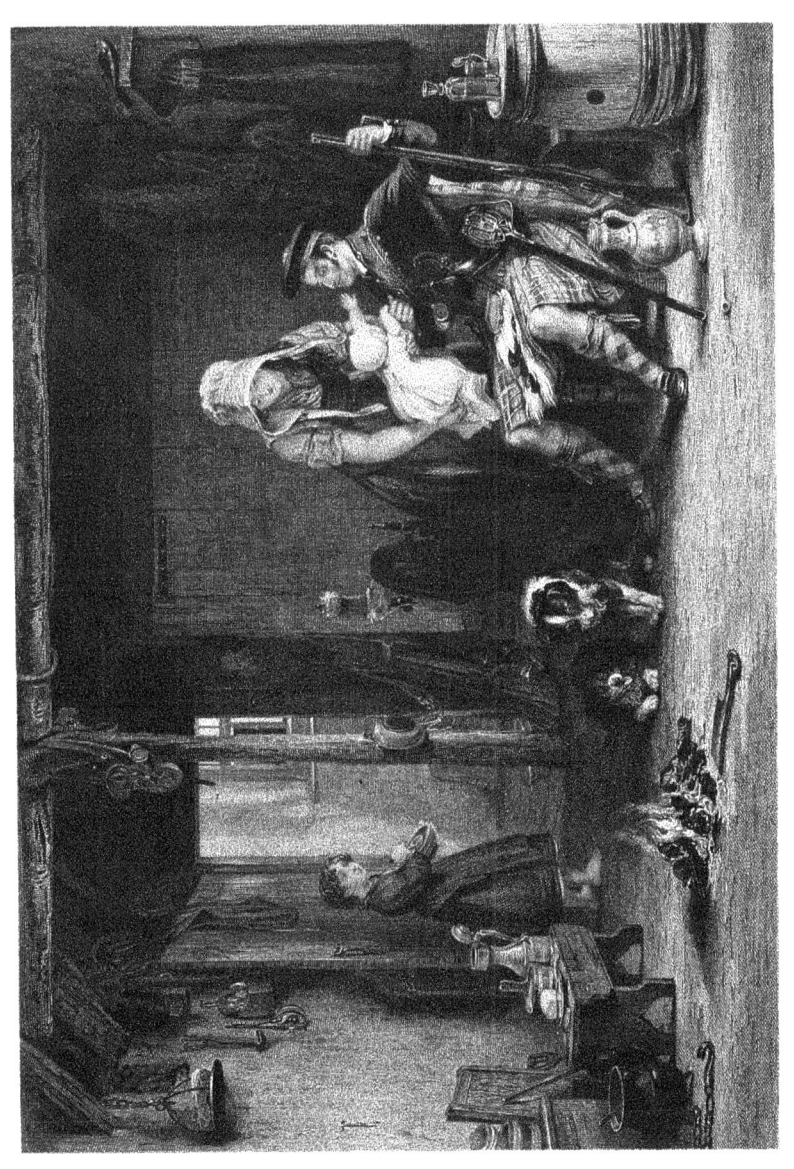

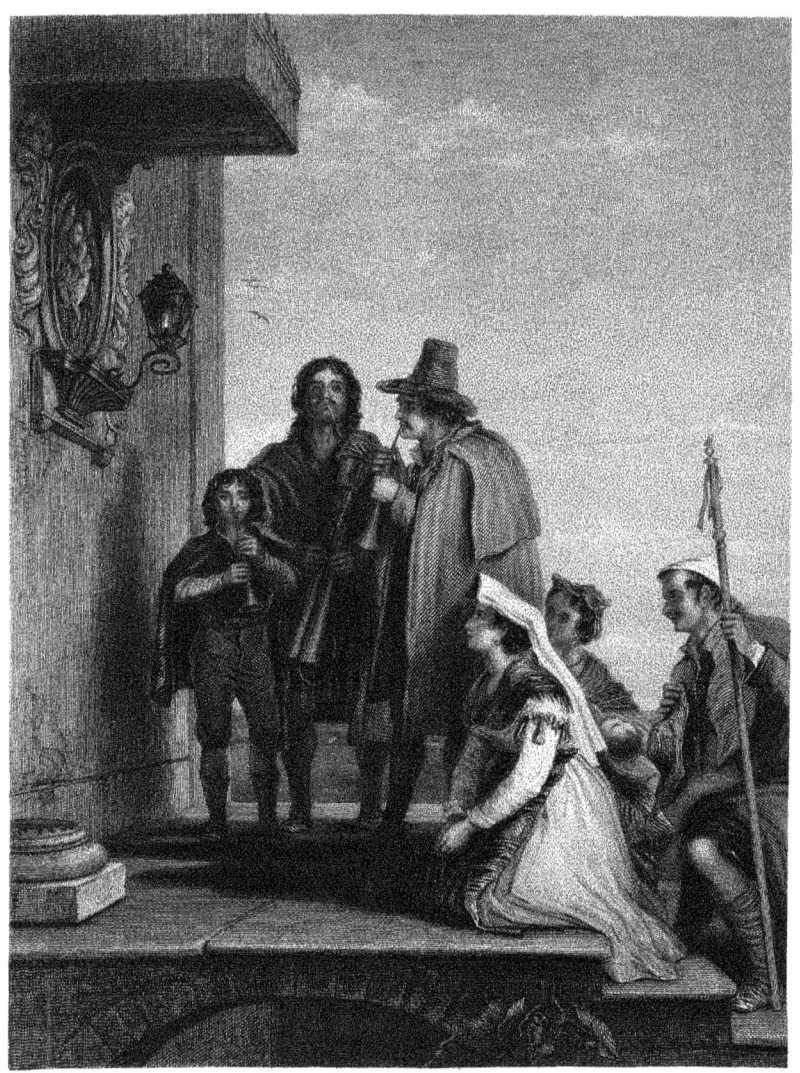

have abstained from entering into any critical discussion as to the change in Wilkie's manner of painting—about which, as well as the varied and more ambitious class of subjects to which he applied it, various opinions will be entertained—were it only for the simple reason that our collection contains so few specimens of his later style. The feeling seems undoubtedly gaining ground among artists and connoisseurs, that, as regards *subjects* at least, he would have acted wisely had the capricious demands of the public taste permitted, to have selected principally those connected with his native country; for a passing visit to a foreign land is hardly sufficient to enable even the most skilful artist to enter thoroughly into its characteristics. Yet, if his Italian subjects are on the whole inferior to those of Eastlake in local truth as well as intensity of feeling they are not without great and peculiar merits. With that now presented as a specimen, " The Pifferari," George IV. was so delighted as to order it immediately for the Royal collection, a proof at least that its beauties were of a marked and palpable character. We have already stated, that Wilkie was much struck when at Rome, with the spectacles of the 'Holy Week.' Multitudes of pilgrims, he observes, from all parts of Italy are assembled in the streets, in costumes remarkably fine and poetical. The dresses of the women are splendid, and not unlike the dresses we were trying to imitate at Kensington in our fancy balls. Each party of pilgrims is accompanied by one whose duty it is to give music to the rest. This is a Piper, or Pifferaro, provided with an immense bagpipe, of a rich, deep tone, the drones of which he has the power of modulating with notes by his fingers, while another plays on a smaller reed the melody or tune, answering the purpose of the chanter. Their music is religious, and resembles in sound the Scotch bagpipe. In parading the streets they stop before the image of the Virgin, whom they serenade, as shepherds, at this season, previous to Christmas, in imitation of the shepherds of old, who announced the birth of the Messiah.

Such is the "materiél" of the composition before us, in which a "pyramidal" style of grouping is very happily adopted; and the broad dark-brown hues of the cloaks of the Pifferari, finely relieve the lighter and gayer costume of the female. The painter has thrown into her countenance all that intensity of devotion (not to be understood by a protestant) which the Italian peasant woman feels towards the "mother of God"—profane but expressive title given to one, who, from her sex and her participation of human feeling and sorrows, is supposed to be as qualified to enter into the trials and troubles of the female heart as to alleviate them by her powerful intercession. " The picturesquely attired peasant woman is from some village on the hills which gird in the Roman Campagna and the Pontine Marshes. The style of the head drapery, which consists simply of a broad linen napkin or towel gracefully folded, and with or without a fringe, is common to many districts throughout the south of Italy. In ordinary cases the fringe is but a loosened part of the linen napkin; but the better conditioned of these Paesane often display on Saints' days and *Giorni di Festa* (holidays) fringes made of gold and silk thread. Although they call it by the very homely and unpoetical name of towel (tovaglia)—whence we have derived our word, or the name of the thing with which we wipe our hands and faces,—or by the name of il pano, (the cloth,) this female adornment figures conspicuously in the popular amatory poetry. The love-smitten Roman or Neapolitan swain sings of it when describing the charms and graces of his bell' idolo, as our primitive English and Scottish song-makers used to sing of the 'flowing auburn hair,' 'lint-white locks,' 'the blue ribbons to tie up the bonnie hair,' 'the snood,' &c. But these southern swains are often very bold, figurative, and almost oriental in their language, making a great deal more of their fair-one's linen towel than our songsters and sonnetteers ever ventured to make of flowing hair or silken ribbon. We have heard them compare the towel to a ship or sail at sea, to a summer cloud, to a comet, a star, the moon, the froth and foam on the sea-shore, the snow on the mountain-top, the glory round the head of a saint, the very head-gear of the blessed Madonna herself, that

> ' Maid, yet mother,
> Goddess, yet woman—like none other,
> That still remembereth in Heaven
> The heart—the hopes—to woman given.' " *

It is doubtful whether the different figures in this picture were painted from *real* characters. There are some of both sexes at Rome who exercise the profession of sitters to painters; and who seem animated by such a kindred spirit of art, as to supply in their *pose* and expression as well as in mere *costume*, everything that the painter could desire, and sometimes even more than he can come up to. There was one individual, whom we remember when in that city, who would come one day in the costume of a monk; the next, as a Piffararo; the third, as a herdsman, or peasant, or fisherman; and, finally, as a bandit. The manner in which he sustained the latter character was really wonderful, so as to create an involuntary suspicion that he had practised the profession before. In a manner he never very clearly made out, he had become possessed of the identical dress and weapons of a celebrated robber chief; and invested in this, he would enact an entire drama, full of the most moving accident. Throwing into his eye the kindling ferocity of a tiger when its prey is in sight he would steal forward, crouching stealthily, like a cat, and aim his gun as at an advancing traveller; and in this position, retaining all the same intensity of expression, would remain fixed as a statue long enough for the painter to transfer to canvass what it would have puzzled him to imagine half as well. He would next, as if beholding the approach of a band of soldiers in pursuit of him, exhibit every sign of mingled hate and terror, and finding himself unable to escape, with clenched teeth, and hands clasping the rock, would shrink convulsively from the fire which he could not avoid, and his yell, as he fell wounded and rolling upon the earth, the curse stamped on his dying countenance, and his expiring convul-

* Penny Magazine.

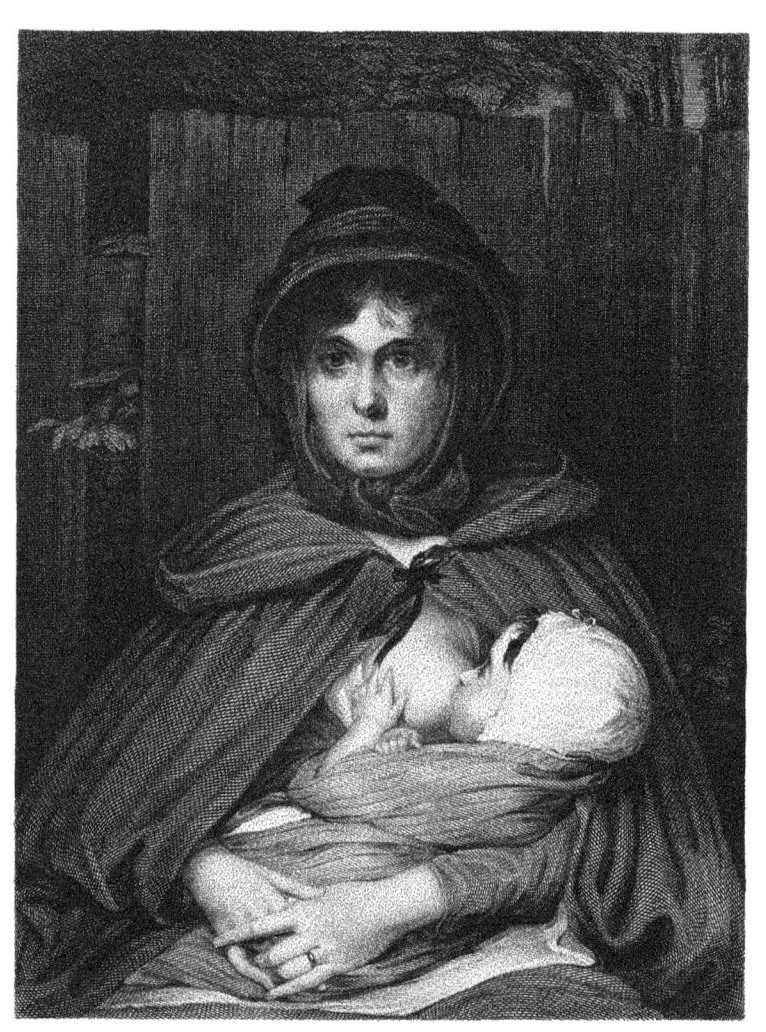

sions were really in the grandest style of attitude and expression, and might, had he lived in his day, have almost saved a celebrated painter the trouble as well as the guilt of the homicide he is said to have committed in his enthusiasm for art, in order that he might catch the appropriate expression of the dying struggles of his victim.

We must not omit to notice Wilkie's claims as a painter of portraits. These, as stated in the outset of this memoir, he took up originally, not from choice, but necessity, to procure him that subsistence, which he could not have obtained by the sale—at miserably inadequate prices—of the finer productions of his genius. In this branch of art Wilkie's success seems, as might have been expected, to have depended mainly on the nature of his subject. As his main excellence lay in the representation of *character*, and as he had little of the purely professional knack of exalting the common-place, and giving a conventional grace to the insipid, it followed necessarily, that when working from a fine original, he would often as much surpass the ordinary portrait painter, as in other cases he would fall below him. At any rate, he himself admits that he was not popular; and least of all with the ladies, accustomed as they were to the elegant and flattering style of Sir Thomas Lawrence. His likenesses are not striking, less from the want of accurate drawing, than from the peculiar artistic treatment; there is a want of the open daylight freshness, and vivid individuality of Vandyke, and a too great preponderance of vague shadow, which, though it may suit some particular subjects, is inappropriate in general. These qualities may be observed in the portrait of Sir Walter Scott, which is contained in this collection. Yet some of his portraits are truly grand, such as that of Daniel O'Connell, and that of the Duke of Sussex, which, as Cunningham observes, throw all neighbouring pictures into the shade. His characters, we must observe, may almost be called portraits, for they are generally copied from originals, with the addition of that particular expression required by the nature of the subject into which they are introduced. "The Gipsy and Child" is no doubt an individual portrait, while it is at the same time interesting as the representative of a class.

Even in our railroad age, there are few who have not fallen in with the curling smoke of the gipsy encampment, in some sheltered nook, amidst regions of woodland and sequestered lanes with grassy borders. That singular race, with all its distinctive peculiarities—the dusky skin, coal-black eyes, and tameless wildness of aspect—yet lingers in the midst of our advancing civilization, unchangeable in their attributes as the Bedouin Arabs, from whom they seem to be originally derived. As in our own country, so are they on the continent of Europe, as mysterious in their origin, appearance, and disappearance, and yet no doubt having everywhere some peculiar organization of their own, such as is depicted in Fielding's novel of "Tom Jones."

The following description of an Italian Gipsy might almost serve as the original of the picture before us. "The only well-known Zingara at Naples,—or the only one that showed herself openly abroad—was a middle-aged woman, that might have stood advantageously to a painter for the picture of her class and race. Her wild dishevelled hair was slightly tinged with grey; but her eyes were the blackest and wildest we ever beheld, and her tongue the quickest we ever heard. We had in our time many of her readings of fortune and predictions, and, the price of the commodity being considered, paid well for them; but we need hardly add, that we found no more truth in her soothsaying than in the extravagantly hopeful dreams of boyhood. She strictly adhered to the few fundamental rules which are common to all fortune-tellers. To the young, she promised the possession of beauty and happy love; to the middle-aged, worldly advantage, with honours and wealth; to the old, more wealth, a far prolonged life, with happy marriages for children, grandchildren, and the rest. In the lines of the hand that gave liberally she always traced the happiest and highest fortunes. In the sparing hand she always saw some crosses and traverses; and she would tell the niggard that would give her nothing, that there was an ominous sign of the gallows in his palm or on his ugly brow. She generally accosted a young man by whispering that she knew a young woman or *lady* (as the case might be) that was absolutely dying for him. In accosting a young woman or young lady, she merely changed the sex of the moribund. Being translated from the broad expressive dialect she spoke, into our vernacular, with a little allowance made for differences of customs and manners, her speeches would pass perfectly well on our racecourses and country fairs, or wherever our gipsy folk ply their trade.

" Several of the old Italian chroniclers relate the sudden appearance of the gipsies towards the end of the thirteenth century, when they came in numerous bands and all at once, as if they had dropped from some dark cloud, or started out of the bowels of the earth. Their complexion, aspect, usages were all new and most strange. The wild robbers of the Apennines were a smooth and civilized set of men compared with these Zingari. As they had no recognisable forms of worship, they were set down as atheists, or as heathens of the worst sort. Two or three centuries later they would have run a chance of being hunted down, savagely persecuted, and even burned; but as yet the inquisition was not.

" The Zingari wandered from state to state, and were seldom long fixed within the limits of one government. It was found out in time that some of them were very knowing horse-dealers, and skilled in all the arts of the farrier; and that some had a decided genius for mending copper caldrons; that some professed a familiar acquaintance with the stars and their influences; and that their old women generally dealt in chiromancy, and other species of fortune-telling. As a faith in astrology was then almost universal, and as even popes and princes of the church entertained these indovini, or soothsayers, these pretended sciences did not expose the gipsies to any particular persecution. For a very long time the palmistry of the gipsy women was allowed to pass without any challenge or interruption, being laughed at by some and believed in by others; which may be said to be the case even now, for every Zingara, or female gipsy, we saw in Italy made an open trade of fortune-telling; but it was of course otherwise, when they proceeded to traffic in philtres and love-potions and hate-potions, and when it was found that poisons were occasionally used in their chemistry. Yet it does not appear that any of the hags who drove this infernal trade to a great length in the fifteenth and sixteenth centuries, and even in a later period, either were Zingara, or had any connexion or intercourse with the gipsy race."*

The following interesting anecdotes of our English gipsies are extracted from an excellent article in a recent number of " Sharpe's Magazine."

" The true gipsy, the real nomadic gipsy, whether traversing the snowy mountains of the north or the burning sierras of the south, yet carries with him distinctive traces of his origin. The flashing dark eye, the long eyelash resting on the sallow cheek, the thin curled lip, the brilliant teeth, the sinewy limbs, not large, rather otherwise, but so totally unencumbered with flesh, giving the idea of suppleness and a power of sinuosity of motion almost as stealthy as that of a snake; these are infallible, and, usually speaking, unfailing tokens of the pure gipsy. We have seen them frequently; and, as far as England is concerned, in Northumberland or in Kent the characteristics are identical.

"There is something exceedingly beguiling in the romance of a gipsy encampment:—the 'lea of the hedge, and the town of the hill,' on a summer's night, with the stars of heaven for canopy, and the grass of the earth for a couch; on a winter's evening, the more tangible comfort of a tarpaulin on poles, and an old rug beneath, with a cheery bonfire at the entrance of the rude hut; unless it be one of the higher-class tribes, who boast of a travelling caravan or two, within which all who are soft enough to care about the weather may be sheltered from its inclemency. To all of them the '*pot au feu*' is an indispensable appendage—it always makes a pretty picture—the cauldron suspended from the apex of the sticks over the flame; it is prettier still in reality. We have seen it many a time; and if we may trust the evidence of our nasal organs, the famous soup with which Meg Merrilies regaled Dominie Sampson is still in fashion among the sisterhood. Only fancy—we address not you, ye pampered sons of luxury, but ye, battered outcasts of fortune, who toil incessantly and fare hardly—only fancy seething in the same kettle, hares, rabbits, chickens, pheasants, and most likely a good haunch of mutton, diverted by these midnight marauders from its original destination, the squire's table! Does not the very idea make your mouths water, ye who are constrained to stale cold meat and boiled rice?

" There are two professions which seem from time immemorial to have been appropriated by the gipsy tribe; that is, tinkering and telling fortunes.

" The latter is decidedly the more liberal profession of the two, and, which is not always the case with 'liberal professions,' not much more dishonest than the other.

" The profession usually, though not universally, assigned to—the fair portion we must not say, but to the female portion of the gipsy tribe, is, if more mendacious, certainly more

* Penny Magazine.

liberal. They consult the stars, and they read futurity: strange to say, we cannot, laugh and sneer how we may, we cannot at all times free ourselves from some inward misgivings as to their vaticinations. Of course, we do not mean those of the gipsy of the half-breed, or the wandering vagrant who cheats nursemaids of their sixpences and silly young ladies of their half-crowns. But there are on record fulfilled prophecies of some of these sybils, which it seems impossible to have effected by connivance, and which, therefore, it is impossible to account for. Nay, such a circumstance occurred but a few years ago, and almost at our own threshold. A gay party, happening to be in the near neighbourhood of a gipsy wife of great repute, in a merry mood adjourned to her tent to have their fortunes told. One after another displayed a fair palm to her, and had the lines of destiny explained. The last was a gay and blooming girl, scarcely twenty years of age. She held out her hand: the gipsy glanced at it, hastily turned away, said she was tired and would not tell any more that day. The young lady remonstrated; when the woman said that she and the rest of her gang were going on one of their usual circuits, but would return there in a month, and then, if the young lady pleased to wait on her, she would tell her fortune. Obliged to be satisfied, the party retired; but one quick-sighted observer slipped away and returned to the woman.

"'What is the reason' she asked, 'that you will not tell Miss F——'s fortune for a month?'

"The sybil would fain have evaded reply; but the lady was firm. At length, but with the greatest reluctance, she said:—'Because, ma'am, ere a moon has run its course, the young lady will be dead and buried.'

"And it was so: the story was told to us by one of the party."

"A professional gentleman of extensive practice was travelling with his daughter in a wild border country, and at a certain point dismissed the chaise, in order to walk a few miles over a romantic tract. Here they fell in with a gang of gipsies; and it was the fortune of the young lady to subdue the heart of a hopeful son of the tribe. It was a decided case of love at first sight, and the lady was well calculated to inspire it; for she was sylph-like in figure, had a profusion of dark silky hair, large black eyes, whose deeply fringed lids reposed on a blooming cheek, a sweetly smiling mouth, magnificent teeth, and manners of most winning kindliness. The young man was decidedly 'done for,' and did not hesitate in demonstrating his affection. It may be that both father and daughter wished themselves elsewhere; but conciliation on their part was highest prudence, and the party sped onward harmoniously.

" At length an elderly gipsy touched the gentleman's arm, and drew him aside.

"'You see,' he said, 'you see that my son is taken with that black-eyed lass of yours; and I like the looks of her myself. Now, what say you? I have got fifty golden guineas for my lad; give your lass the same, and let them make a match of it.'

"The offer was declined, much, as it seemed, to the disappointment of the old man, who was, however, too proud to persist. A very short time afterwards, certainly not more than two or three years, this young lady, who had resisted the inducements of the flashing black eyes, coral lips, white teeth, and fifty golden guineas of the gipsy youth, was walking in the train of our young queen at her coronation, a peeress of the realm."

Might not Charles Lamb have had in his mind's eye the very picture that Wilkie has here placed tangibly before us, when he wrote that strange wild poem, which, as he complains, was rejected by the Editor of a hot-pressed annual, for fear that it should "shock all mothers?"—

1

"'Suck, baby, suck! mother's love grows by giving;
Drain the sweet founts that only thrive by wasting:
Black manhood comes, when riotous guilty living,
Hands thee the cup that shall be death in tasting.

2

"'Kiss, baby, kiss! mothers' lips shine by kisses;
Choke the warm breath that else would fall in blessings:
Black manhood comes, when turbulent guilty blisses,
Tend thee the kiss that poisons mid caressings.'

"So sang a wither'd beldame energetical,
And bann'd the ungiving door with lips prophetical."

Although it *is as* a painter that Wilkie will go down to posterity, we shall form but an inadequate estimate of his talents and character unless acquainted with his writings. His letters and notices of his travels display his literary abilities, no less than they show the richness of his mind and the excellence of his heart: besides these, his "Remarks on Painting" will be perused with great interest by the professional student. These, as well as Wilkie's journals and correspondence, from which alone a full impression of all that he was can be gained, are *exclusively contained* in Allan Cunningham's admirable Biography, from which our meagre outline of the occurrences of Wilkie's life is principally derived. From this invaluable collection it would not be right to avail ourselves of any lengthened quotations; but the following brief passages, suitable for the general reader, will sufficiently show Wilkie's ability in composition.

"Art," as he finely describes it, "*is only art when it adds mind to form;* whatever is high or happy in thought, or skilful and gracefully natural in touch, whatever speaks to the feelings, or appeals to the judgment, will, if seen in the most distant corner of the earth, or in the remotest period of time, be as truly felt and as rightly judged as in the day and hour when it first passed from our hands."

.   .   .   .

He might himself well remember, that true genius is of no particular time or country—

that passing from the schools of Italy, she selects, he observes, " the uncouth but mighty Rembrandt as the disciple of her choice; a draughtsman without style, a painter of wondrous brilliancy, where all else is subdued; adding lustre, by the poetry of his touch, to the mystery of darkness and obscurity; giving splendour to poverty, sublimity of expression to the most homely countenance, majestic motion to the most abject form; while in the choice of subject, use of materials, illusion of effect, he stood alone, unlike all, and surpassing all, as if nature in creating him *desired to lavish her rarest gifts only to prove the unlimited variety of her power*, and the poverty of those artificial assistants which in the excess of talent can be dispensed with." The truth of this is attested by the inimitable originality and variety of his own productions, and by the manner in which he sprung, self-formed, into excellence, amidst such a variety of disastrous obstacles.

In another eloquent passage he laments the hard fate of so many in the highest ranks of his profession:—" The divine and captivating Correggio, from the very doubts thrown upon his history, is supposed to be of the ill-requited and neglected class; a like cloud of doubt and obscurity hangs over the story of Rembrandt; the days of Wouvermans were ended, if not passed, in bitterness; and those of Brouwer were numbered in prison. Morales, the divine Morales, was found at Badajos by Philip the Second, in extreme poverty as well as old age; nor were the powers of art nor a name denied to the modest Pareja, who was born to the inheritance of slavery, and whose ransom from servitude was the sole reward that his success procured him."

The following remark must, we think, come home to every true lover and patron of art:—

" The possessor of a picture regards it not in reference to the hand that produced it, nor as one whose view of it has been hasty and fleeting: he thinks alone of the sentiment and feeling of the work, and the lasting impression which it makes on his mind; and regards it as possessing matter for thought, as a companion of the leisure hour, holding up in its solemn stillness an image which he loves, perpetuating the *vanished smile* and the *never-to-be-forgotten glance* of one perhaps long since past and gone, or the *hue of the changing foliage*, or *the lustre of the fleeting cloud*, beauteous

' As if an angel, in his upward flight,
Had left his garment floating in mid air:

all of which, and much more, *arrested and rendered abiding by the sorcery of art*, are kept treasured in the reflecting mind, affording to the possessor materials of pleasure, and a permanent source of pure enjoyment."

The impression that should be produced by a truly noble work of art upon the cultivated but unprofessional spectator, to whom the technicalities and artistic arrangements connected with a picture are unknown, is thus finely described:—

" To one who knows art only by the impression it makes, and to whom the mode of speech and thought of the artist are as dark as the book of the Sybils. a picture should be as a mirror held up, in which he might see the true impress of nature, preserving the glow of health and beauty, the wisdom and the gravity of matron looks, and *fixing in unfleeting outline and colour the choicest images which appear in our waking dreams, or in the visions of a fine imagination.*"

Were we at liberty to quote further, we might extract his most discriminating and graphic sketches of different painters and their works:—Michael Angelo—Vandyke—Velasquez, and others; but for these we must again refer the reader to the original volumes of Mr. Cunningham.

Of the character of Wilkie, it is not the object of this work, confined as it is principally to critical remarks, to speak at any length; moreover, unavoidably scanty as has been our memoir of him in the preceding pages, the various traits we have related will have sufficiently displayed the soundness of his mind as well as the excellence of his heart. He was a man so devoted to his profession, upon the pursuit of which he concentrated all his faculties and desires—and his peculiar excellencies, like those of Burns, were so native and spontaneous, arising out of his moral and intellectual idiosyncracy—that 'he may be said to be so identified with his works, as that they are not only the lasting memorial of his genius, but the truest exposition of his character. In reading them we seem to converse with the Author himself. Wilkie had none of the fiery and impetuous nature that formed at once the inspiration and the torment of Burns; his passions were all moderate; and no one better appreciated or knew how to put in practice the maxim of his poet-countryman, that—

"Prudent, cautious self-control,
Is wisdom's root;"

but his social and domestic affections were not the less concentrated and profound. There is something almost of a primitive and scriptural character in the intercourse of Wilkie and his parents—a feeling of mingled reverence and affection towards them is manifest in all his actions—their anxiety and sacrifices on his behalf, his cheerful self-denial and gratitude, their mutual confidence in and reliance upon each other, present us with the brightest aspect of human nature. What can be a more beautiful sight than the domestic fireside of the Painter who had attained fame and distinction, not that he might neglect, but cherish and soothe with his filial attentions, the declining days of a mother to whose influence he was indebted for the opportunity to follow out his inclinations? How many traits of tenderness towards her appear in his letters! How constant his care for, and delightful his familiar correspondence with his sister! What interest he took in the improvement of her mind! And though rigidly economical and conscientious in his own affairs, how cheerfully did he take upon himself the losses and responsibility of an embarrassed brother— to an extent, indeed, that seriously preyed upon his health, and perhaps shortened his existence! "His attachments." says Cunningham, "were calm, kindly, and constant; he was faithful to his friendships, and it was not for a slight offence that he weighed up the anchor of his regard." He had much of that exclusive, peculiar love of his country which the natives of the North maintain ever warm and glowing, when compelled to live and labour at a distance from their own soil; but there was nothing offensive in its manifestation. Amidst all the seductions of the world (and that of artists is seldom distinguished for its superior morality) Wilkie continued to maintain the seriousness of feeling and propriety of conduct which he learned at the parental manse. The practical good sense, cool deliberation, and steady perseverance of his countrymen, their noble self-denial, maintaining and giving birth to as noble a liberality, were ingrained in his character; and their patient perseverance and untiring industry, which he himself exemplified, he considered as more essential to success in art, than what is called mere genius. No one more thoroughly detested the talking professors of his art; or the cant and pretension of a false criticism, so often used as a cover for real ignorance. When teased in this way, his dry and characteristic reply was, "Let us be doing something." Clearness and precision were the qualities, which, as a student, he aimed at himself; and he required them of students when he had become an academician. His attention to their studies was conscientious; he would not allow them to execute anything in a style devoid of meaning; but would insist that the appropriate expression and sentiment should be carefully discriminated. He took pleasure in welcoming a spirit of patient industry akin to his own, and, far from discouraging and disparaging the rising talent of young aspirants, far from "bearing no brother near the throne," he delighted to foster those who promised to do honour to the profession he loved. In his general intercourse he was kind and conciliating, his gentle humour untinctured with bitterness, and his disposition free from envy, hatred, and uncharitableness. He was one of the least assuming of mankind; he never courted applause, and detested flattery; and his love of art was so genuine and absorbing, that he seems to have ever felt his deficiencies far more than he prided himself on his attainments. With all the distinctions which his genius had procured him, and all the refinement he had acquired by study and experience, there ever lingered about him somewhat of his early and native simplicity, which carried with it a singular charm. His appearance was stamped with the qualities of his mind and heart. His person was tall and handsome, with light sunny hair, and the clear bright intelligent eye of Scotia. "His goshawk eye," as Cunningham says, "which beamed with a wild light, was subdued as he advanced in life;" but traces are to be seen of its expression in the portrait appended to this work, as well as in his other likenesses, one of which is preserved in the collection of portraits of Sir Robert Peel's contemporary friends and worthies, in his splendid gallery at Drayton Manor. In the statue by Mr. Joseph, erected by subscription, and now placed in the entrance to the National Gallery, the expression is serious and profound, such as we may suppose the painter to have assumed when lecturing on art.

No one was ever more thoroughly devoted to his profession than Wilkie; he possessed the true soul of the artist. His studies were not confined alone to the particular walk for which nature had gifted him; his ambition to enlarge the boundaries of his acquirements was ever on the increase. Far from being satisfied with the high position which the public voice assigned to him, and from repeating the principal characteristics of his early works, till he fell into a mannerism, he was continually scrutinizing the finest productions that departed genius has bequeathed to us, in order to reach, if possible, the secret of the peculiar excellence of each, and thus to form a style of his own, containing as many of the highest qualities of art as could be combined with one another. Whether he was successful in this aim, there may be a difference of opinion; there can be none as to the nobleness of the endeavour. Some indeed have considered certain of his historical productions as constituting almost a new era in art; and of the "Knox preaching" it has been said in particular, that it unites the "high qualities of the Italian school with the lower but still valuable qualities of the Dutch." We are left very much to conjecture in what degree Wilkie might have succeeded in the last and highest aim of his career as a painter; that, namely, of producing a new class of scriptural pictures, in which all the lights and assistances derived from a study of local costume and character should be combined. His stay in the Holy Land was too brief; his sketches are too few and slight, to enable us to form an opinion. There is a peculiar interest in these last sketches, these final memorials of the career of a great painter, whose enthusiasm for his art seemed but to increase as his bodily strength decayed, till he was consumed by his self-forgetting ardour in the very prime of his existence.

We had already penned and sent to press our concluding observation, when a fortunate accident enabled the publisher to obtain possession of " these very same last sketches, and final memorials," alluded to, as well as those executed in that journey into Spain, of which we have already given a brief description. This will enable him to add to what we must ever consider the standard productions of his genius a varied selection of the most striking of these later productions—which besides having all the charming freshness and first vigorous impression of original sketches from nature, will enable the reader to form his own judgment as to what might have been realized by Wilkie in the walk of art to which he aspired, had his life been spared. These, as they successively appear, will be accompanied by further notices of the travelling adventures which originated them, and also such brief descriptions of the objects themselves, as may be required to explain their peculiarities and beauties.

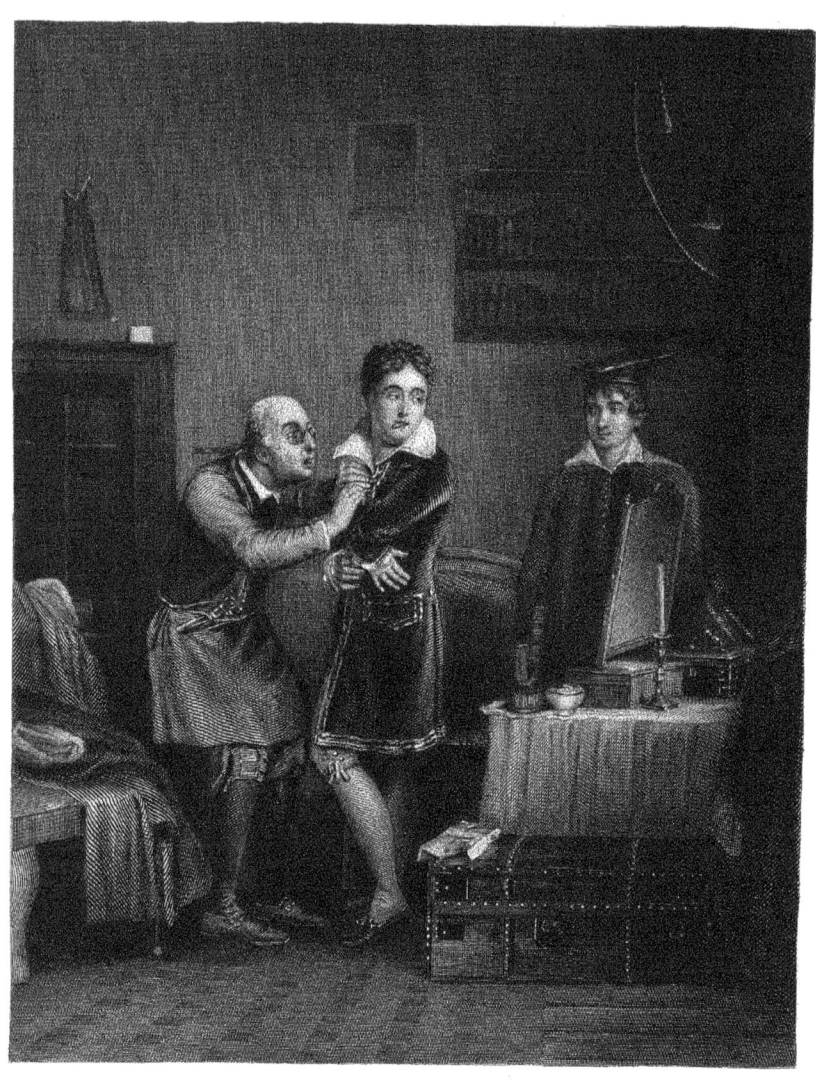

SR DAVID WILKIE, R.A. ENGRAVED BY W. GREATBACH

THE NEW COAT.

This is some early picture of the painter's, nor is there need to say much about it; although it is interesting as developing his gradual progress. The subject is trivial, and did not admit of any great display of the painter's powers. "A hobbedehoy—neither man nor boy"—is apparently about to be sent forth to school, or from thence into the wide world—for the life of us we cannot divine which. He is being invested in a new coat, or perhaps his first. Who of us does not remember the important event, the feeling of dignity it produced, overcoming the irksomeness occasioned by an unaccustomed garment,—the pride in its tight fit, in its buttons and all its belongings, especially the pockets, in its superfine cloth and its silken lining? The painter has well entered into all this. The youth is complacently admiring himself in the mirror, and smoothing with the back of his hand the glossy smooth-sitting waist; his companion is looking on in silent admiration and envy at his gallant appearance. In all this, however, there is nothing that an ordinary artist might not very well have accomplished. But the old tailor richly deserves to be reckoned among Wilkie's gallery of life-like characters. He is evidently a portrait, and yet a type of his class. We may imagine him the very individual upon whom the blustering Petruchio poured forth such a torrent of appropriately contemptuous epithets.

> "Thou liest, thou thread,
> Thou thimble,
> Thou yard, three-quarters, half-yard, quarter, nail,
> Thou flea, thou nit, thou winter cricket thou —:
> Brav'd in mine own house with a skein of thread!
> Away, thou rag, thou quantity, thou remnant;
> Or I shall so bemete thee with thy yard
> As thou shalt think on prating, whilst thou liv'st."

Let us observe, notwithstanding, that Shakspeare, who rose in all things above common prejudices and delighted to combat them, has, in his delineation of another knight of the thimble, run counter to the well-known saying, that a "tailor is but the ninth part of a man." When Falstaff is raising recruits for the wars, and Bullcalf, Mouldy, and Wart are disposed to fight shy of the business, Feeble, a *woman's* tailor too, is determined, as he

THE NEW COAT.

says, "to bear no base mind," but to go boldly to the wars. "Wilt thou," says Falstaff, "make as many holes in an enemy's battle, as thou hast done in a woman's petticoat?"

"FEE. I will do my good will, Sir: you can have no more.
FAL. Well said, good woman's tailor! well said, courageous Feeble! Thou wilt be as valiant as the wrathful dove, or most magnanimous mouse. Prick the woman's tailor well, master Shallow, deep, Master Shallow.
FEE. I would, Wart might have gone, Sir.
FAL. I would thou wert a man's tailor, that thou might'st mend him, and make him fit to go. I cannot put him to a private soldier, that is the leader of so many thousands: Let that suffice, most forcible Feeble.
FEE. It shall suffice, Sir.
FAL. I am bound to thee, reverend Feeble."

Have we not before us here, in this painting of Wilkie's, the very impersonation of the magnanimous tailor, bent with fifty years sitting at the board, slight as if the first gust would carry him away like a feather, yet fulfilling, in strictly professional language, the well-known saying, "the mind's *the measure* of the man?"

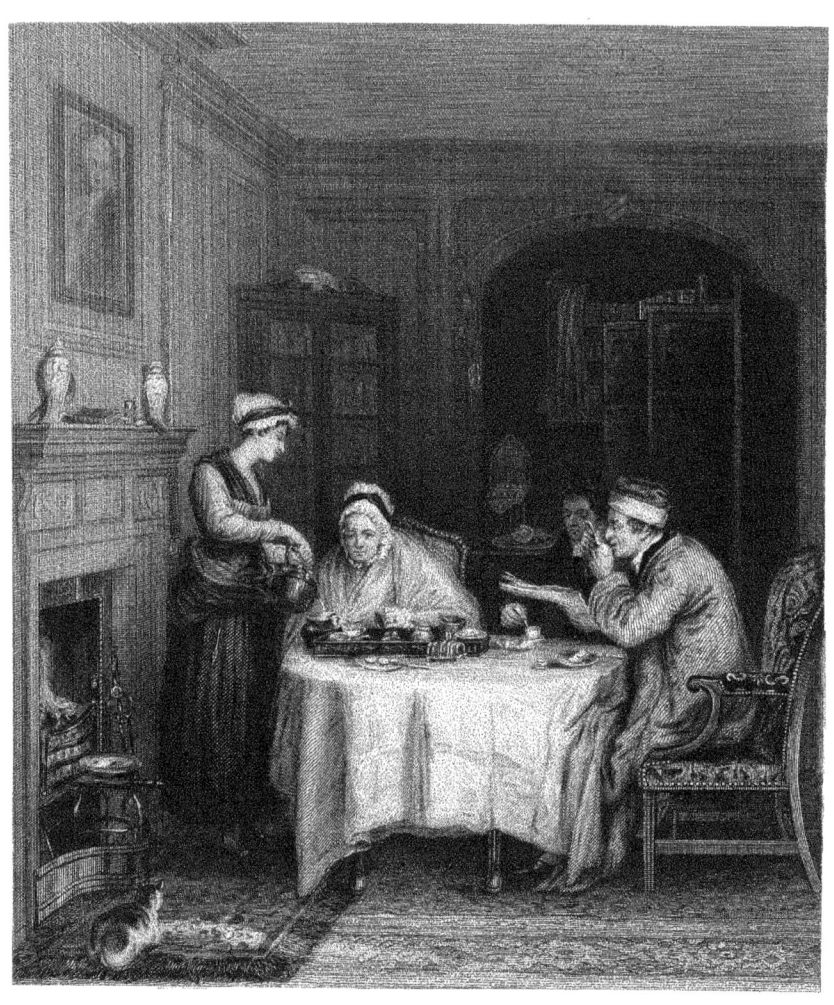

PAINTED BY SIR DAVID WILKIE, R.A.—ENGRAVED BY W. GREATBACH

THE BREAKFAST-TABLE.

THE STAFFORD GALLERY is, we believe, the most magnificent *private* collection of the Old Masters in the metropolis, unrivalled for its Titians and Claudes; and the admission of a picture by a modern painter is justly regarded, as Allan Cunningham observes, as "a crowning proof of reputation and a security against forgetfulness." Wilkie was of course desirous of taking his place among the recognised masters of modern art, and the noble proprietor of the Gallery, who was one of its most liberal patrons, had given him a commission, but from the number of works he had undertaken, he was long unable to fulfil it. At length he took up the subject of the "Breakfast-Table," which gave such high satisfaction to the marquis, that he behaved on the occasion with a degree of liberality, which, it is to be regretted, was not always evinced by those who complained of Wilkie's descending to portraiture, to which he was driven as a source of pecuniary profit. In a letter of thanks, the painter observes: "The groom of the chambers has paid me, by your lordship's desire, £400 for the picture; a sum which, as it exceeds the price 350 guineas I engaged to paint it for, I have received as a liberal mark of your lordship's approbation of the work." Had such conduct as this been more general, Wilkie would have been better enabled to pursue his proper walk of art without the fear of being withheld by ruinous embarrassment.

"The Breakfast-Table," without being one of the most remarkable of Wilkie's works, has a certain charm to our national habits and feelings. It has a quality into which we can all enter—a look of delicious comfort, snugness, and peace. It seems to do one's heart good to look at it. There is about it the atmosphere in which the best of our domestic and social qualities are nurtured—the "sweet security," of home—the look of order which supremely distinguishes an English fireside. The old-fashioned panel room, with its cabinets and china, and family portraits, the Turkey carpet and rug, the shining fender and fire-irons are all scrupulously clean. The ample damask tablecloth, of snowy whiteness, tells of the stores of family linen, the pride of the old lady who is presiding over the table. She is herself the very picture of nicety, and there is the careful but kindly expression that marks her out for a good housewife and strict but considerate mistress. The maid-servant seems long established in her place, from the neatness and propriety of her appearance. Commend us to that old lady for brewing a good dish of tea; it is a matter she evidently understands. She watches the stream of boiling water, as it issues from the shining copper kettle, with a wary and experienced eye; and well knows the exact moment to arrest its course. "The heart of her husband," as Solomon says, "can safely confide in her;" she will not spoil his breakfast, nor disturb his digestion and temper by a flavourless, washy decoction. And the old gentleman in the cramoisie gown is evidently not a little particular in his tastes. With his nose to his egg, he is hesitating whether it is immaculately fresh, before he ventures to take a spoonful. We can fancy him very sensitive about his linen—almost as testy as Touchwood himself, and with all his kindness too. We must not forget poor puss. She is sleek and indulged, but not presuming withal— the very picture of a model cat, and one that knows her place.

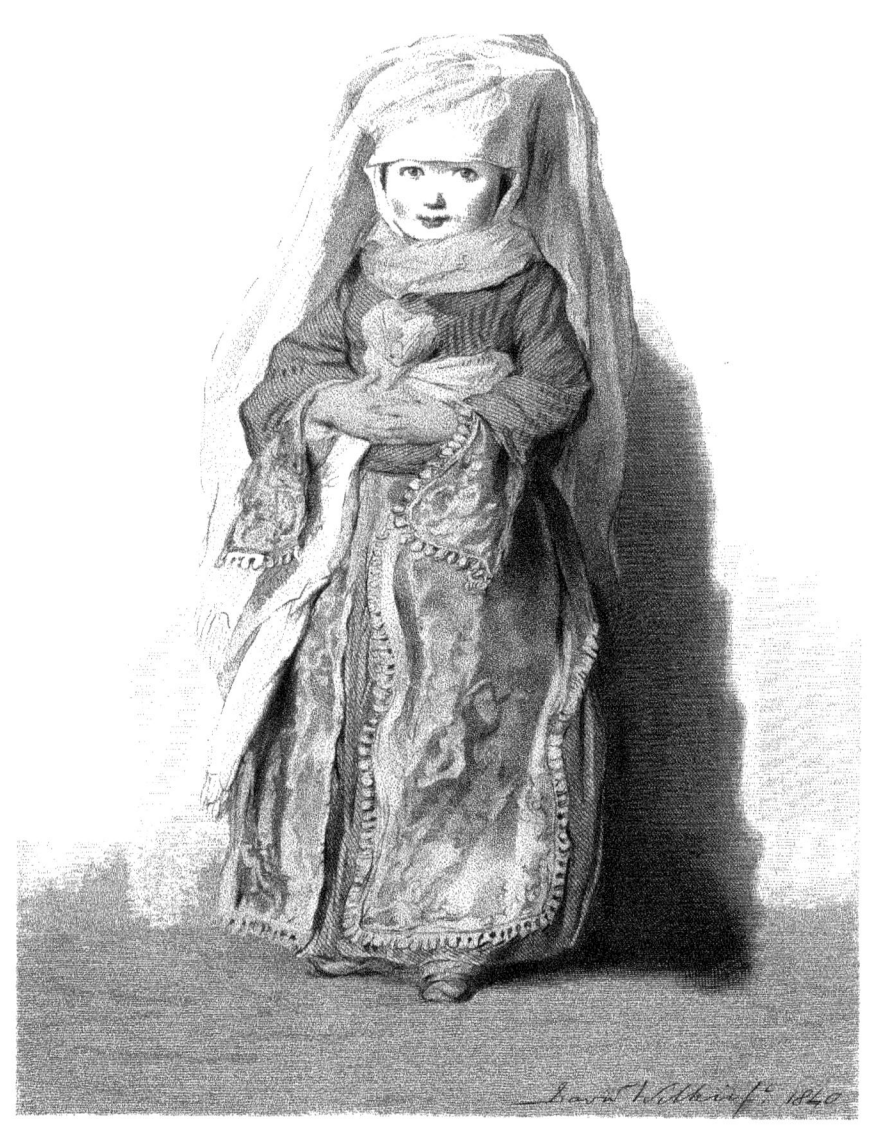

THE DAUGHTER OF ADMIRAL WALKER.

SKETCHED BY SIR DAVID R.A. ENGRAVED BY T. W. HUNT

THE DAUGHTER OF ADMIRAL WALKER,

IN A TURKISH DRESS.

PROFESSOR LESLIE, in his recent "Lectures on Painting," delivered at the Royal Academy, has the following remarks upon Wilkie; which, as will be seen upon comparison, agree so entirely with the estimate given in the preceding part of this Biographical and Critical Notice, that we are glad to fortify our own remarks by quoting such excellent authority. "I believe all opinions will concur in placing Wilkie's subjects from familiar and rustic life, with few exceptions, *highest* among his works. Such were the pictures that made his first reputation—'The Village Politicians,' 'The Blind Fiddler,' 'The Rent-Day,' 'Duncan Gray,' &c. Of this class, however, the most elaborately painted and the fullest in subject, 'The Village Festival,' in the National Gallery, is certainly *not the one* to which I should give the preference. For though that exquisite delicacy of touch, which marks more or less every period of Wilkie's art, is here seen in the greatest perfection, yet the picture seems to me, in all respects, the most artificial of his earlier productions. It was a picture which gave him great trouble to paint, as is evident from his diary." After alluding to the change of style in his later works, Mr. Leslie goes on to say:—"The masterly sketches made in those countries from which he was not destined to return, shows how actively (too actively indeed) his fine mind had been engaged to the very last. Among them, I remember one of the most fascinating representations of childhood I ever beheld—the young daughter of Admiral Walker, in an Eastern dress. It was as beautiful as anything of Reynolds or Gainsborough, and yet quite unlike either."

The copy of this sketch we here present to our readers (in which the engraver has felicitously preserved the style of the original) will delight alike the most exacting critic and every one who, though unacquainted with art, has a natural feeling for the beautiful. Any common painter would have been gravelled by the costume, but a genius like Wilkie's could make its very singularity and quaintness set off by contrast the beauty of the living subject. The trusting look of childhood—the intense gaze of its pure pearly eye, as if into the very heart of the spectator—was never better conveyed by mortal pencil. None but a great artist could throw off, apparently without an effort, a work so consummate in feeling, and so ethereal and graceful in touch and handling. There is, if we may use such a word, a sort of inspiration about it.

THE DAUGHTER OF ADMIRAL WALKER.

The father of this fine little girl was one of Wilkie's most intimate friends at Constantinople. He arrived there just after the fall of St. Jean de Acre, which was wrested from the Pasha of Egypt by the combined English, Austrian, and Turkish fleets, and restored to its original master, the sultan. "Constantinople," he says in his Journal, "shows far more than common excitement. We see daily both prisoners and successful warriors, fresh from the scene of action. We have made, among the latter, a most excellent acquaintance in Admiral Walker, who was commander of the Turkish fleet, and bore an important part in the taking of Acre, and brought here to the Sultan the news of the victory. He is a fine-looking man; becomes the Turkish dress well, and his wife is a most ladylike woman. They have a house here, and we see them frequently." We find, on the 7th December, the following entry in his Journal:—" Was occupied to-day in making a drawing of the child of Admiral Walker in the Turkish dress.—Mrs. Redhoun and the Greek governess having come to attend the young lady. Had a note from Mr. Pisani to say the Sultan would sit to me on Thursday morning." The sketch of the Sultan turned out but a common-place affair; that of the little child—hit off "*con amore*"—a gem of the finest water, and one of the happiest efforts of the painter.

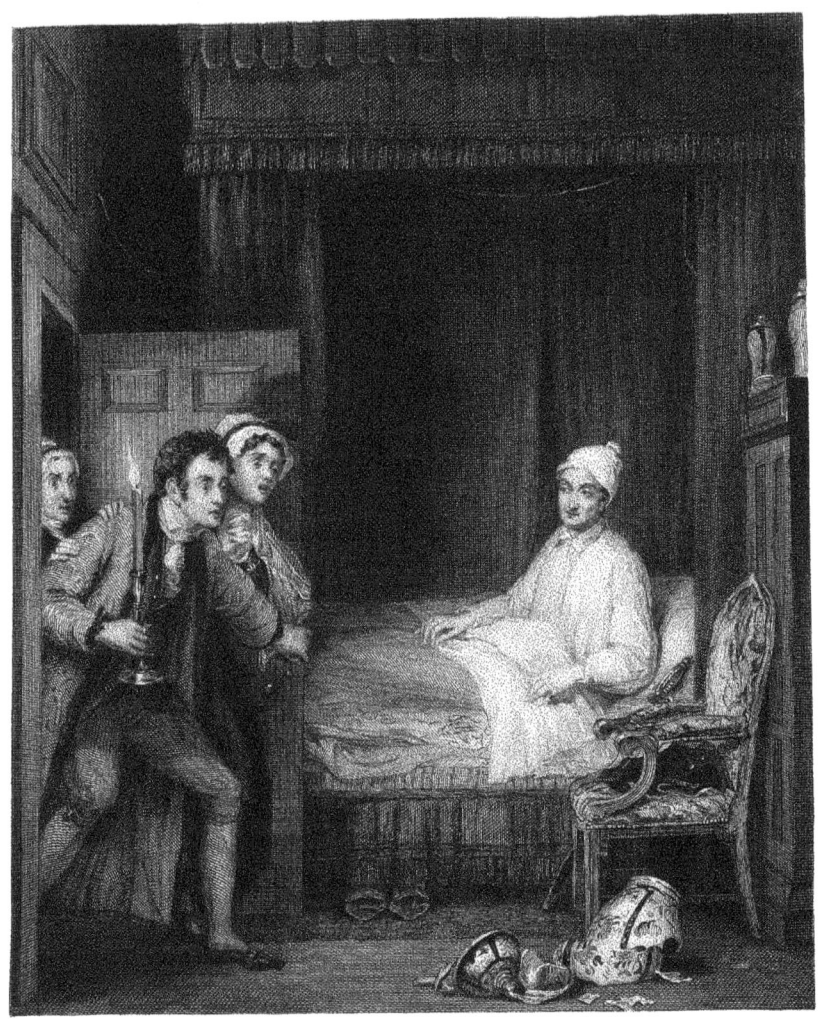

PAINTED BY SIR DAVID WILKIE, R.A. ENGRAVED BY W. GREATBACH.

The Original Inserted by Chas Cone, Esq.

THE BROKEN CHINA JAR.

IN this picture Wilkie has embodied a story in a poem called the "Social Day," by Peter Coxe, which was distinguished rather by its then novel and expensive illustrations, than by any vast merit in the composition itself. A benighted wanderer—an old soldier, as it seems—has found shelter at a country mansion, when, after hospitably entertaining him, the host conceives the project of playing off upon him a practical joke. He is put into the "Haunted Room," the only one, as he was told, untenanted in the house. To bed he accordingly goes:—

> "'Twas now that awful noon of night
> When shadows timid mortals fright,
> The Laird, and a selected few
> Close to the haunted chamber drew,
> And at the door, (with crouchen ear,)
> Listened, th' effects of fright to hear.
> . . . . .
> By strings through secret places run
> The work of mischief is begun;
> The windows shake, the curtains rattle,
> And chair meets chair in furious battle.
> The veteran waked from slumber sound,
> Surprised, but calm, and look'd around:
> His eye acutely roamed about,
> To find the skulking spirit out.
> . . . . . .
> Thus rapid mused the gallant tar,
> When he beheld a porcelain jar,
> In China's richest colours bright,
> Such as give tasteful eyes delight,
> On antique cabinet that stood,
> Strong contrast to the sable wood:
> Fast to the jar he fixed the string
> That had embraced the curtain's ring;
> And when again, in idle play,
> They thought to drive his sleep away,
> This pride of aunts, this boast of nieces,
> This favourite jar was dashed to pieces!

THE BROKEN CHINA JAR.

The crash was great, and instant spoke
Mischief attended on the joke.
Conscious the scheme had brought disgrace,
They hastened from their hiding place.

" Hurrying beyond the chamber-door,
They saw the fragments on the floor:—
It was a great and sad surprise,
They scarcely could believe their eyes;
And, singular—the stranger's face
Show'd not a sign that fear had place.
No guests in future were afraid,
And from that hour the ghost was laid."

Such is the story, as compressed from this very diffuse and tedious poem. Wilkie's genius was here in trammels, but he has done all that an able artist could to give interest to so very poor a subject. The picture, albeit not one of the painter's best, possesses nevertheless many of the peculiar beauties of his style, which enriched whatever it was employed upon.

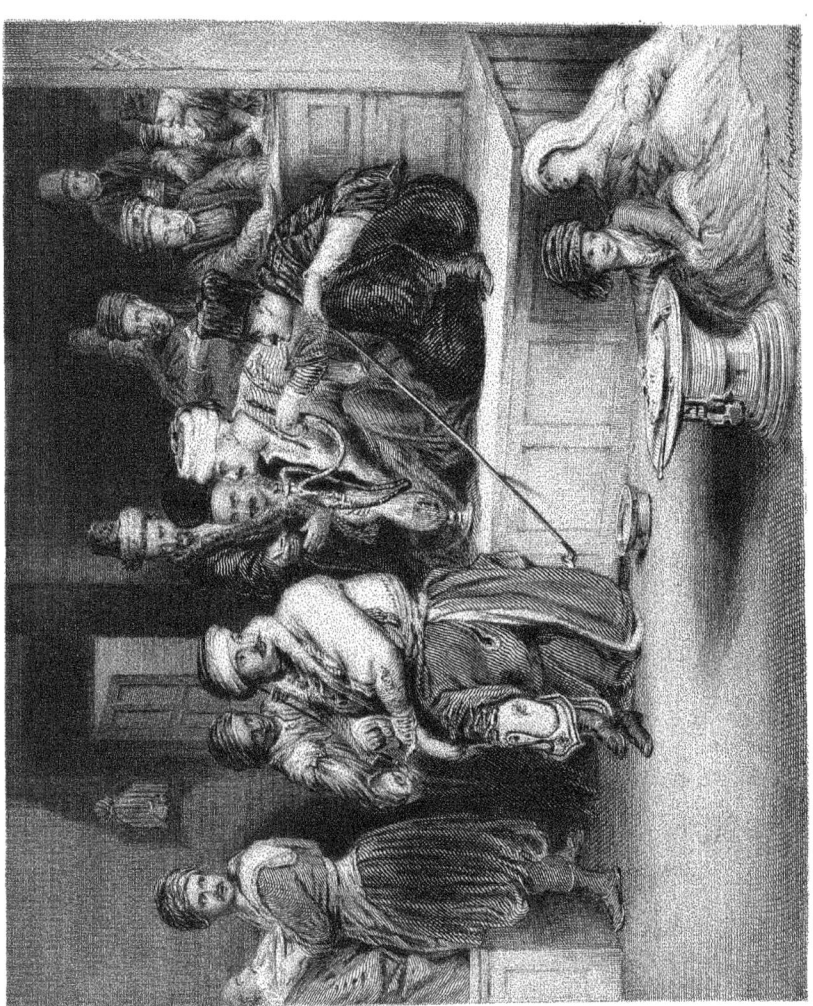

THE TURKISH COURIER RELATING THE NEWS OF THE CAPTURE OF ACRE IN A CAFÉ AT CONSTANTINOPLE.

It has been already mentioned in our memoir of Wilkie, that he arrived at Constantinople at a time of great excitement among both Mussulmen and Christians. The domination of Mehemet Ali, in Syria, had assumed such a character that England considered herself called upon to expel him from that country, and restore it to its original master, the Sultan. Whatever may be thought of the policy of this interference on her part, it created a feeling of enthusiasm in favour of the English at Constantinople, which rose to the greatest possible height upon the receipt of the intelligence that the combined British and Austrian fleet had in the space of a few hours bombarded and taken the famed fortress of St. John of Acre, which, when in a far less effective state of defence, had, by the heroism of Sir Sidney Smith, baffled the power of Napoleon; and which Mehemet Ali had only wrested from the Sultan after a bloody and protracted siege. Regarding it as the key of Syria, he had strengthened and garrisoned it with such care, that it was considered by the Turks to be impregnable, as it would no doubt have proved to the utmost efforts of their own arms. The news of its capture, says Wilkie, spread over Constantinople like wildfire, gladdening every one, and exciting the young Sultan to a frenzy of joy. The painter gave a royal feast to celebrate the event, at which were present Austrian, Russian, and English naval officers; and the last sounds that caught his ear as he retired from the deepening mirth, were the resounding cadences of the " Good Old English Gentleman."

We do not learn from his journals whether he happened to witness the incident that he has made the subject of this clever picture—most probably not. But in his rambles about the Turkish capital in search of character and incident, the coffee-house would naturally be the first place to afford him an easy opportunity of witnessing and transferring to his sketch-book the traits of the different classes of the population who are accustomed to assemble there, and there alone: for neither theatres nor public gathering places of any kind there are met with in this drowsy Oriental capital. We may add, what indeed will strike every one, that the café is the only place for the circulation of private gossip or public intelligence. And in order fully to appreciate the merit of Wilkie's sketch, we must endeavour to figure to ourselves a population destitute of any further intellectual life than what may be derived from the pages of the Koran, who, with all their old traditions and prejudices hanging about them, are isolated from the world around,.the movements of which, in the absence of public journals, reach them only in confused and exaggerated rumours, growing more and more marvellous as they circulate from mouth to mouth. Add to this that the belief in magic is universal through the East, and to this cause, in great measure, the wonderful doings of the Giaours, or Christian infidels, are, or till lately were, attributed. Indeed the process of taking likenesses is looked upon by the passing generation of Mussulmen, as a half-magical and decidedly heterodox proceeding, from which they shrink, under the notion that it conceals some subtle device of the infidels, in order, to use Mr. Weller's favourite expression, to "circumvent" the faithful. Among the Turkish part of the population, to which we are principally alluding, Wilkie had therefore to catch as he could the more characteristic traits of expression. And it must be admitted that he has done so with no small degree of skill. A circle of wondering hearers are listening to an account of the astonishing deeds of the English, as narrated by one of the Tatar couriers, who ride with surprising speed, sleeping or dozing by night on horseback, over plain and mountain, without pause, till from the furthest bounds of the empire they have carried their dispatches to the Turkish capital. His costume is peculiar; his jacket, of furred leather, and ornamented riding boots, with his bronzed and hardy face, would at once stamp his occupation. Behind him the servant of the coffee-house, who is, as usual in Cairo and Constantinople, a grinning negro-boy, is bearing his full or perhaps replenished pipe. We may suppose the Tatar to have been well acquainted with the formidable nature of the defences of Acre, and to have witnessed the scene of the bombardment—the continuous discharge of the thundering artillery—the shells flying with destruction and death in their train amidst the streets of the devoted town, and finally that tremendous explosion of the magazines which shook the new walls, and hurried into eternity some hundreds of the unfortunate besieged. At this climax of his tale he has apparently arrived, and the faces of his auditory reflect the powerful emotions with which the news is received by them. On the same bench as the courier are three figures, of whom the two nearest are Turks, one invested in the old national turban, the other in the "fez" or red cloth cap, which, worn by the Sultan himself, is now substituted for it in both the Egyptian and Turkish armies, and often among the population at large. The former is smoking the "narghile," or water-pipe, with a glass vase and a long flexible tube; while the other is using the ordinary one, a cherry-tree stick with a bowl. Both have withdrawn their amber mouth-pieces, and are listening to the stirring tale with a feeling of astonishment not unmingled with awe. The latter expression is powerfully stamped upon the countenance of the heavy-browed Armenian just behind the Tatar, (quite a type of his class,) who is attired in their usual costume of a furred robe and a black cap, in shape like an inverted kitchen kettle, a figure so familiar to every traveller to the city of the Sultan. On a higher bench is another group, and the admirable style in which it is dashed in, shows with what quickness Wilkie was enabled, after his long study of character, to catch and stamp upon his canvass the peculiarities of foreign as well as native expression. For instance, how

THE TURKISH COURIER RELATING THE CAPTURE OF ACRE.

thoroughly has he pourtrayed the thin, high-browed, and high-souled old Turk, one of a race that is fast passing away, who had not yet received the conviction that the infidels were destined, at no distant period, to obtain the ascendency over the faithful, one which is now embraced with all the force of inevitable fatalism, by the rising generation, to whom the wonders of European civilization are more familiar! There is a start almost of terror on his countenance as the deeds of the infidels are narrated: the idea seems for the first time flashing over his mind, how easily the same prowess might, in a few hours, lay at their mercy even Stamboul itself. And how finely has the painter hit off and contrasted with this true type of the old Mussulman, the flabby, obese, sensual "bon vivant!" a sort of Turkish Falstaff, upon whose fat body the news that thrills through every body else seems— like his English prototype at that of the civil wars that were convulsing the island—to operate only as a subject for a passing jest, or a philosophical argument for making the most of the good things of this life. Nor let us forget the figure of the dervish, with his fanatic eye and flowing beard, and high conical cap of white felt, nor that of the barber, who fills his customer's mouth with lather, as he turns away to catch the news; all of whom are familiar figures in the Eastern capital.—The children, around the brazeer filled with charcoal for lighting the pipes, are added to supply in some degree the deficiency of female faces, which could not be correctly introduced in such a place.

A GROUP OF FIGURES ENTERING MADRID.

WILKIE reached the capital of Spain in October, 1827. He found himself there, he says, with a feeling almost of surprise, and was at first rather disappointed. "Even if I should find nothing worthy of the journey, one point I shall at least ascertain, namely, the quality of the pictures yet remaining in this capital: they have been so long celebrated, but no artist of our own country has seen them. At the American Consul's I have had the good fortune to meet Mr. Washington Irving, whose surprise at seeing me was extreme. I found him, with his brother, whom I knew in Paris, and the Consul, all willing to assist me in every way: they promise me a rich treat, and I feel at once at home with them." Nor were these expectations disappointed; the treasures of art collected at the Escurial and elsewhere, the famous pictures of Titian, Murillo, and Velasquez, and other Spanish masters, were as important to the painter who was studying a new style, as the original character and social peculiarities of the Spanish people were suggestive of a new class of subjects for his pencil. These peculiarities have been admirably depicted by Borrow. "I have visited most of the principal capitals of the world; but, upon the whole, none has ever so interested me as this city of Madrid, in which I now found myself. I will not dwell upon its streets, its edifices, its public squares, its fountains, though some of them are remarkable enough; but Petersburgh has finer streets, Paris and Edinburgh more stately edifices, London far nobler squares, whilst Shiraz can boast of more costly fountains, though not cooler waters. But the population! Within a mud-wall, scarcely one league and a half in circuit, are contained two hundred thousand human beings, certainly forming the most extraordinary vital mass to be found in the entire world; and be it always remembered that this mass is strictly Spanish. The population of Constantinople is extraordinary enough, but to form it twenty nations have contributed—Greeks, Armenians, Persians, Poles, Jews, (the latter, by the by, of Spanish origin, and speaking among themselves the old Spanish language;) but the huge population of Madrid, with the exception of a sprinkling of foreigners, chiefly French tailors, glove-makers, and perruquiers, is strictly Spanish, though a considerable portion are not natives of the place. Here are no colonies of Germans, as at St. Petersburgh; no English factories, as at Lisbon; no multitudes of insolent Yankees lounging through the streets, as at the Havanna, with an air which seems to say, the land is our own whenever we choose to take it; but a population which, however strange and

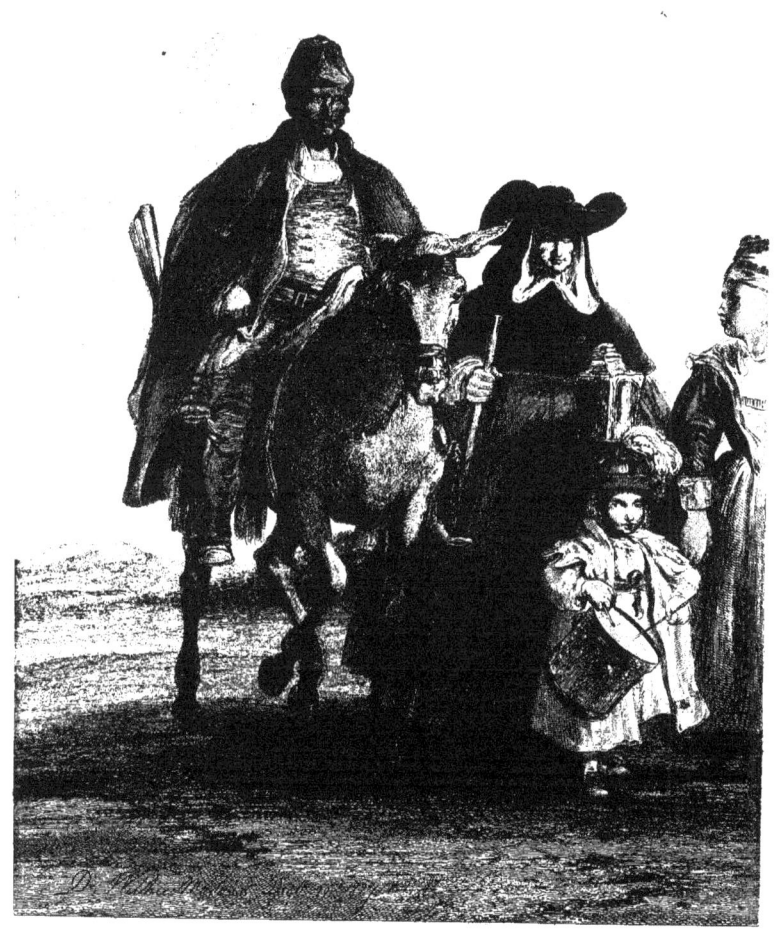

SKETCHED BY SIR DAVID WILKIE, R.A — ENGRAVED BY COUSEN

wild, and composed of various elements, is Spanish, and will remain so as long as the city itself shall exist."

It is not surprising that such a people, so little visited by foreigners, should, as Wilkie observes, be rather shy of them; consequently he saw little of them but what the public places afforded. He witnessed, however, one of their great public amusements—the Bull-Fight: this took place in an area like a Roman amphitheatre: six bulls were combated, and finally killed; six horses were gored to death, and two men severely wounded, to the great delight of the people.

It was in the Prado, the principal promenade of Madrid, that Wilkie chiefly amused himself with the characteristics of its inhabitants. The spot was celebrated in old Spanish romance, as the scene of duels and intrigues, till Don Carlos the Third turned it into a grand public walk—the resort of all who desire to see and to be seen. The whole extent is about nine thousand seven hundred feet. There is a broad carriage-road in the middle, and shady avenues on each side; and it is adorned with splendid fountains and statues. Each class has its separate haunt—the convalescents,—the elderly folks,—the country people,—and the fashionables. For the latter, the "Saloon" is the great place of attraction. Here a *frulling* sound, like the chattering of birds in a cage, reigns in every direction, produced by the tremulous shake, and opening and shutting of innumerable fans of all colours and sizes—so many eloquent tongues, speaking an intelligible language to conscious observers. Even as flowers are "the language of love in the East, there is nothing in the soft science which may not be explained by a Spanish lady with her fan." In the other parts of the promenade may be seen groups intent on a very prevalent pastime; viz., a most assiduous and persevering examination of their own and their children's heads. Fat wet-nurses from the mountains of Santander, with showy handkerchiefs tied about their heads, tight cloth jackets, and gorgeous laced petticoats, are seen with their squalling charges. Such was the spectacle of national character that met the eyes of Wilkie, some traits of which he has consigned to his inimitable sketch-book. The group before us consists of a Guerilla and his Child, accompanied by a Priest, apparently a favourite with the painter, for we find the same head in other of his Spanish compositions.

A GROUP OF CAMELS.

WILKIE first fell in with the camel at Smyrna; and he has recorded the impression made upon him by the sight. To such a mind the groups of these animals and their Eastern conductors were suggestive of a whole train of romantic associations, reminding him of their long journeys over hill and sandy wilderness, through the vast interior of Asia. He set to work immediately, and with his accustomed skill has set vividly before us this very characteristic group.

Recent travellers have rather reversed the custom of praising the camel. Its unwillingness to receive its load, its impatience of any interruption of its course, its hideous groaning when distressed, and sometimes its savage fury when provoked, have called down their unreasonable animadversion. They overlook its endurance of long toilsome marches without water, such as would destroy any other animal. Even its old proverbial patience is denied, or stigmatized as the patience of stupidity alone. Its very appearance is considered by some as most uncouth and ugly. Beautiful it certainly is not: and yet who is there that has beheld it pacing its native sands under the transparent sky of the East, and has not been struck with its picturesque and even majestic gait. And who has not been delighted with its full, dark, expressive eye, as depicted in the well-known works of Vernet, or in such masterly sketches as the one before us? We have delighted to watch it when the animal, after a long day's march, is reposed in almost sculpturesque stillness, browsing the desert shrubs, and have thought its expression singularly beautiful.

It is a popular error that the camel is only suited to the level sands of the desert, when, in fact, it has ever been accustomed to the most toilsome and rocky passes. It subsists upon very little, and we have seen it go without water for three days together. It makes its grave as well as its home in the wilderness; the line of road across the sands taken by the caravan to Mecca is marked out by a line of whitening camels' bones, and the traveller meets with it in every stage of decay, from the moment when the vultures have but just fleshed their beaks in its fallen corpse, till, stripped to the last integument, the wind whistles through the ghastly framework of its naked ribs, and its bones, falling asunder and bleached by the heat and wind, serve to mark the appointed track upon which its strength was spent.

The following sketches from the life are extracted from a recent work by the writer:—

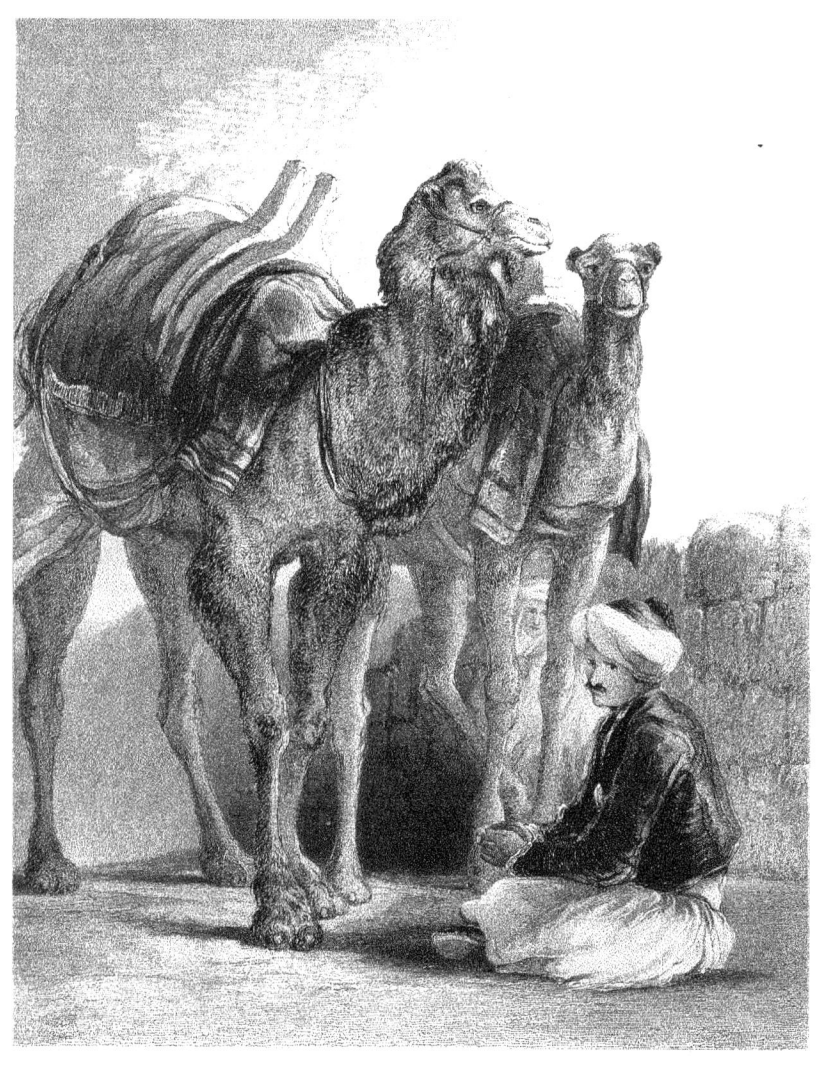

A CAMEL

SKETCHED BY SIR DAVID WILKIE R.A.— ENGRAVED BY C. COUSEN

LONDON, PUBLISHED FOR THE PROPRIETORS BY GEO. VIRTUE 26 IVY LANE.

A GROUP OF CAMELS.

CAMEL RIDING.

" A singular and half-dreamy sensation is that of first riding a camel, the very opposite to that quickening of the pulse which comes to us on horseback. Your seat on a broad pile of carpets, is so easy and indolent, the pace of the animal so equal and quiet,—instead of the noisy clatter of hoofs, you scarcely hear the measured and monotonous impress of the broad soft foot on the yielding sand,—the air fans you so lazily as you move along ; from your lofty post your view over the Desert is so widely extended, the quiet is so intense, that you fall by degrees into a state of pleasurable reverie, mingling early ideas of the East with their almost fanciful realization. And thus the hours pass away till a sense of physical uneasiness begins to predominate, and at length becomes absorbing. It now appears that the chief and only art in camel-riding lies in the nice poising and management of the vertebral column, which seems to refuse its office, though you sustain its failing functions by a desperate tightening of your belt. To sit quite upright for a length of time is difficult on account of your extended legs : you throw your weight alternately to the right or left, lean dangerously forward on the pummel, sit sideways, or lounge desperately backwards, all in vain. The *beau sexe* have, for obvious reasons, decidedly the best of it in this exercise. To lose your sense of weariness you seek to urge the animal to a trot ; but a few such experiments suffice,—fatigue is better than downright dislocation ;—and you resign yourself perforce to the horrible see-saw and provoking tranquillity of your weary pace, till the sun's decline enables you to descend and walk over the shining gravel."

THE CARAVAN.

" It is a truly oriental spectacle, the most characteristic that exists, transporting the beholder back to the very earliest historic times, and even into the clouds of tradition and fable that precede it ; for there can be no doubt that this mode of travel was practised from a period long lost in obscurity, that it would naturally be resorted to in these regions in the very infancy of the world, and that the organization of these migratory hosts must besides ever have been nearly the same. My thoughts went back to the time of Joseph and the Patriarchs, to the days of wealthy Tyre and Petra, and the later magnificence of Palmyra, all connected with this primitive unchanged mode of travel across the vast interior of Asia, all indebted for their splendour to the patient Camel, the ship of the desert, so wonderfully adapted by an omniscient Providence for ministering to the wants of the Eastern world, both in its earliest and advanced stages, equally needful to the migratory camp of the Bodouin wanderers, and for the requirements of the luxurious trading cities of Egypt and Syria, which have for ages dispensed the riches of the East throughout the Western world. Those cities and their commerce have passed away, but the same mode of travel still subsists, and ever must throughout those extensive regions of the world, to which it is exclusively suitable.

A GROUP OF CAMELS.

The long procession, with its face set towards distant Mecca, defiled slowly away, the most advanced portion disappearing over the sandy swell, where we had first encountered it. I could not but follow it in imagination to its destined bourne, through the many perils which hovered about its painful track,—the Bedouins of the Great Desert, the fearful Simoon, the terrible destitution of water, and often of necessary food, under which many, at least of the more poorly provided and infirm, must sink : I thought too, of the fate which, even now, might be hovering over the gayest and best furnished of these splendid pavilions, whose delicate tenants, unequal to the struggle with protracted fatigue, must then be committed to their last homes in the wilderness, to form a fellowship in the grave with the broken-down straggler, whom the departing host has heartlessly left behind to perish, to dig with his expiring strength his own shallow grave in the sand, and await the passing of the angel of death."

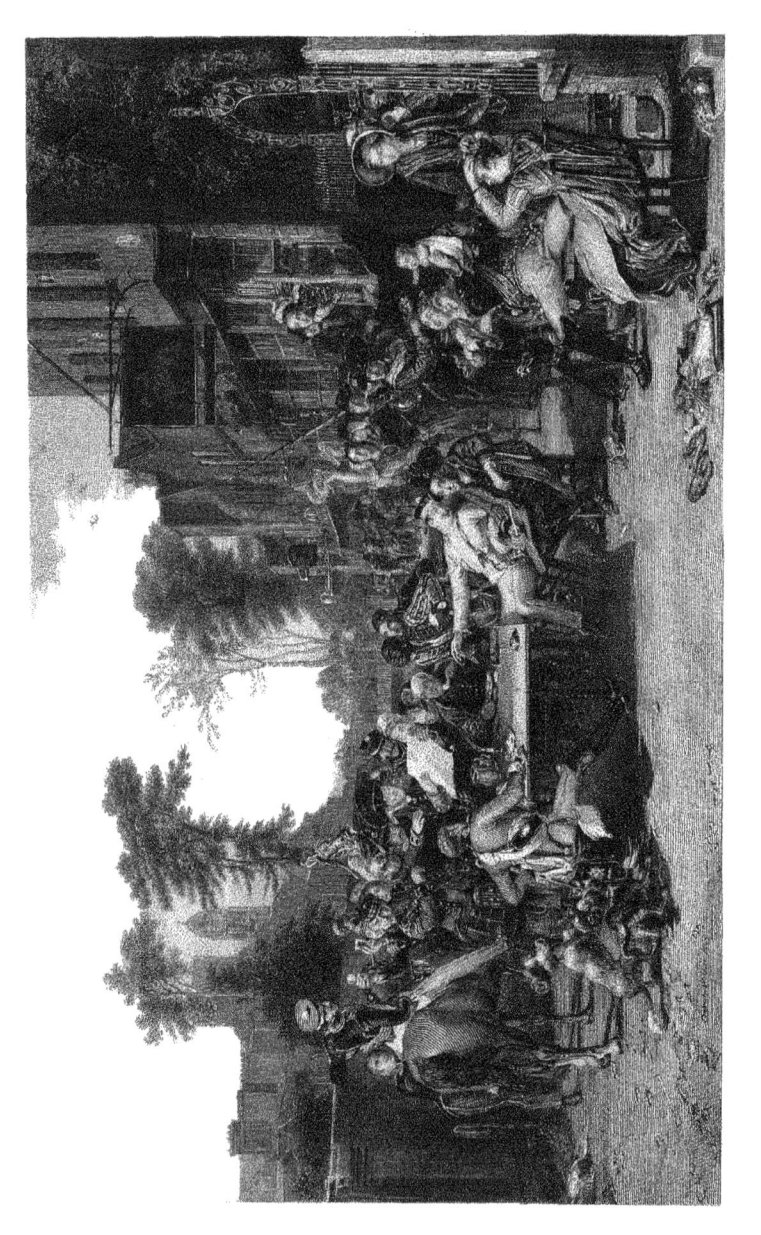

THE CHELSEA PENSIONERS READING THE GAZETTE OF THE BATTLE OF WATERLOO.

THE first notice of this important picture that we meet with is in a letter from the painter, dated 12th December, 1816, to his friend Sir George Beaumont, describing certain scenes and impressions during his tour in Flanders. Among these, the Field of Waterloo, he says, "was to himself, as it must be to every Englishman, a subject of the deepest interest. Whatsoever one's pursuits might be, it was impossible to visit such a place but with the keenest associations." He then goes on to say, "As I know you will feel interested in any circumstance of a pleasing nature that occurs to me, I cannot refrain from mentioning that the Duke of Wellington has commissioned me to paint him a picture; and that, when he was last in England, he called upon me with some friends to give me the subject. He wants it to be a number of soldiers of various descriptions, seated upon the benches of the door of a public-house, with porter and tobacco, telling over their old stories.

Wilkie resolved to turn this commission to account, and to make the picture a memorial of Waterloo; and, with this design, in December, 1818, he first submitted the sketch to the Duke of Wellington. We find, from his journals, that it was some time before his Grace could satisfy himself as to the arrangement of the materials. With an eye to variety of character, the painter had introduced many pensioners of half a century ago; the Duke, very naturally, wished to have more of his confederates in arms. The final decision was made on the 12th of July, 1819; his Grace, Mr. Long, and the painter being of the council. The Duke pointed out, in the two sketches submitted, what he liked and disliked, and thought that out of them a picture might be made that would do. He preferred the one with the young figures; but as Mr. Long remonstrated against the old fellows being taken out, the Duke agreed that the man reading should be a pensioner, besides some others in the picture. He wished that the piper should be put in; also, the old man with the wooden leg; but he objected to the man with the ophthalmia. He then said the picture might be immediately proceeded with.

During the whole of the year 1821, this picture, as Allan Cunningham observes, "was like a spell upon the mind of Wilkie." His visits to Chelsea were unintermitting. "At that time," says Mrs Thimson, (wife of Dr. Anthony Todd Thimson,) "we lived on the road from Kensington to Chelsea, and remember Wilkie's frequent and toilsome walks to that low region called Jews' Row, the Pall Mall of the pensioners, to sketch an old projecting house, under which some of his groups were placed." He usually drank tea on his return, and showed the little bits of tinted paper, the materials of his picture. Altering the composition from time to time, he at length satisfied himself with it; and in February, 1822, had the honour of a call from the Duke of Wellington, to see his progress. His Grace seemed highly delighted with it, " took notice of the black's head and old Doggy, and the black dog which followed the Blues in Spain ; was interested with what I told him of the people, and where they had served." The picture, at length completed, was transferred to the Exhibition of the Royal Academy, where the sensation it created was almost unexampled. The " crushing and crowding" was tremendous; and the painter, one morning, was witness to such a scene as convinced him that his picture was in imminent danger: he wrote, therefore, to Sir Thomas Lawrence, to request as a particular favour, that he would order a railing to be put up without delay. On going to Somerset-House the next morning, he found that the accomplished President had been already there to superintend the operation. Shortly after he received a note from the Duke, asking what he was indebted for the picture. It contained sixty figures, and besides months of previous study, had taken for its execution sixteen months. Wilkie fixed 1,200 guineas as the price, with which the Duke was entirely satisfied, and requested the painter to call at Apsley-House, counted out the money to him in bank-notes, on which Wilkie expressed his sense of the handsome treatment of his Grace throughout the whole affair.

Let us now turn from its history to the picture itself. The truth of the localities is as great as their composition is skilful. The old towers of Chelsea Hospital, the groups of lofty elms, and the antique gabled architecture of "Jews' Row," with its variety of signs, all referring to different military exploits and leaders, are admirably arranged as a frame-work to set off the living characters. Of these the variety is remarkable. On successive visits Wilkie had collected together all the originals he could pick up, the wrecks of old campaigns; and these he has intermingled with the stalwart forms of heroes in their prime, and has relieved the composition with the grace and animation of women and children. The story almost tells itself. A group of persons is carousing, when one of the Lancers rushes in with the Gazette of the Battle of Waterloo. The eager excitement occasioned by the news is diffused over the assembled groups with surprising skill; we seem to catch the joyous spirit of the scene in gazing upon it. The principal characters are portraits. The old pensioner who is reading the Gazette was with Wolfe at the Battle of Quebec. The negro was formerly servant to General Moreau, and behind him is a soldier of the Indian army, who fought with Wellington at Assaye. The feeble veteran, whose senses are blunted with age, and who catches imperfectly the report shouted into his ear by the joyous young Irishman at his side, is one of the most remarkable of Wilkie's gallery of characters. The rest of the central group, the Lifeguardsman seated on a barrel, the Lancer on horseback,

READING THE GAZETTE OF THE BATTLE OF WATERLOO.

who has brought the Gazette, and the sturdy Highlander, a Glengarry Macgreggor, who fought at Barossa, with other soldiers, if less remarkable, are equally true to life. On the right-hand side we have in the foreground a soldier of the Blues, who had fought at Vittoria, lifting up his infant; at his feet is a black dog, called the "Old Duke," already alluded to, which followed the regiment in Spain. Behind him is the old oyster-woman, a sort of "Femme du Regiment," and a wooden-legged veteran, pipe in mouth, and with a keg which he is about to replenish. These prominent characters are intermingled with the rest with great skill. We have before remarked upon Wilkie's talent in blending the pathetic with the lively; and here, a striking instance, is the face of the soldier's wife, looking over the Gazette with trembling eagerness, to watch whether the name of her husband is among the slain. Her very life seems to hang upon the issue. These are traits of feeling and expression which stamp the great master.

We cannot conclude our sketch without bestowing the highest praise on the admirable manner in which the engraver has rendered, on so small a scale, even the subtlest details of the original composition. Little except colour is wanting to give us a perfect idea of this masterpiece of our great national painter.

THREE GREEK SISTERS OF THERAPIA.

WILKIE has given in his journals and letters many lively accounts of his impressions of Constantinople, and its unequalled environs. He familiarly describes the city as divided into districts, rising precipitous from the water, as if Highgate and Hampstead were planted close to the Thames on one side, and Greenwich and Richmond Hills on the other; at the same time, the heights here rise far higher than these, and the suburbs are so extended as to appear, save London, the largest city he had ever seen. The quarter he lived in, Pera, is allotted to Europeans of all sorts; Galata, next to it, is the place for bankers and merchants; while Stamboul or Constantinople, divided from them by an arm of the sea, is the real Turkish quarter, where the Bazaars, the market for slaves, the ancient Hippodrome, the Mosque of St. Sophia, and the Seraglio of the Sultan are situated. On the other side, the Southwark side, and the only part Asiatic, is Scutari, all of which, extending for miles along the Bosphorus, give to this city its celebrated character for magnificence of situation.

Almost the first thing Wilkie did was to repair to Therapia, to visit the English Ambassador, Lord Ponsonby, who received him most kindly, and gave him much information respecting the state of the Ottoman Court. To this delightful resort he paid more than one visit, sometimes going by land and returning by water. "Therapia and Buyukdèrè," says Miss Pardoe, "are the summer residences of the European Ambassadors, and consequently the occasional focus of the Frank aristocracy. Both are beautifully situated. Buyukdèrè stands boldly near the very junction of the two seas, while Therapia is less exposed to the tempest blasts of the 'storm-vexed Euxine.' It is backed by a richly-wooded hill, on which the houses of the upper town have, however, very considerably and very picturesquely encroached. And here the English and French embassies, since the great fire of Pera, when the ambassadorial residences were destroyed, have entirely established themselves, only occasionally visiting the city; and hence the commerce of the place has become very respectable, and the appearance of its inhabitants acquired no slight tinge of the restlessness and businesslike manner of their Frank visitors."

It was during one of his visits to Therapia that Wilkie made the annexed sketch of three young Greek ladies, friends of Mrs. Bankhead. There is a very considerable Greek population at Constantinople, the Patriarch usually residing there. A particular quarter, called the Fanar, is appropriated to them. The Greeks have ever possessed considerable

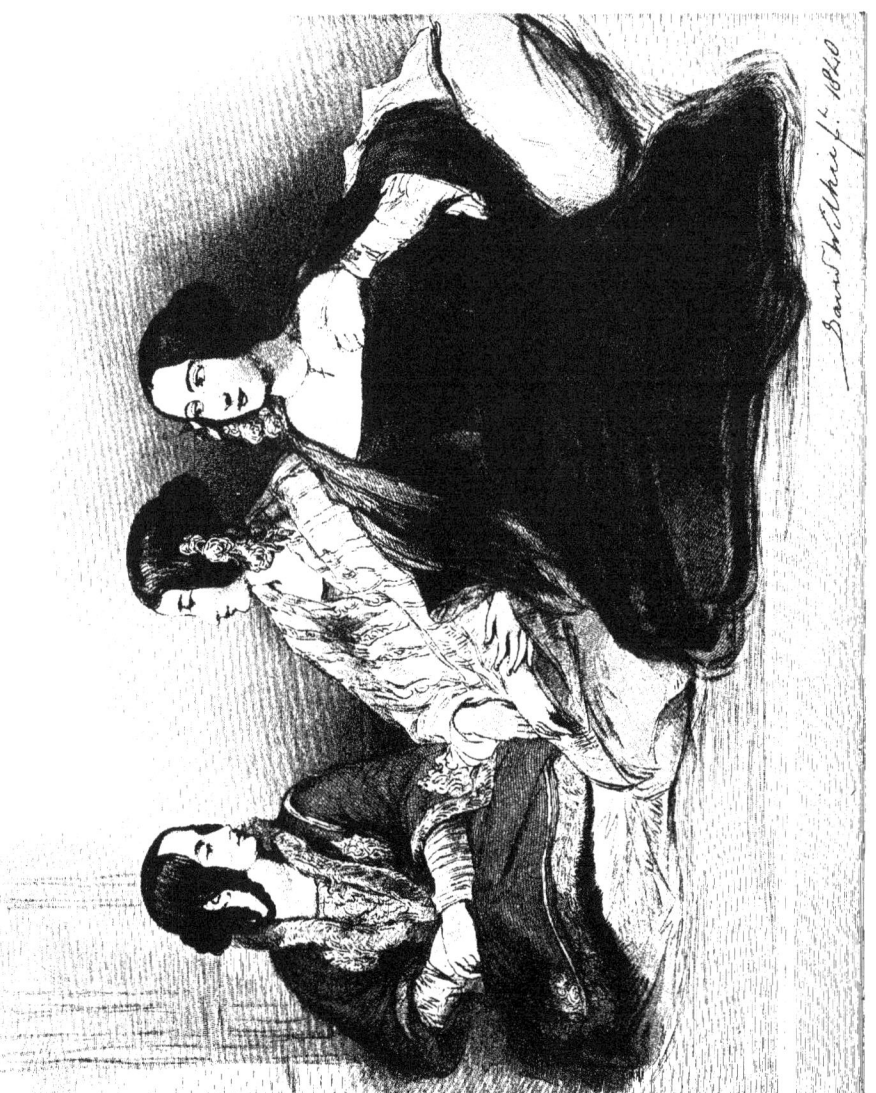

THE GREEK SIS E API

SKETCHED BY SIR D

influence in the Ottoman capital, from their restless intriguing character, and superior talents. Some of them have amassed considerable riches, but before the independence of their country they were afraid to display it. The lawless will of the Sultan, like the suspended sword of Damocles, ever threatened them in the midst of enjoyment; and notwithstanding the care with which they sought to conceal their wealth, the edict of arbitrary power too often arrested their career, and pounced upon their possessions. Therapia and the other beautiful villages that line the shores of the Bosphorus, are their favourite retreats. The Greek women have ever been celebrated for their charms, not always of the severe and Minerva-like character usually imagined, but displaying at least as much of the softer beauties of Venus; and, unless they are greatly belied, they still display the graceful levity (without much of the intellectual seasoning) of the celebrated favourites of Alcibiades or Pericles. Not a few of them contrive to fix and fascinate the natives of the severer north — English and French merchants, who are fixed by their interests in the Levant. This is particularly the case at Constantinople and Smyrna, the principal families of the latter city being almost all related. Few travellers in the Levant but have to remember Smyrna for its open-hearted hospitality and its light-hearted gaiety. It is the very paradise of Mediterranean "middies," who have not a few tender souvenirs connected with pic-nic parties to the neighbouring villages, where the merchants have countryhouses — and with moonlight dances under the beautiful sky of "soft Ionia." And those who, like the writer, have experienced the vicissitudes of Eastern travel, and have been laid prostrate by sickness, know how to appreciate the feeling attentions of the Greek women.

Of the malicious archness of these Levantine belles the following instance was narrated to us at Smyrna. A certain Count and diplomatic functionary, with no small sense of his own pretensions, consulted a young lady upon the subject of his marriage. His heart was not engaged, and all he wanted was to make a desirable match. Hereupon his confidant, aware of his immeasurable vanity, persuaded him to write three offers at the same time, to as many young ladies, whom she suggested for his choice, from whom, when duly accepted, as he could not fail to be, he might afterwards pick at leisure. He greedily swallowed the bait, and dispatched the triple proposals. Upon this his adviser went round and *confidentially* told all three of the ladies. Although each might perhaps have accepted the Count, had she been left in ignorance of his offers to the rest, yet, under the circumstances, very shame compelled them to reject him; and thus he received at the same time an indignant refusal from the trio, and, worse than all, the story got abroad through Pera. Well indeed might the Arabian say, that "the wit of women surpasses the cunning of man."

Wilkie has represented these young women in the European dress, which is a pity—since their national costume of the graceful short jacket and red cap with its pendant tassel is infinitely more elegant. But the belles of Pera think it more distingué to wear the Parisian costume, which in general is anything but becoming to their face and figure.

To improve the education and moral training of the Greek women has for many years been an object of anxious solicitude to the lady of the Rev. Mr. Hill, an American missionary at Athens. She has laboured to produce female teachers, qualified to carry on the work among their young countrywomen, and with no small degree of success. The good work was, however, suspended at the time of our visit, by the jealousy of the Greek church, who feared lest the influence thus obtained might be directed towards proselytism,—a suspicion which was entirely unfounded.

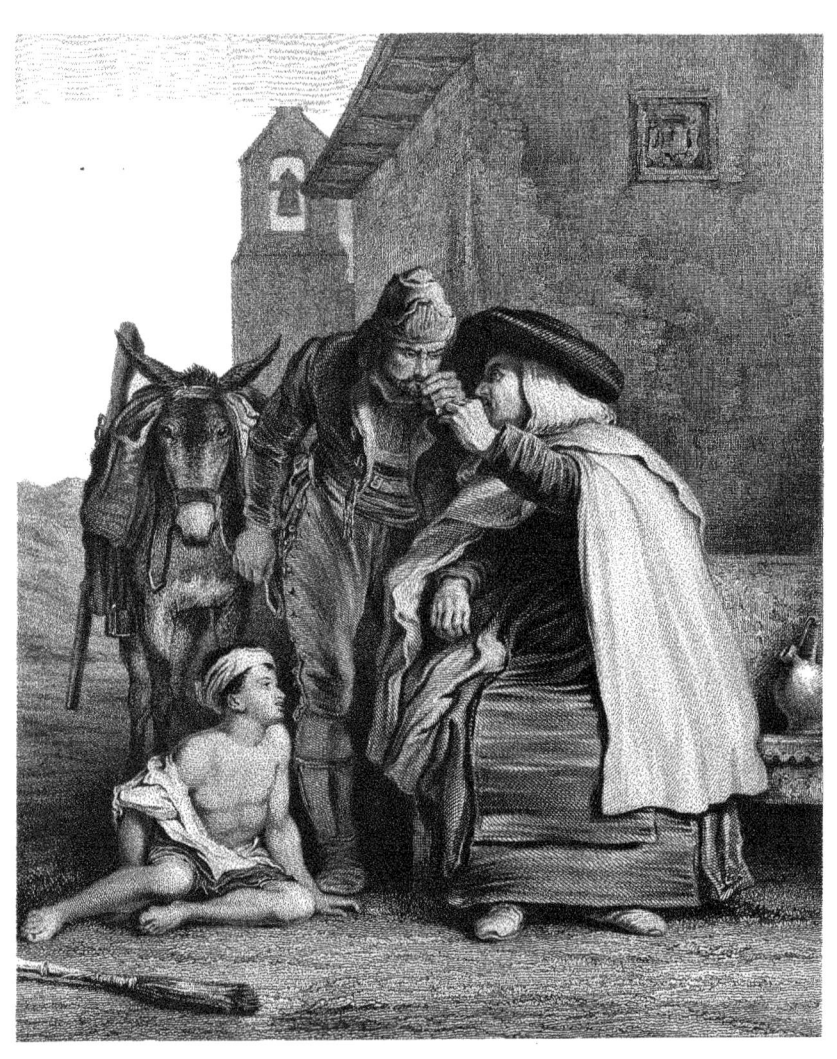

THE GUERILLA TAKING LEAVE OF HIS CONFESSOR.

This is another of the fruits of Wilkie's tour in Spain. The troubled state of the country at the period of his visit suggested his painting scenes from the previous struggles with the French. He arrived at Madrid, his portfolio stored with sketches taken on the road, and immediately set to work with such ardour that, to use his own words, "pictures grew up under his hands, with even more rapidity than they used to do at Kensington." The works thus produced have all the stamp of truth; they are evidently painted from recent observation of character, and are full of freshness and originality. Let us take, for instance, the subject before us. "The Guerilla, or Peasant Soldier," is departing to engage in the struggle against his country's enemies; his mule is saddled, and his small bag for provisions with his gun slung from the saddle. He has just confessed, and doubtless received absolution, like Benvenuto Cellini, for all the homicides he ever had committed or ever should commit, in the service of the church. This business over, he is gravely lighting his cigarro by that of his reverend confessor; a curious illustration of the national habit. Each figure in this sketch is full of character. The Spanish peasant, by the concurring accounts of travellers, is a truly noble being. "With respect to the Spanish aristocracy," says Barrow, "the ladies and gentlemen, the cavaliers and senoras, I believe the less that is said of them the better. I would sooner talk of the lower class, not only of Madrid, but of all Spain. The Spaniard of the lower class has much more interest for me, whether mavolo, labourer, or muleteer. He is not a common being, he is an extraordinary man. He possesses a spirit of proud independence, which it is impossible but to admire. He is ignorant, of course; but it is singular that I have invariably found amongst the low and slightly educated classes far more liberality of sentiment than amongst the upper. Amongst the peasantry of Spain I found my sturdiest supporters." This description of Barrow is entirely borne out by the pictures of Wilkie. The same eminent writer has given us many traits of the Spanish clergy, of whom, in the main, his account is highly unfavourable. Yet there are undoubtedly many noble exceptions; and if the influence of the priest is unfavourable to the progress of intellectual enlightenment, yet we cannot doubt that, on the other hand, it is often exercised for good. Wilkie seized almost intuitively upon the character of whatever presented itself to his notice, and thus we find among his sketches many striking portraitures of the Spanish priests, stamped with all the austere bigotry of the inquisitor—the resolute hatred of innovation. "A tribe of beings

THE GUERILLA TAKING LEAVE OF HIS CONFESSOR.

can scarcely be found with a more confirmed aversion to intellectual pursuits of every kind. Their reading is confined to newspapers; but they prefer their chocolate and biscuits, and nap before dinner, to the wisdom of Plato and the eloquence of Tully." While the majority are thus sunk in the sleep of ignorance and prejudice, there are not a few of the higher rank of ecclesiastics, who, externally the most bigoted in profession and austere in appearance, lead in secret the most dissolute lives, pride themselves upon being illuminati, study Voltaire and the Encyclopedia, and make a mock among themselves of everything in the shape of religion. These facts are revealed to us in Blanco White's memoirs. Such extremes may naturally be looked for under such a system.

The half-naked boy, though undoubtedly sketched from nature, appears almost like a transcript from one of Murillo's Spanish boys, a correspondence which attests the truth of both. The roguish countenance of this urchin and the peculiar cast of his features proclaim his Moorish origin. Every reader of Spanish history is acquainted with the splendour of the Moorish kingdom in Spain, its overthrow by Ferdinand and Isabella, and the final expulsion of the race from the soil. Yet the Arab blood is largely intermingled with the Spanish; this little urchin is almost a counterpart of the Donkey Boy of Cairo.

We must not forget to notice the Spanish mule, the breed of which is remarkable: its good qualities are vaunted by Barrow, who declares that its steady and fast walk will tire down a trotting horse.

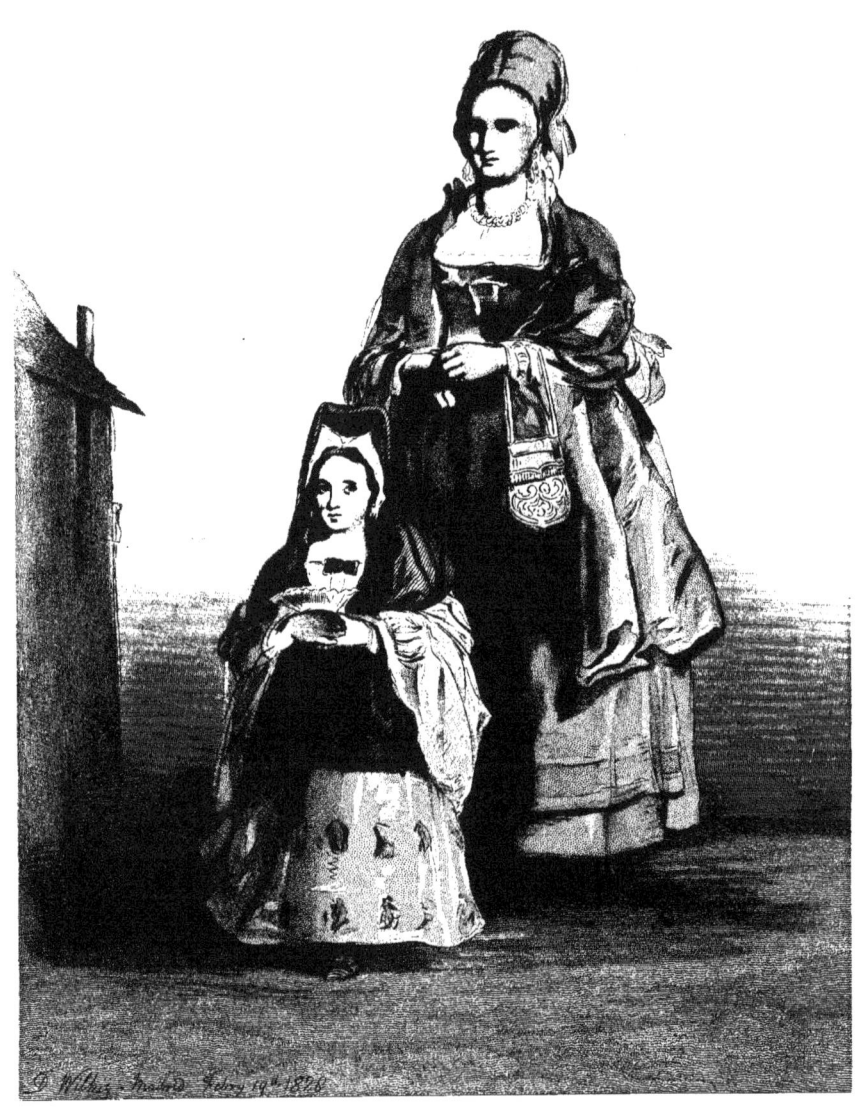

THE SENORITTA AND HER NURSE.

In Wilkie's " Remarks on Painting," he observes of Vandyke, that his representations of the children of Charles I. are painted at that age when the simplicity of inexperience shows them in most engaging contrast with the power of their rank and station, and that, like the infantas of Velasquez, they *united all the demure stateliness of the court, with the perfect artlessness of childhood.* The punctilious etiquette and the grave aristocratic hauteur of the court of Spain is indeed curiously stamped upon all the youthful portraits of their great national painter, and the same ceremonious gravity seems to descend through the different gradations of society. The poor and proud hidalgo, with a long pedigree, a threadbare cloak, and an empty stomach, is inimitably painted by Cervantes, who makes the meanest personages of his immortal fiction address each other in an almost courtly style of compliment. There is little or no change in this respect in our own times, as may be seen from the lively pages of Borrow. There is an old proverb that "the French are wiser than they seem, and the Spanish look wiser than they are." The sketch before us may well be called *delicious*, for its perfect comprehension of this peculiarity of the national character, as well as for its vivid look of life; and its airy, graceful, and masterly style of handling. We have had very beautiful representations of childhood from Wilkie's pencil, among which that of the "Infant Daughter of Admiral Walker" is the most perfectly *natural* and *artless;* but here we have the child in leading-strings; the little lady of birth, brought up in all the pride of station, and taught to assume the court air from her very cradle—to wear gracefully the fascinating mantilla, and to handle betimes the expressive fan. Thus trained, she is taken to the Prado for a promenade by her nurse, who follows at a respectful distance, and reflects in her own demeanour all the gravity and the conscious importance of her miniature mistress. The charm of the performance is, that through all this artificial exterior peeps out the sweetness of nature—the child is seen through the assumed garb and manner of the full-grown lady. To seize and convey this peculiarity required no less moral discrimination than artistic skill.

No subject could be more uninteresting or unmanageable in the hand of some common painter—we should have had all its stiffness without its redeeming character and grace. It is the true artist alone who is gifted with the exquisite perception of the slightest shades of character, with the marvellous faculty of stamping them in living reality upon the senseless canvass.

THE SENORITTA AND HER NURSE.

Wilkie made no long stay in Spain, but the results of his industry were prodigious. He was but just reviving from a low state of health, which had for many months almost interdicted him from following his professional avocations. His journal details the many efforts he made, during his stay in Italy, to resume his beloved pursuit, but in every instance he was overcome, after a short application, by unconquerable lassitude and mental confusion. His temporary abstinence from painting appears to have worked a salutary improvement; for we find him at Madrid resuming his labours with renewed vigour and "gusto," while the number and variety of his productions not only surprised the Spanish connoisseurs, but also the world of art in England, to which he returned to execute some of his very finest works.

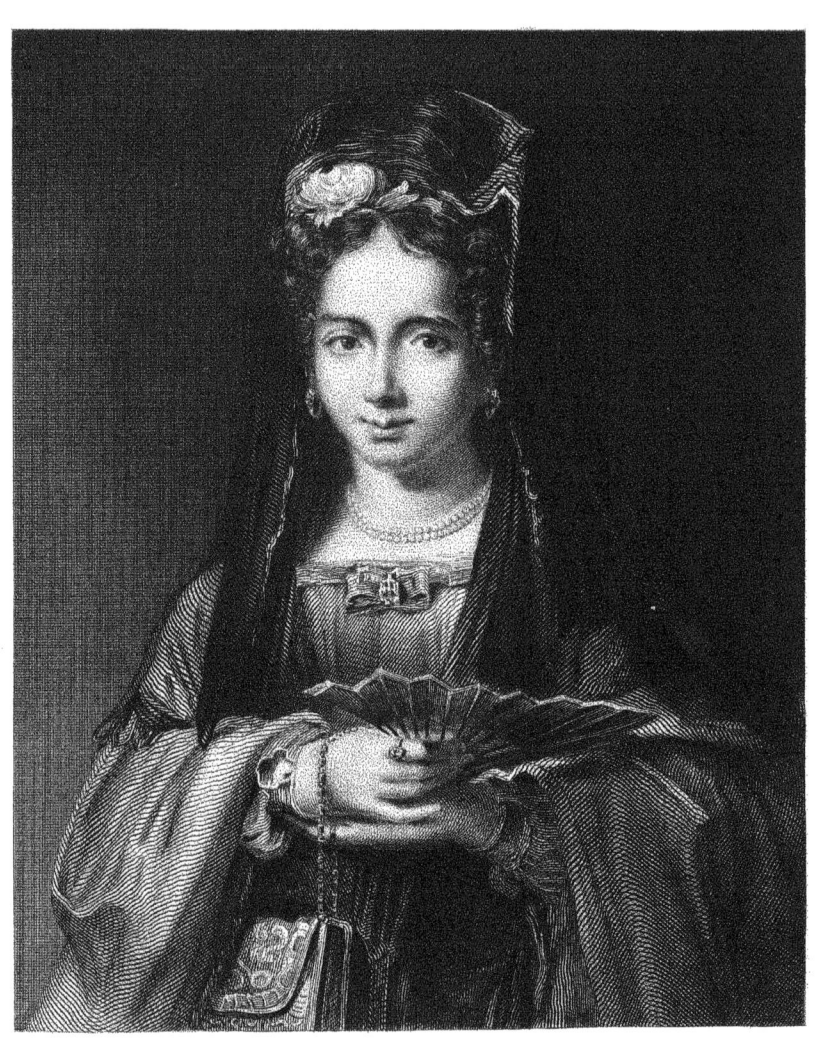

THE SPANISH LADY.

PAINTED BY SIR DAVID WILKIE R A.- ENGRAVED BY W GREATBACH

THE SPANISH LADY.

ALL travellers have expatiated upon the peculiar fascination of the Spanish women. The author of "A Year in Spain" declares that the most stubborn morality is not proof against their seductions. But no one has described them in terms more glowing than Lord Byron, in a letter to his mother: "Long black hair, dark languishing eyes, clear olive complexions, and forms more graceful than can be conceived by an Englishman, used to the drowsy listless air of his countrywomen," (with whom, be it said, his lordship was not just then in the best of humours,) "added to the most becoming dress, and at the same time the most decent in the world, render a Spanish beauty irresistible." And again, in "Don Juan," he breaks out thus rapturously, speaking of the women of Cadiz:—

> "And such sweet girls, I mean such graceful ladies,
> Their very walk would make your bosom swell,
> I can't describe it, though so much it strike,
> Nor liken it, I never saw the like.
>
> An Arab horse, a stately stag, a barb
> New broke, a cameleopard, a gazelle,
> No, none of these will do; and then their garb,
> Their veil and petticoat—alas! to dwell
> Upon such things would very near absorb
> A canto—then their feet and ankles—well,
> Thank heaven, I've got no metaphor quite ready,
> (And so, my sober muse, come, let's be steady,)
> Chaste muse! (well if you must, you must)—the veil
> Thrown back a moment, with the glancing hand,
> While the o'erpowering eye, that turns you pale,
> Flashes into the heart:"

and so on. The sober painter was not the man to be carried away like the poet; but he was doubtless not insensible to attractions like these, while the costume appeared to him better suited for the purposes of his art than those of England and France. The colours adopted by the Spanish ladies are grave,—a black mantilla and veil drawn over the head, with the flashing and eloquent fan, give them a semblance at once "mystical and gay," and particularly piquant. Of the effect thus produced, the specimen before us gives a fair idea. The hair and eyes are relieved by a single flower, and by the graceful and flowing headdress, certainly better than they could be by all the refinements of a Parisian toilette. As to the fan—it is almost part and parcel of a Spanish beauty—in her skilful hand it seems to express every phase of the tender passion, from lively coquetry to amorous langour; it is indeed a potent instrument, and well she knows how to wield it. In judging of the moral character of the Spanish women, we must not accept the tales of passing travellers, without a grain or two of reservation. Byron tell us, that "the business of their life is intrigue," and in another letter to his mother, he observes, " At Seville, we lodged in the house of two Spanish unmarried ladies, women of character; the eldest, a fine woman, the younger, pretty. The freedom of manner which is general here, astonished me not a little, and in the course of further observation, I find that reserve is not the characteristic of the Spanish belles. The eldest honoured your unworthy son with very particular attention, embracing him with great tenderness at parting, (I was there but three days,) after cutting off a lock of his hair, and presenting him with one of her own, about three feet in length, which I send, and beg you will retain till my return. Her last words were, '*Adios, tu hermoso! me gusto mucho!*' Adieu, you pretty fellow! you please me much!" Whatever may be the truth as to these points, the Spanish women, it is allowed on all hands, have, when aroused, often displayed the highest heroism and self-devotion, as well as all the virtues which can adorn and dignify the sex.

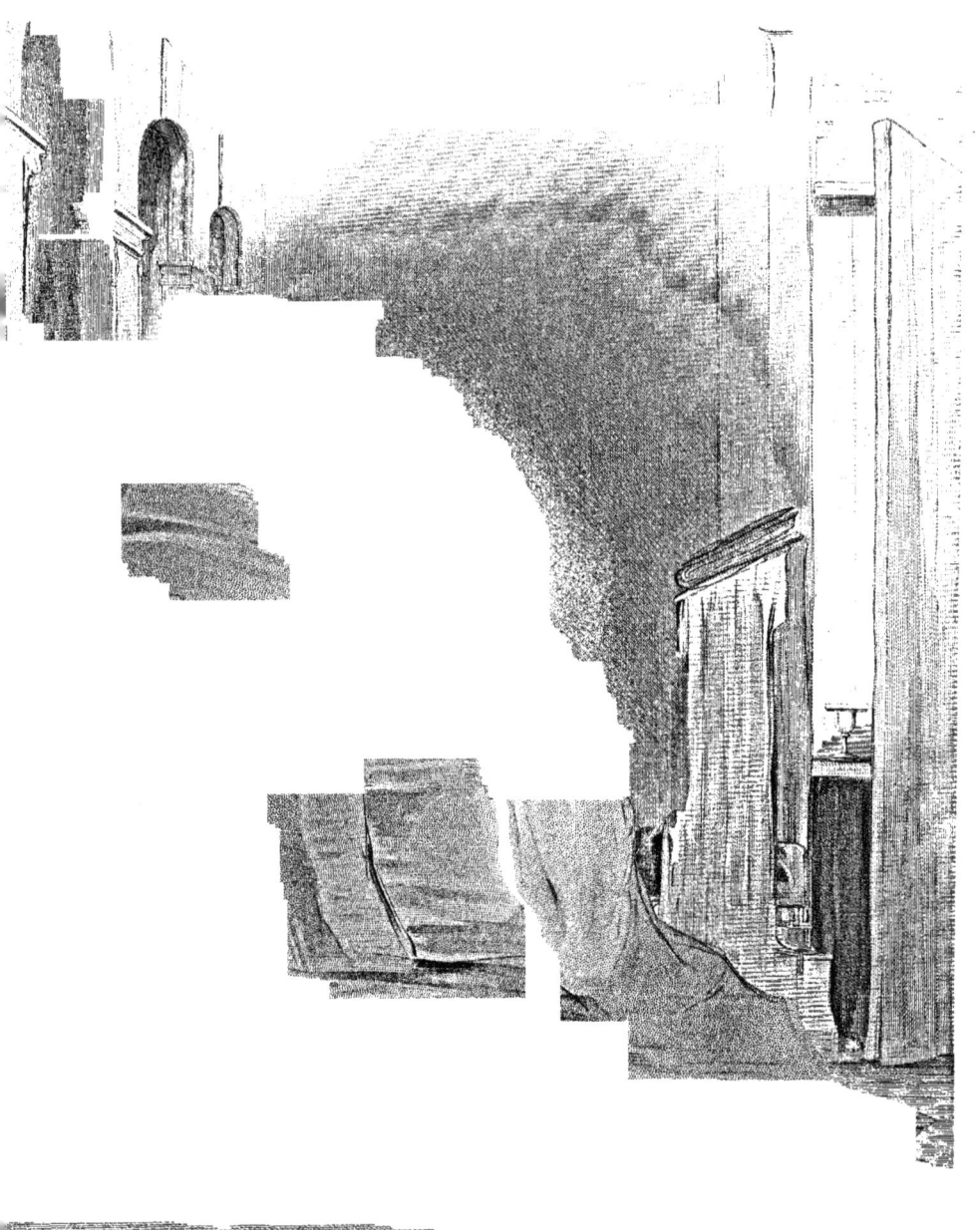

SCENE AT TOLEDO.

A SCENE AT TOLEDO.

THE CONFESSIONAL.

WERE we required to select any *one* subject from the works of Wilkie, numerous and varied as they are, which should give the highest idea of his powers, it would be that now before us. It is one of those happy things struck off in a moment of inspiration; full of that feeling and fervour which is beyond the ordinary efforts even of a man of genius. The painter at the time of its execution was doubtless under the influence of the striking scenes that he witnessed in the catholic churches of Spain, as well as of the marvels of art wrought by the painters of that country, often from the same materials. If the time invoked by Beckford should indeed ever come, when "the tiara with its train of scaring terrors shall vanish like a feverish dream," the Spanish painters will have preserved to future ages all the phenomena of a bygone religious enthusiasm, from the self-tormenting austerities and penitential agonies of the lonely monk to the rapt enthusiasm and ecstacy of the triumphant saint.

This work of Wilkie's is one in which the art is most consummate—the noble simplicity of the composition, the masterly ease and breadth of the style, the judicious contrasts of form, and extraordinary force of expression produced by means so simple, were perhaps never thus conspicuously displayed in any of the painter's productions. But these remarkable qualities are almost overlooked by us in the intensity of the pervading sentiment.

The confessional!—what a host of almost fearful associations arise as we think of this discipline of the Catholic church! terrible alike to the frail being, whose every lawless thought must be bared to inspection, and to the no less frail depository of the darkest secrets of the human heart. What is it that wrings the frame of that pale young monk with so woeful an agony? Some passion, perhaps, the indulgence of which would be a deadly crime, but which he finds it impossible to subdue — some sad confession echoing the complaint of the miserable Abelard, "that the conflicting inclinations, of which St. Paul speaks, distracted his soul, and that of loving God ever proved the weaker; who, without the love of virtue, without regard to the vows he had taken upon him, suffered at once the pains of vice and virtue, without the hope of being recompensed by either."

Finely has Wilkie conceived and marvellously depicted the damp brow and the fevered cheek, the agitated frame and the convulsive and confiding grasp of the poor young monk, which all tell of this wasting and unnatural struggle with himself, the confession of which seems to be to him at once a torture and a relief. And that grave and noble head of the old man—what an expression has the painter thrown into it!—as of one who is overshadowed with the solemn responsibility of his office, and who has learned to sympathize profoundly with the mental woes which, though he is called upon to soothe, he feels that a higher power alone is able to heal, and that in the deep agonies that convulse the spirit, "man with his God must strive."

THE PRAYER OF THE DESPONDENT MONK.

* * * * " I am one, whose spirit,
From its first hour of fatal consciousness,
Hath with the saddening shadow of despair
Been overcast: nor have I e'er prevail'd
To burst the chain which mocks my cries for light,
Though I have agonized with earnest prayer,
With burning tears, and frenzied utterance,
For peace—that cometh not. * * *
Oh, then, at length have pity on me, Lord !
Thou canst not mock my cries—heal thou the wounds
That the sore galling of my chain of torment
Hath worn so deeply.—Oh, in mercy heal
The energies that sin hath brought so low—
My worn and wasted heart—else, with long brooding
Upon the fearful brow of cold despair,
I fall in fixed and hopeless fascination
Before his awful gaze, and wear his chain
Through that dread night which hath no hope of dawn."—ANON.

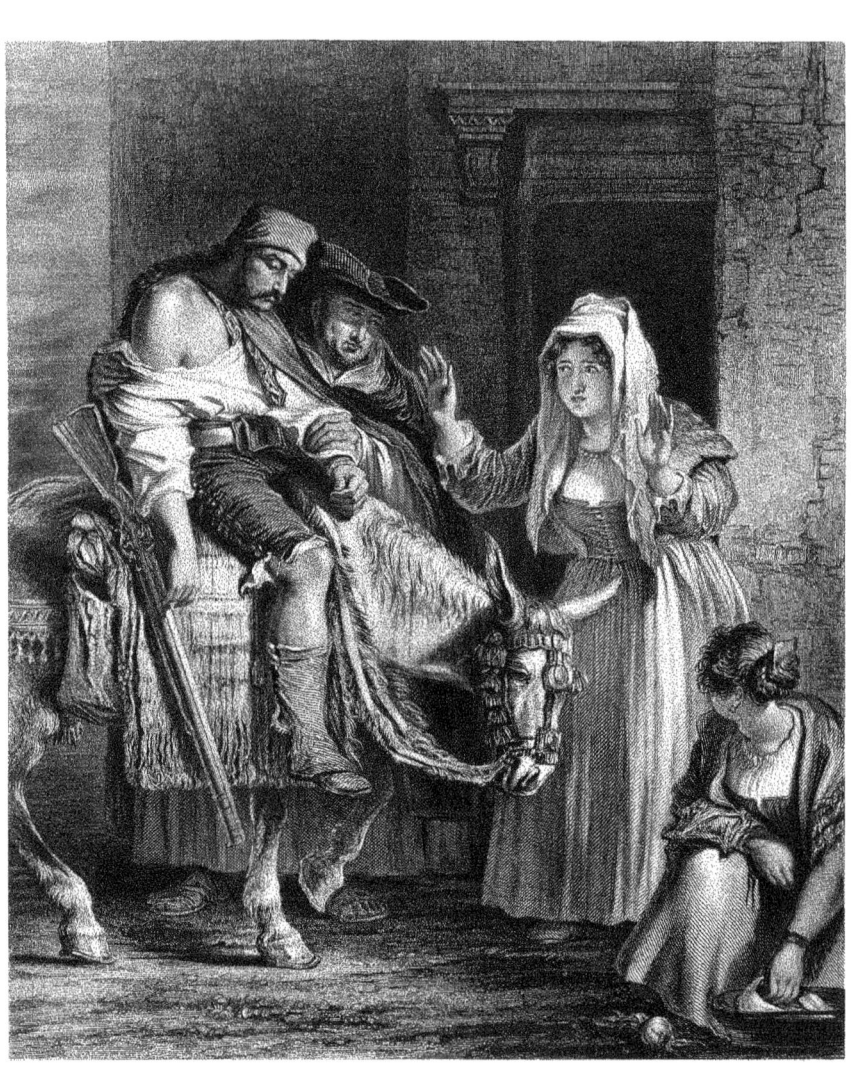

THE WOUNDED GUERILLA.

OVER this subject, one of the series painted at Madrid, Wilkie has contrived to throw a pathetic interest. In another sketch he gives us the Guerilla, in all the vigour of determined manhood, about to go forth to risk his life in an unequal struggle with the invader of his native land. In comparing the two pictures, the contrast of expression is painful. The countenance of the one is full of animation, that of the latter fallen and sunken. The strong man has become helpless as a child, and is with difficulty supported upon his mule by a sympathizing priest. He seems but feebly conscious that he has reached his own door, from which he is too probably never again destined to go forth alive, and scarcely recognises the distressed wife, who comes forward to receive him. This figure of the wounded Guerilla may be considered as one of the masterpieces of Wilkie. The noble, manly head, sunk on the robust chest, wears an expression of suffering, and in its deep pallor, like that of death, its different traits appear more marked and touching than in the fulness of life and health. The listlessness of the once vigorous limbs is portrayed with a master hand. The other figures are certainly less happy. The wife is too pretty and commonplace, both in character and attitude, and the girl in the corner adds nothing to the expression of the subject.

A brief notice of the circumstances that led to the Guerilla warfare are almost necessary for the appreciation of this and other sketches of Wilkie's, connected with the subject. Not long after the battle of Trafalgar, Napoleon resolved on obtaining the crown of the Spanish Bourbons for one of his own family; and accordingly fomented the strife between the king, Charles, and his eldest son Ferdinand. Some serious disturbances having taken place, the former felt compelled to abdicate in favour of the latter. Napoleon now appeared in Spain, summoned both father and son to appear in his presence, upbraided Ferdinand, and released Charles from his promise; whereupon the latter resigned the crown for himself and descendants into the hands of the French emperor, who forthwith invested his brother Joseph with the royal dignity. It was the old fable of the oyster realized in politics. The grandees passively acquiesced in the deposition of their hereditary monarchs; not so, however, the Spanish people; they rose against the foreigner, assembled the provincial juntas, proclaimed Ferdinand, and ordered a general levy. They next sent deputies to England to solicit assistance, which was cheerfully afforded them. Our limits forbid us to detail the well-known incidents of the Peninsular war, principally waged between the

French and English, for the Spanish regular troops were of little service in the struggle. It was very different with the Guerilla bands, chiefly composed of the peasantry, who, intimately acquainted with every nook and corner of the country, were enabled to attack the invaders to the greatest advantage. Concealed among the mountain passes, or among the covert of rocks or bushes, they hung upon the skirts of the French armies, cut off their foraging parties, intercepted their messengers, destroyed their provisions, waylaid their recruits, and caused them to suffer in detail the worst evils that an army in an enemy's country can endure. Thus they proved most powerful auxiliaries to the English, who, as is well known, at length compelled the French to evacuate the Peninsula, and rolled the tide of conquest back to the very capital of the invaders.

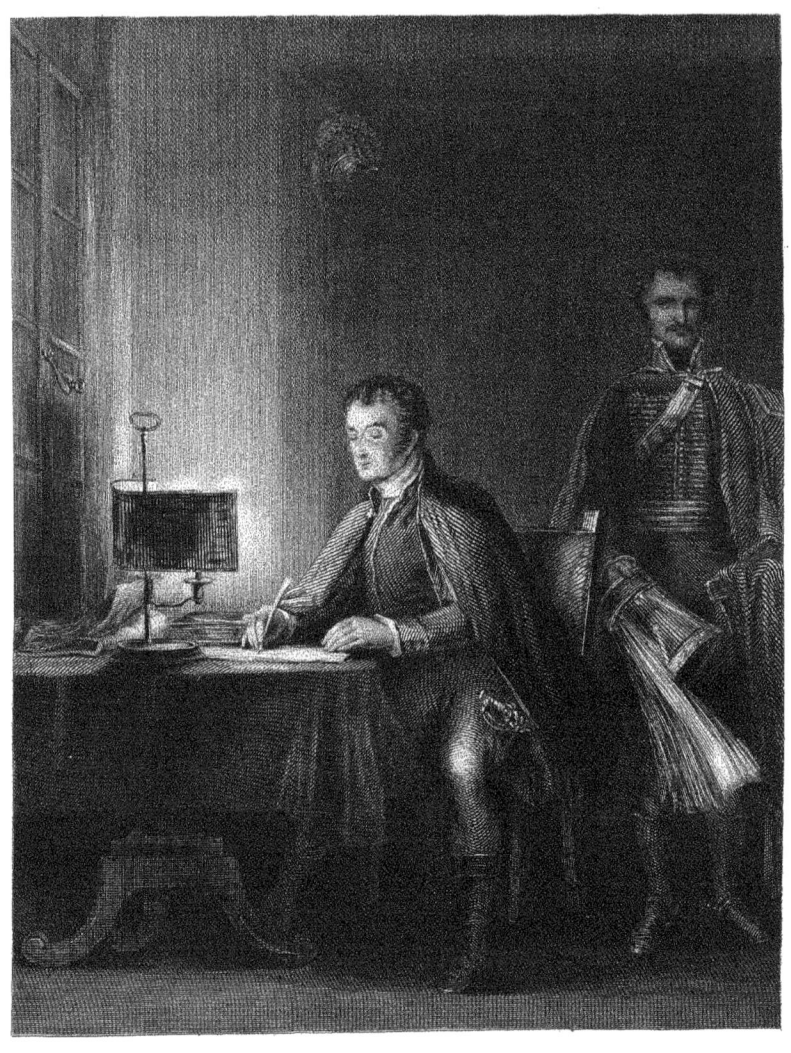

DUKE

SKETCHED BY SIR DAVID WILKIE R.A. — ENGRAVED BY W. GREATBACH

THE DUKE OF WELLINGTON WRITING HIS DESPATCHES.

THIS is the sketch of a picture painted for Sir Willoughby Gordon. Wilkie visited Strathfieldsaye to paint a portrait of the Duke of Wellington and the Charger on which he rode at Waterloo, for the Merchant Tailors' Company. He had the opportunity of observing the Duke almost in absolute solitude, there being no one but himself and Lord Charles at the place; besides that, his Grace, with his usual system, gave him regularly two sittings a day. This enabled him to give both to the head, hands, and accessories the utmost possible truth; and the picture thus carefully completed was highly satisfactory both to the parties who had commissioned it and to the Duke himself. From the same materials he no doubt composed his characteristic cabinet picture.

It was objected to this picture that it did not tell its story; there was nothing to show that the despatch was written on the eve of the Battle of Waterloo, as the painter intended. It is certainly singular that he should have selected the *eve* of the battle rather than its glorious termination, as the subject of the duke's despatch. There is a collected calmness in the features, which, however characteristic in general, is hardly reconcilable with the expression of those emotions which, even in one whose self-command is so habitual, must, one would suppose, have appeared on his countenance on so momentous an occasion, when the proud consciousness of having achieved immortality must have been dashed with sorrow at the price by which it had been purchased—the best blood of his brave troops, and the loss of many a cherished personal friend.

This great man has not been without his detractors. Let us hear the opinion of a foreign writer and statesman, who will not be suspected of any English partialities:—
"There is no use in denying it: every circumstance considered, the Duke of Wellington was the greatest general whom the late wars have offered for human contemplation: his mind was so equally poised, notwithstanding the vivacity of his genius, that he was always ready, and equally prompt, on every occasion. He united the powerful combination of Napoleon to the steady judgment of Moreau. Each of these mighty captains was, perhaps, in some degree superior to Wellington in his peculiar walk. Napoleon may have had more rapidity of view and plan upon the battle-field, and could suddenly change his whole line of battle, as at Marengo. Moreau everywhere understood better the management of a retreating army before an exulting enemy. But the exquisite apprehension and intelligence of Arthur Wellesley served him instead of both, and took at once the conduct

and the measures that the occasion required. Many of our military men have contested his genius, but no man can deny him the most equable judgment that was ever met with in a great soldier. It is this admirable judgment, this discerning wisdom of the mind, which has misled Europe as to his genius. * * * * * Men do not expect to see in the same person the active and the passive spirit equally great; nor does nature usually bestow such opposite gifts in the same person. In Napoleon a steady judgment and an endurance of calamity were not the concomitants of his impulsive genius and tremendous activity; while Moreau had all his passive greatness. But the Duke of Wellington has united the two qualities. Nay, more: the noble army he had so long commanded had gradually learnt to partake of the character of their leader. No soldiers in the world but the English could have stood those successive charges and that murderous artillery, which they so bravely bore at Waterloo."—THIERS.

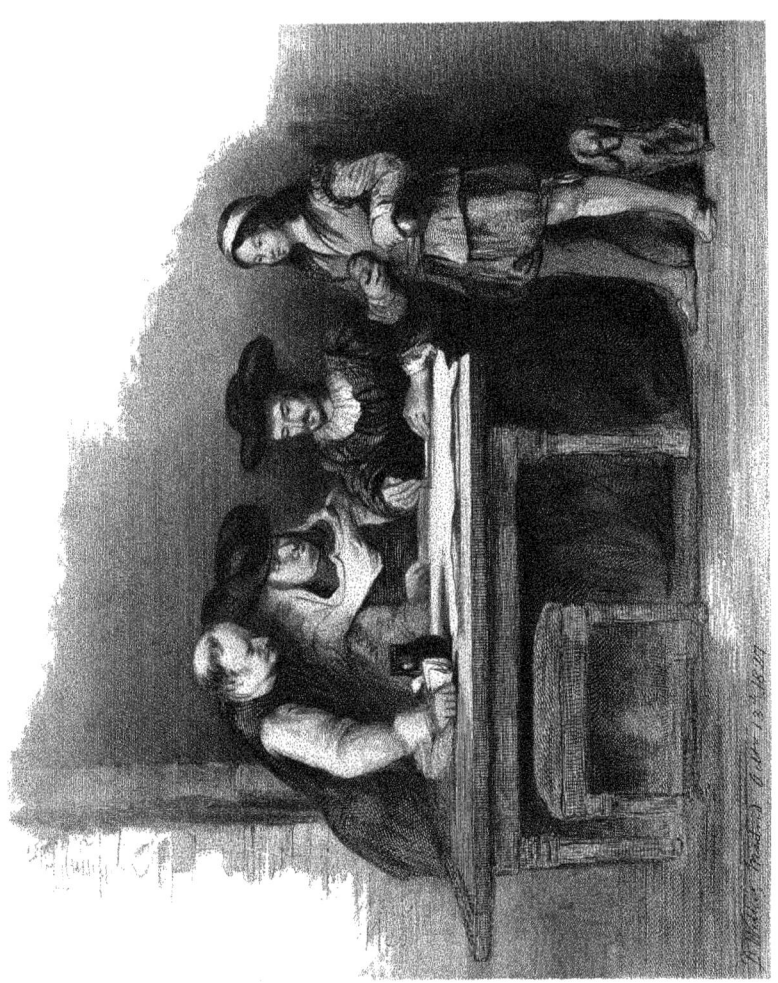

CHRISTOPHER COLUMBUS AT THE CONVENT OF LA RABIDA.

ALLAN CUNNINGHAM gives us an interesting account of the origin of the picture of which this is a sketch. Soon after Wilkie's return from Spain, he called upon him in company with a friend, a Mr. Ritchie, to look over his portfolio of sketches. Among them was this subject, with the character and interest of which Cunningham was so much struck that he advised the painter to expand it into a subject the size of life. Calling Wilkie aside, Ritchie whispered to him, "Do what Allan says; name your price, and I will buy the picture." His friend unfortunately did not live to see his commission complete. The utmost pains was, however, bestowed upon it by the painter, who sent it to the exhibition of 1835, where it attracted considerable attention. It is certainly one of the most striking of his Spanish pictures.

The incident here illustrated is a very remarkable one—perhaps the turning-point of the fortunes of Columbus, and the immediate cause of the discovery of the New World. "A stranger," says Washington Irving, "travelling on foot, and accompanied by a boy, stopped one night at the gate of a convent of Franciscan Friars, and asked for bread and water for his child. Friar Juan Perez de Marchena happening to pass, was struck with the appearance of the stranger, and observing from his air and accent that he was a foreigner, entered into conversation with him—that stranger was Columbus." In the interview which followed, Columbus submitted his ideas to Perez. Up to this period the illustrious discoverer had been endeavouring to engage some of the princes of Europe in his plans. He had first applied to the Senate of Genoa, his native city, and afterwards to the King of Portugal, while he sent his brother to Henry VII. of England, who had listened to his overtures, and he was about to visit that country, when the momentous conference with Juan Perez decided him upon postponing it till he had sought for the patronage of Ferdinand and Isabella. Satisfied of their practicability himself, Perez, for whom Isabella had a great respect, recommended Columbus to her very warmly. He also secured the friendship of the Duke of Medina Celi, who laid the plan before Cardinal Ximenes. Twice, in consequence, was Columbus called to court; but the proverbial caution of Ferdinand, and the expensive war which he was then carrying on for the expulsion of the Moors, caused him to listen but coldly to the project. The conquest of Granada achieved, another effort was made by the persevering friends of Columbus. The moment was well chosen, and the issue successful. After eight years of constant solicitation, he at length attained his object, and on the 17th of April, 1492, entered into a formal agreement with the Spanish sovereign. Having taken leave of the queen, Columbus marched in solemn procession with all his company to the monastery of La Rabida, the scene of this first interview with Perez, who after the ceremonies of confession and absolution were over, administered to them the holy sacrament, and joined in prayers for their success. Next morning, being Friday, the 3rd of August, the little fleet got under weigh from the adjacent port of Palos. The success of Columbus, his vast discoveries, his return to Spain, his subsequent humiliations and imprisonment, are known to all our readers.

The painter has evidently felt his subject, and has thrown into the treatment an appropriate intensity. At the table, with maps and charts spread out before him,—wayworn and travel-soiled, but of noble and commanding mien,—sits Columbus. He is entirely wrapped up in the mighty scheme over which his spirit had been brooding for years. His absorbed expression, his earnestness of conviction as he traces with the compasses the line he proposes to follow, and explains to his hearers the reasons which lead him to expect success, is finely rendered by the painter. His object, it should be remembered, was the discovery of a shorter passage to the Golden East than that around the Cape. "After revolving long and seriously," says Robertson, " every circumstance suggested by his superior knowledge in the theory as well as practice of navigation ; after comparing attentively the observations of modern pilots with the hints and conjectures of ancient authors, he at last concluded that, by sailing directly towards the west, across the Atlantic ocean, new countries, which probably formed a part of the great continent of India, must infallibly be discovered." As the attempt to discover a north-west passage to these desired regions led shortly after to the discovery of the northern continent of America, so did this western line of navigation accidentally reveal the southern. To return to the picture— the other figures are full of expression, though subordinate to the principal one. The friar on the right of Columbus appears to be listening with mingled surprise and admiration, while the physician, Garcia Fernandez, of greater scientific acquirements, is looking on with a more scrutinising look, yet evidently no less satisfied and convinced by the arguments adduced. The boy on the right relieves while heightening the predominant expression. The concentrated and somewhat Rembrantesque arrangement of the light and shade is entirely in harmony with the rest of the treatment.

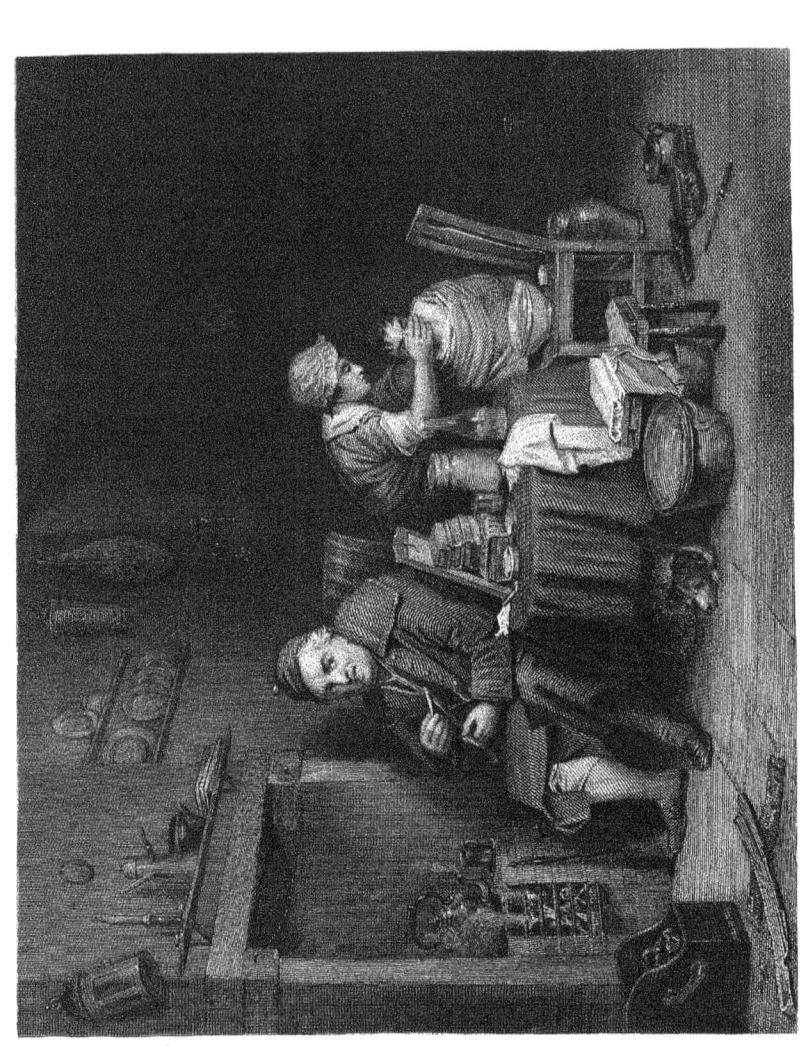

SATURDAY NIGHT.

WE are unable to discover any particulars respecting this picture in Allan Cunningham's Life of the painter, but from the manner and subject suppose it to be one of his earliest class of productions, illustrative of the domestic habits of his native country, and studied in every particular from actual models. It looks like a first instalment of that originality of style which reached its highest excellence in "The Village Politicians" and "The Blind Fiddler." The subject is unambitious, but characteristic of the habits of the humbler class in Scotland. There is, perhaps, no country in the world where the mass of the people are so imbued with a serious regard to religion, and so punctilious as to the fulfilment of its ordinances— where, in particular, the Sabbath-day is kept holy, in a manner so exemplary, and with so much of that spirit of rigid Puritanism which came in with the Protestant Reformers, and which combines that spirit of minute observance peculiar to the Mosaic law, with the additional sanctity derived from the doctrines of a better dispensation. The picture before us is a curious exemplification of this national habit. In England, as we all know, Saturday is a day distinguished by scrubbing and cleaning and preparation for the quiet of Sunday. But few, however, would think it necessary to shave themselves over night, lest they should entrench upon the sacredness of the morrow. But in Scotland it is otherwise. The following anecdote was communicated by the late Mr. G. F. Robson, the well-known and, perhaps, unequalled painter of Highland scenery. In the pursuit of materials for his pictures, he had wandered away from the track till night overtook him, and he began to fear that he should have to pass it supperless and with nothing but heather for a couch. At length he perceived a distant gleam of light, which betokened the welcome shelter of a peasant's hut. At a knock, so unusual at that hour in a lonely solitude, arose a loud barking of dogs; almost instantly the door was thrown open, and three or four men, each with a glittering weapon in his hand, looked eagerly out into the darkness—an apparition at the first glance so formidable, that the painter almost repented him of his summons. But a moment's reflection dispelled his uneasiness. It was "Saturday night," and the glistening blades which had so startled him proved to be merely the razors of the inmates, who were occupied in getting rid of their beards over night that they might not be guilty of a violation of the day of rest. It is almost unnecessary to add that hospitality and piety went hand in hand with these simple people, and that the wandering artist met with a frank and kindly welcome.

SATURDAY NIGHT.

The interior before us, then, is the true presentment of a Scottish household of the humbler class on Saturday night. The details are all painted from nature—the plain walls and stone floor of the cottage, with its few articles of furniture neatly arranged. Every thing has the look of decent poverty and pious contentment. The gudeman is calmly and methodically preparing for business. The family looking-glass is propped up against a pile of books, the well-thumbed library of the cottage; the water is boiling, the shaving-pot and lather-box ready, and the razor receiving its finest edge. The old fellow is evidently a portrait—one of the painter's darling oddities; he has the true northern expression of shrewdness and caution, not without traits of a more genial character, seen through his more predominant, habitual qualities.

In the background operations are going on more actively. The bairn is undergoing a thorough scrubbing, which is to obliterate every trace of the week's dirt. The mother is evidently going through it with conscientious rigour and determination of purpose. The victim is swaddled round so as effectually to preclude any struggling, and from the contortious of his countenance is evidently getting to the climax of the operation. It is a predicament that most of us can probably remember to have been placed in, in our juvenile days, and the smart of the yellow soap and the inexorable scrub of the rough towel revive in memory, as we gaze upon this comic representation of what then appeared to us to be no laughing matter.

In addition to the shaving and scrubbing, the shoe-blacking is also to be attended to. When all these preparations are concluded, we may figure to ourselves the graver scene, so beautifully described by Burns. Thankful for the week's mercies and anticipating the day of rest from its toils and cares, the gudeman reads a portion of Scripture, and the humble group, with minds composed and grateful, unite in family prayer—a practice which it is to be hoped no social changes or increasing refinement will ever succeed in banishing from the homes of the Scottish peasantry.

"The cheerfu' supper done, wi' serious face,
    They round the ingles form a circle wide;
The sire turns o'er, with patriarchal grace,
    The big ha' Bible, ance his father's pride;
His bonnet rev'rently is laid aside,
    His lyart haffets wearing thin an' bare;
Those strains that once did sweet in Zion glide,
    He wales a portion with judicious care,
And, "Let us worship God," he says, with solemn air.

The priest-like father reads the sacred page,
    How Abram was the friend of God on high;
Or Moses bade eternal warfare wage
    With Amalek's ungracious progeny;

SATURDAY NIGHT.

Or how the royal bard did groaning lie
    Beneath the stroke of Heaven's avenging ire;
Or Job's pathetic plaint and wailing cry,
    Or rapt Isaiah's wild seraphic fire;
Or other holy seers that tune the sacred lyre.

Perhaps the Christian volume is the theme,
    How guiltless blood for guilty man was shed,
How He, who bore in Heaven the second name,
    Had not on earth whereon to lay His head;
How His first followers and servants sped,
    The precepts sage they wrote to many a land.
How he, who lone in Patmos banished,
    Saw in the sun a mighty angel stand;
And heard great Bab'lon's doom pronounc'd by Heaven's command."

THE GUERILLA COUNCIL OF WAR.

THIS subject is one of four painted at Madrid, and afterwards purchased by George the Fourth, who decidedly preferred it to the others; and there can be no question that in point of truth and variety of character it is the *best* of Wilkie's Spanish pictures. He picked up the materials for its composition on his road from Bayonne to Madrid, as he jogged along in the slow-going vetturino, to put up for the night at the wayside " posada," or roadside inn, which deserves a particular mention. The badness of these Spanish caravanseries was proverbial in the days of Cervantes, who makes Dorothea observe, "that it is their proper peculiarity to be destitute of all conveniencies." Witness also Sancho's amusing dialogue with an innkeeper touching the contents of his larder, which is no doubt another quiz upon their notorious state of disfurnishment. On his demanding what there was to eat, the host replied, " 'Anything that you please; ask for whatever you fancy; for whether it be with birds of the air, animals of the earth, or fish from the sea, this hostelry is abundantly provided.' 'There is no need of so many things,' observed Sancho: 'a pair of roasted chickens will be enough, for my master is delicate, and eats but little; and I myself am not gluttonous to excess.' The host said that there were no chickens, because the kites infested the country. ' Well, then,' returned Sancho, 'let the signior host roast for us a capon that is tolerably tender.' 'A capon! holy virgin!' exclaimed the host; 'in truth 'twas only yesterday that I sent more than fifty to the market. But, with the exception of capons, your grace may ask for whatever best pleases you.' 'At that rate,' resumed Sancho, 'there can be no lack of veal, nor of kid neither?' 'For the present,' replied the host, 'there is none in the house, because the stock is exhausted; but the ensuing week there will be a fresh supply.' 'An odd game this we are playing,' said Sancho; 'but I will wager that all these missing provisions are well made up by a great abundance of bacon and eggs.' 'Pardieu!' responded the host, 'your grace has really a singular memory. I have just said that I have neither hens nor chickens, and now you want me to find eggs. Think, if you please, of some other delicacies, and give up asking for eggs.' 'In the name of Christ, then, come to the point,' cried Sancho; 'say at once what you really *have* got, and let us have done with this skirmishing.' 'Signior guest,' then,' said the innkeeper, 'what I really *have* got are two ox-feet that are very much like calves' feet, or two calves' feet that are very much like ox-feet. They are cooked with their seasoning of peas, onions, and bacon; and seem at this present moment,

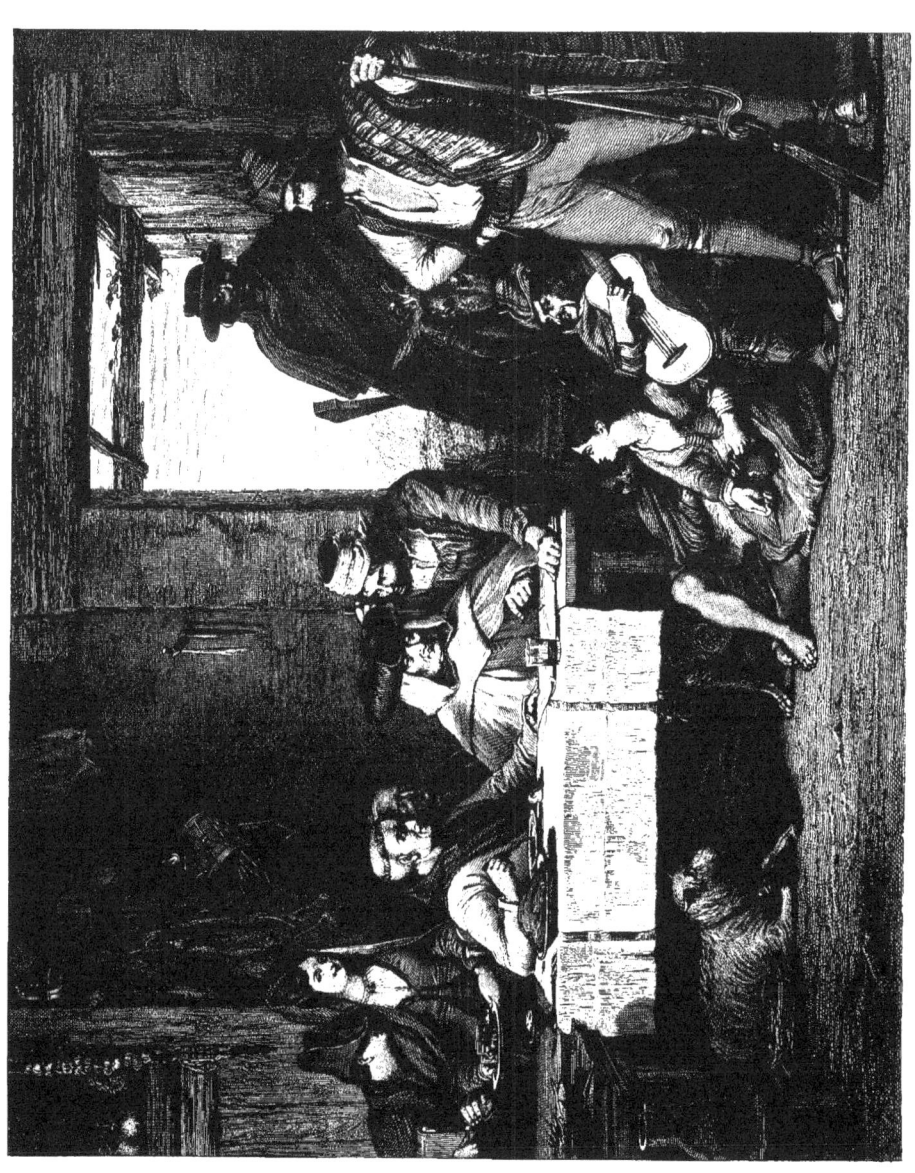

while bubbling in the pot, to cry, Come eat me—eat me!'" This satirical description, which, after all, was perhaps an experience of its author's, is intended perhaps to apply to the more remote of the hostelries; but even the best are but indifferently stocked. The chief standing dish is still Sancho's favourite, "olla podrida," in which he recommends to the cook to tumble anything whatever, provided that it is but eatable. It is commonly composed of beef, mutton, bacon, hens, partridges, sausages, pudding, vegetables, and all sorts of ingredients, stewed down till the different elements are confounded together in an unctuous and indefinite richness of flavour—a composition of which a recent traveller speaks in terms of high commendation. The ground-floor of the "posada" is a large room, serving as a sort of stable and kitchen, allotted to horses, mules, muleteers, contrabandistas, (smugglers,) and all sorts of wandering wayside characters, strolling beggars or musicians, who compose a motley assemblage that is enchanting to the painter. From this you ascend to the habitable first-floor, where the more civilized strangers are accommodated; and where the painter says, that for four nights they were sadly put to it, there being a French gentleman with his wife, a mademoiselle, a young man, and himself all stowed into one room, with four beds, making recess-beds, with curtains and other contrivances for decorum, like the scene described in the last chapter of the "Sentimental Journey." But such things must be, he observes, if we will travel in Spain.

The country was besides in a distracted state at the period of his visit. "One night, a party in arms arrived after supper, of whom the principal was a robust young man, with moustaches, dressed somewhat like an officer, with a sword and epaulettes, who said he had just received orders to march against some armed men who infested the hills; and as he proceeded he met two hundred of the king's troops in search of armed peasants, and saw a placard requiring these marauding parties, not much unlike his friends of last night, to return to their allegiance under pain of high-treason." But it is doubtless some scene in the then recent patriotic struggle of the Spanish peasantry with their French invader that the painter has set so vividly before us. The priests, with a map before them, are concerting with the guerilla, or armed peasants, some plan of surprise or defence. In the direction of this resistance the clergy were the principal agents, entertaining, as they did, a very natural abhorrence of the contagious liberalism of the French; they not only excited the religious and patriotic enthusiasm of their flocks, but lent all their skill to the successful carrying out of the details of the struggle. This group of monks seated at table is a masterpiece of character. The head of the principal reminds us, in its mingled expression of intellect and benevolence, of the finest characters of the Spanish priesthood; such might have been a Ximenes or a Las Casas. The bland look of this distinguished ecclesiastic admirably contrasts with the cold and stern expression of the other monks, which almost creates a shudder: men in whom the very spirit of bigotry seems incarnate—genuine types of inquisitorial sternness, of jesuitical craftiness, which keeps no faith with heretics, and regards the lighting of the Auto da Fé as a pious service to the cause of God and the church. The force of these fearful heads is increased by the contrast with the sunny faces, black eyes, and espiégle looks of the pretty Posadara, to whom a poor Salamanca student, (such, we may presume, as Cervantes has depicted, who though " far advanced in Latin," caused such an increase of kindred among certain of his cousins, and those who were no cousins at all, that a fabricator of genealogical trees could not see his way through it,) is whispering some evidently welcome flattery. The fine figure resting on his gun is a type of the noble peasant of Spain, and the wild armed Contrabandista, or smuggler, familiar with every nook of the Guadarama mountains, which are seen in the background, is entering his accustomed haunt with an expression of distrust at the holy personages assembled there. It is not too much to say that the dwarf musician tuning his guitar is worthy of Murillo himself, as well as the goatherd and girl, with the muzzled house-dog and pet lamb of the family. The accessaries, too, are beautifully put in. In this fine work are combined, besides the detail and clearness of his early pictures, the bold and masterly style that he had adopted after a diligent study of the Italian and Spanish painters.

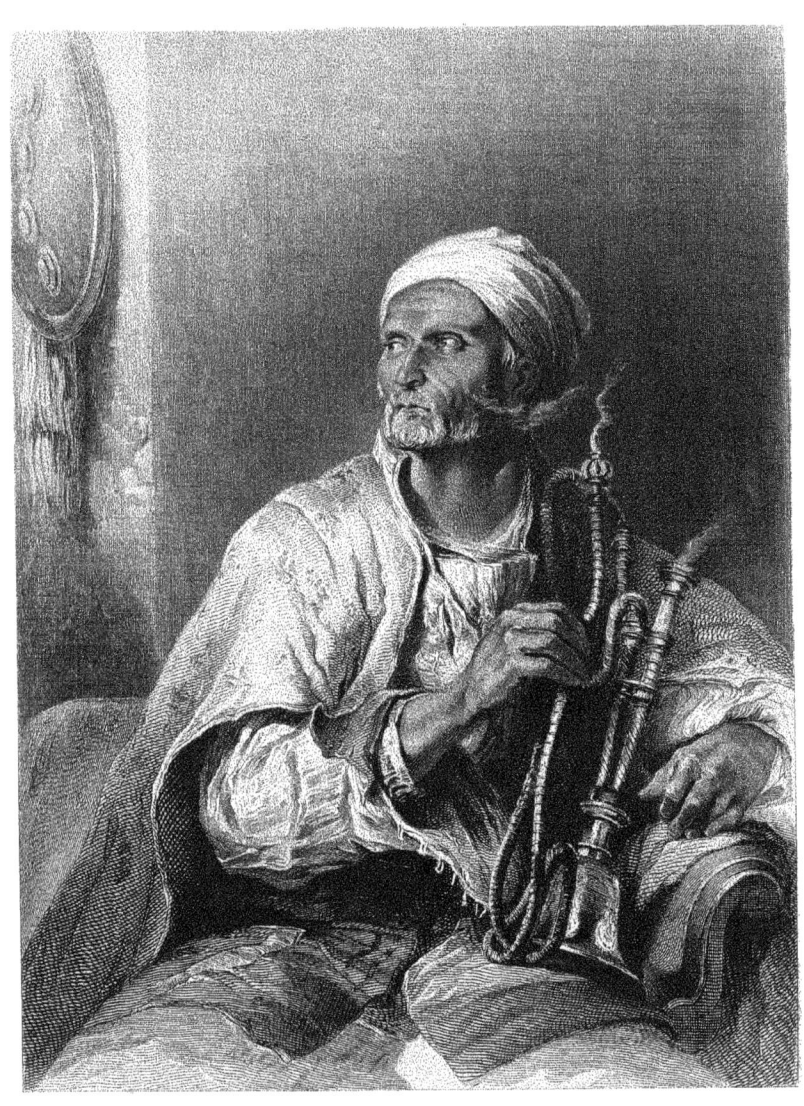

SKETCHED BY SIR DAVID WILKIE, R.A. — ENGRAVED BY

THE HOOKA-BADAR.

THIS is one of the most powerful and finished of the painter's studies from nature. The subject is very sketch-inviting, full of the picturesque in character and costume, and we have no doubt that Wilkie revelled in it. We are inclined to think that he must have fallen in with this fine old fellow at the India House, when he visited it for the purpose of obtaining sketches of character and costume, for his great picture of "Sir David Baird at the finding of the body of Tippoo Saib." He writes to Lady Baird, "In the course of the spring, I made various studies from native Indian soldiers now here; but when they came to discover for what subject they were wanted, a sort of superstition seized them at once, and now they will no longer sit." In another letter, he says, "I was told that there were three Hindoo cavalry soldiers at the India House, who had come overland, to complain of some grievance. I obtained their consent to sit to me, and they came—a Jemidar and two inferior officers—in their native dress. I explained to them, by the interpreter what I wanted, and put them on a platform in a group, the Jemidar, as Tippoo, reclining with his head supported by one of his lieutenants, and his hand held by the other, with his finger on his pulse to know if he were alive or dead. The group was magnificent, and I was all ecstacy to realize such a vision of character and colour. It was indeed a vision, and a vision only; for all of a sudden the youngest of them said, 'Me no Tippoo!' and sprung from his position, while the others repeated, 'No Tippoo I! No Tippoo I!' and to my surprise, left their places also; and no persuasion I could use could induce them to resume them." Such are some of the minor tribulations of painters. The same suspicion of "glamour" is very common in the East, and renders it almost impossible to get a comfortable sitting from a Turk. Many a traveller has cunningly availed himself of this to get rid of some troublesome, intrusive individual, by taking out his tablets and threatening to take note of him.

But to return, this old Hooka-badar, or Hookah-bearer, (who seems to have been a much more patient sitter,) is a very characteristic figure. In India, as in the East, the number of servants necessary to form a complete establishment is very numerous, and the subdivision of labour very minute. The pipe is a most important item in the catalogue of Oriental luxuries, or to speak more correctly, necessaries, and when we consider the number of pipes kept in a large house, the office of preserving them clean and of presenting them to visitors, is not so insignificant as we might at first suppose. There is a dignified expression about the old Hooka-badar, as though he was aware of the importance of his functions, and prided himself, not a little, on their punctilious fulfilment. Wilkie has well depicted the soft dusky skin, the delicate and nervous organization of the Hindoo, and has treated the flowing costume with inimitable taste. The silken sleeve is touched in with the hand of a perfect master. The breadth and power of the style must delight every one who has any knowledge of art; and, indeed, this sketch must be regarded as one of the most striking and effective that its painter ever produced.

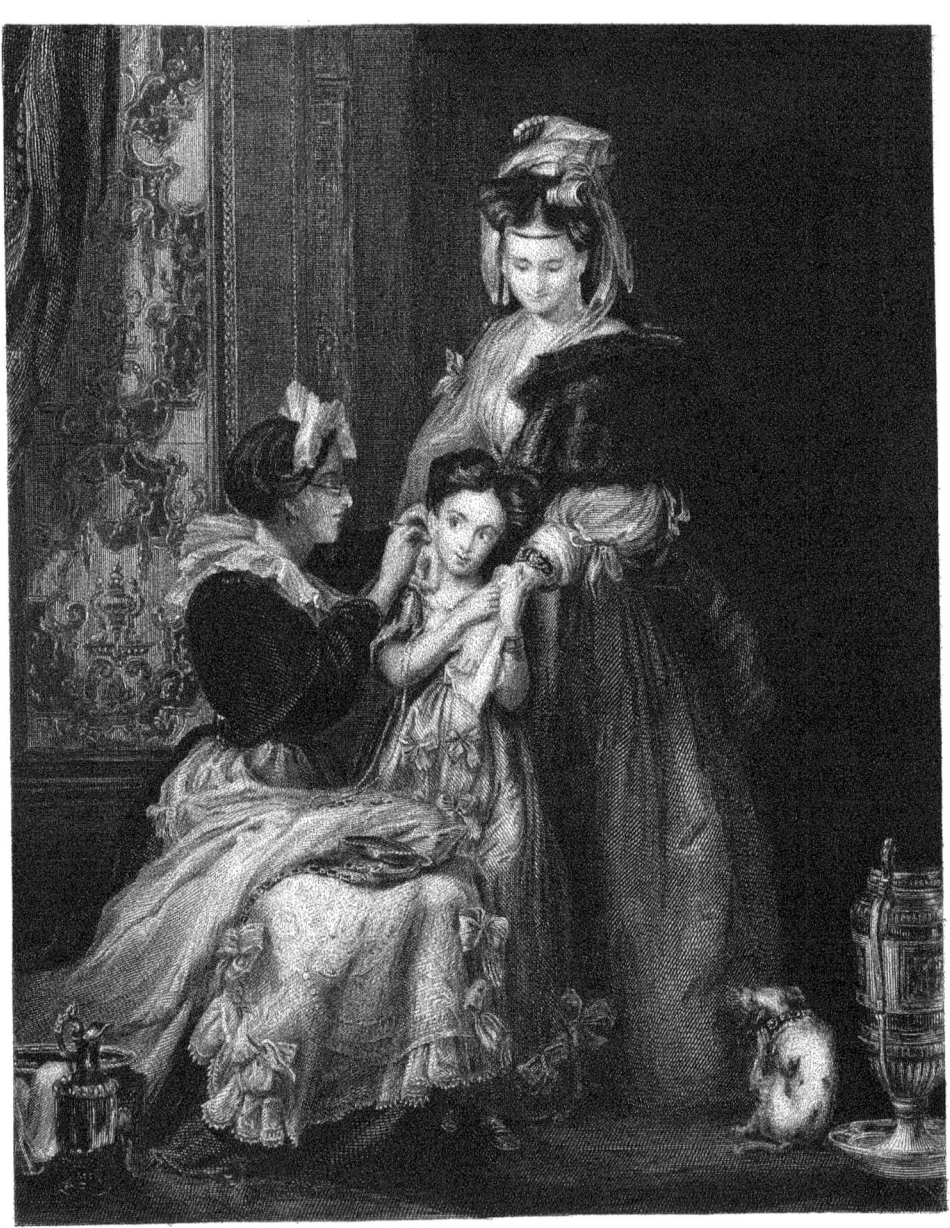

SIR D WILKIE, R A PAINTER

THE FIRST EARRING.

THIS picture was first exhibited at the Royal Academy in 1834, soon after Wilkie's arrival from Spain, when his mind was stored with the peculiarities of the different Spanish and Italian masters, by which it was his intention to profit in the formation of a New School—bolder and broader in effect, and with far less minuteness of finish, than in his earlier pictures. To this change of style he was prompted, it would appear, no less by economy than taste. The immense labour bestowed upon his first class of compositions—the number of figures with which they were crowded, the infinite variety of expression, and the conscientious elaboration even of the minutest details, had been but ill repaid, even at the highest price he had ever succeeded in obtaining. Less labour, with a more rapid result, was, therefore, in a merely pecuniary sense, exceedingly desirable. Neither the public, however, nor the artists, were altogether satisfied with this change in Wilkie's manner; and indeed it must be admitted that many works executed at this period of his career are far from bearing a comparison with those by which his reputation was established. Among them, notwithstanding the favourite opinion of Allan Cunningham, we should be very much disposed to place the specimen before us; not that it is without considerable merit; but there is none of that originality of conception and felicitous—almost, we might say, miraculous—skill of execution, by which so many of his *chef-d'œuvres* are characterised.

The subject, trivial in itself, is calculated to display the skill of the painter, since by *finesse* of expression alone could it be redeemed from commonness. Here Wilkie rarely or never failed; whatever the comparative interest of his subject, he was almost invariably successful in seizing the true character of the incidents and personages he depicted. The general style of this composition is exceedingly ornate, the costumes are rich, the background and accessories elaborate, affording much scope for colour and handling. A little girl, at that age when personal vanity and the love of decoration begin to develope themselves in the sex, is about to undergo the half-dreadful, half-delightful operation of the fixing of her first Earring. There is a struggle between alarm at the expected pain, which is magnified by imagination, and the anticipated delight of becoming like Mamma—of emerging from childhood, and putting on the adornments and airs of a little lady in her teens. The calm, complacent look of the mother, smiling at the short-lived apprehensions of the child, and the quick, eager expression of the dexterous operator, are exceedingly well represented. Wilkie well understood the great art of contrasted expression in giving interest even to subjects comparatively barren.

In this picture the richness of the reflected lights and the mellow tone of the background finely relieve the lights, most of which, as in his later pictures, are subdued and toned down.

We ought not to forget to notice the dog: decorated in all the pride of a pet poodle, he is lifting his paw to his ear with a sympathetic movement, as if threatened himself with the piercer. Indeed everything is highly ornamented in this picture—vases, ewers, gilded looking-glasses, rings, jewels, earrings, laces and ribbons, furs and silks, are blended together into a general effect—rich, even to gorgeousness. The costume is apparently Spanish; the heads probably portraits of some of the painter's acquaintances in Madrid.

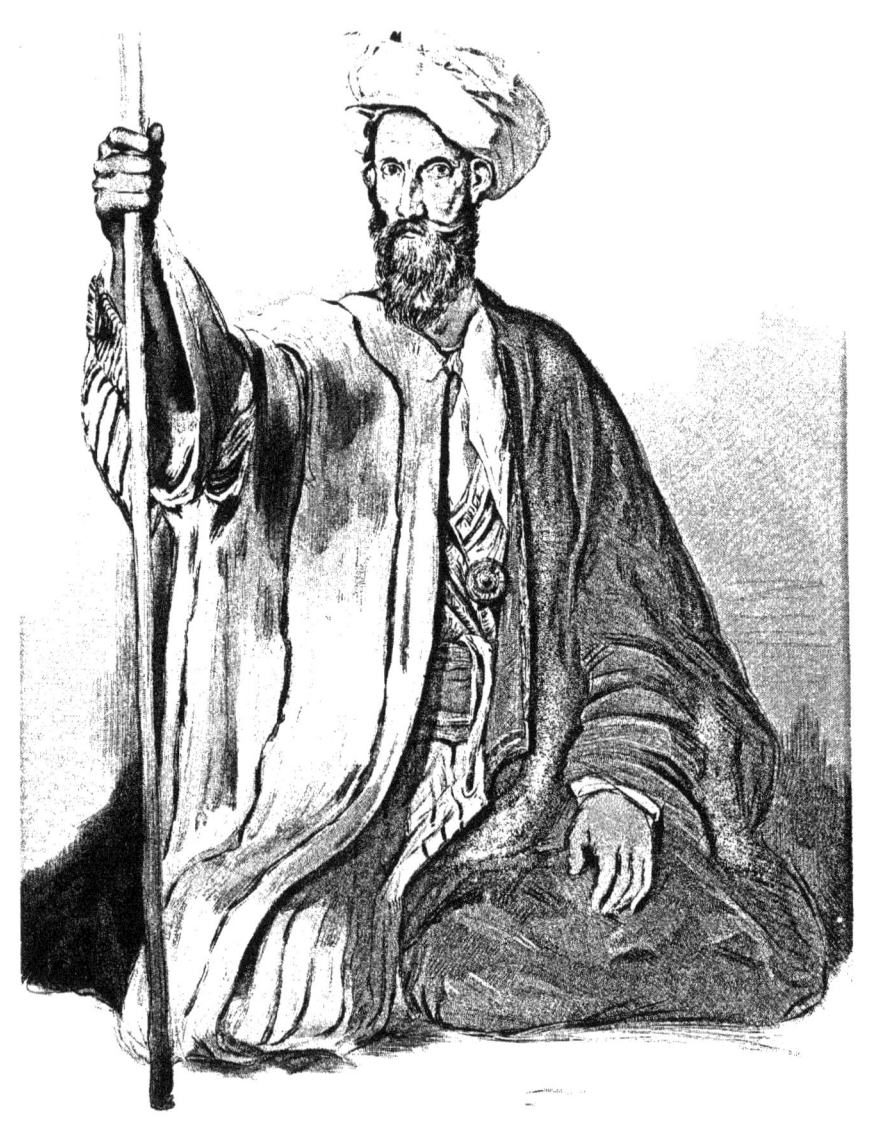

AN ARAB SHEIK,

WHO ESCORTED SIR DAVID WILKIE TO THE DEAD SEA AND THE JORDAN.

THIS, to our thinking, is one of the most surprising and life-like of Wilkie's sketches, and shows that, wherever he turned his steps, he was on the look out for character, and from long practice had a wonderful skill in seizing it. To the fidelity of this portrait we can personally testify, as doubtless can many other travellers who have availed themselves of the services of this Sheik, who is a well-known character at Jerusalem, a very respectable man, (if such a term can be applied to a wild Arab,) of his particular confraternity.

At the sight of that tall gaunt figure, that high and peculiar cast of face, and the wild light cast over it by the expression of a half-insane and restless eye, one might have supposed that the knight of La Mancha had doffed his antiquated armour for the costume of the Arabs, to commence a career of adventure among the tribes of the burning wilderness.

But nothing can be less like this than the reality. This Sheik is simply an influential man among certain tribes around the Dead Sea; and as the state of Syria was convulsed and uncertain at the period of Wilkie's visit, his party gladly availed themselves of his services in the double capacity of guard and guide; in short, to go before them to feel the way in dangerous passes, and bear the brunt of any open attack or secret ambush. There is not much fear of either, but to witness the amusing gyrations of these escorting vagabonds, one would suppose there were a robber in every bush. Few things are more amusing or picturesque than the lathy figure of our Sheik, in his long robes flaunting to the breeze, his scraggy neck and head surmounted with an enormous turban, when with a view of enhancing the value of his services, he poises his long spear, and flourishes about on his Arab steed to the right and left, as if in momentary apprehension of attack from some imaginary troop of marauding Bedouins; an exhibition he carries through with a degree of gravity that renders it irresistibly ludicrous. Nothing can well exceed the truthfulness and vigour of the sketch. The voluminous turban, the simple and flowing Arab drapery, are put in with the hand of a master; and such is the look of life, that we almost expect, as we gaze upon him, to see the tall sinewy Sheik leap up in his full proportions, and stalk before us in all his grotesque ragged dignity.

Wilkie's excursion to the Dead Sea was the most exciting of his whole journey, and he dwells upon it in various letters to his friends at home, among the last he ever composed.

AN ARAB SHEIK.

Upon leaving Jerusalem he plunged at once into the wilds of the Kidron, and reached, by precipices the most dreadful that can be imagined, the extraordinary convent of Santa Saba, of which he gives, as we can testify, a very truthful though brief description. "Our object was now to gain the monastery of St. Saba for the night. In our progress we were favoured with the breaking through of the moon, a great help; for as the dells and glens began to deepen and get more rocky, nothing could exceed the terrific appearance of the path we had to descend. Our horses, however, proceeded with miraculous care; our lengthened procession seemed to slide down what appeared to be absolute precipices, some of which required the whole party to dismount. At last we reached the convent, which, with high towers and massive walls, filled up the gorge of the adjoining cliffs of the torrent. Here we dismounted, and entered by a small wicket, where, after descending multitudes of stairs and terraces, and passing through a garden, we were shown into a saloon covered all over with rich Persian carpets, and surrounded by divans, as if made on purpose for the repose of fatigued travellers." Next morning, preceded by the ragged escort, they descended to the Dead Sea, which, in its awful dreariness, was aptly compared by the painter to "the Valley of the Shadow of Death." Here he made some interesting barometrical observations, and then passed on to the Jordan—"rapid, deep, and muddy." On his way home to Jerusalem by Jericho, he pitched his tents, as did the writer, by the beautiful fountain of Elisha. "A fire was lighted, refreshments cooked, and as night came on, the strange appearance of our companions and the newness of the situation gave it," he says, "completely the air and impression of romance. We awoke before dawn, and found the Arabs outside with a blazing fire, and all preparing to start; their dress, arms, and horses relieved by the darkness of the night, produced the wildest effect." These are indeed scenes that can never be forgotten by those that have been privileged to witness them; and had the painter been spared, we should doubtless have had some vivid representations of them from his inimitable pencil.

The motives which induced Wilkie to visit the Holy Land are well explained by the following extract from one of his letters:—"Whoever has been accustomed to walk through the streets and lanes, or by the walls, rocks, hills, valleys, brooks, and fountains of Jerusalem, where the Scripture events have taken place, will be convinced he sees before him a part of the original material from whence the inspired writers have drawn their narratives; at once satisfying him of the accuracy, while it gives a perfect idea of the situation of the details. From the arrival of Jesus Christ from Jericho, his entrance before the feast of the Passover to the time of the last supper, his cruel crucifixion and resurrection, every movement and resting-place may be traced with scarce a doubt of any leading point of that eventful period: yet, strange to say, the art of painting in Italy has arisen and triumphed in her devotion to such scenes, with scarcely a reference or resemblance to these obvious localities.

AN ARAB SHEIK.

While the world was shut out from the Holy Land, this want of knowledge could not be felt; but when travellers now are, by the facilities of steam-boat navigation, conveyed so readily here, my impression is, the future painters of Scripture pictures must stir themselves to be on a par with those who are to appreciate them. Being impressed with this, and seeing that a number of clergy and students of divinity have been making this journey, allow me to state to you, who are so great and so influential, a want that to us as a nation is now, in the sacred land, so obviously felt." But Wilkie was prevented, by an untimely death, from realizing the views here laid down.

THE TURKISH LETTER-WRITER.

This is a character very familiar to those acquainted with Constantinople. Shortly after his arrival there, Wilkie was walking about Tophana, below Pera, when he noticed in the outer court of a mosque a scribe of the most venerable appearance, engaged in reading over to two young Turkish women a letter or paper he had been composing for them. The group struck him as very characteristic, and suitable for a picture; but he has varied the monotony of the costume by the introduction of a *Greek* girl instead of two *Turkish* ones, which, while it certainly adds to the picturesque variety of the composition, is rather inaccurate as to local usages, since a Turkish and Greek girl would hardly be listening together to the same letter. Moreover, the headdress of the Greek girl is, if we mistake not, an indoor costume, and copied, in fact, from the same "lady at Pera," of whose beautiful profile he has given us a sketch in this collection.

The letter-writer is generally to be seen in a quiet corner of the outer court of some mosque, under an arabesque piazza or a shadowy plane-tree; and we have especially remarked several of them in that of Bajazet, which is a considerable thoroughfare. With a small wooden table and box, a copy of the Koran, a reed pen, and very primitive paper, and a Turkish inkstand tucked into his ample girdle, he awaits the arrival of his customers, for whom he provides one or two stools; having the soothing pipe at hand to fill up the intervals of his labours, and perhaps to inspire him with a greater variety of ideas. His dress is always neat, though often poor; his bearing is grave, and even reverend, and he looks like a depository of secrets. His functions are, of course, very much in request in a city where education is at the lowest possible ebb, especially among the Turkish population. It would be a rich treat, with our Western notions, could we get hold of some of his epistolary compositions, dictated by the requirements of manners and ideas so widely different from our own, yet with the same human nature everywhere peeping through the crust of national peculiarities. Wilkie, in his journal, says that it is a "love-letter" that the scribe is reading over to his fair customers. How he arrived at this knowledge we are left to conjecture; (flowers and other objects are, as is well known, common love interpreters;) but the expression he has thrown into the face and figure of the Turkish lady is, at any rate, dictated by his conviction. She seems as though her feelings were not satisfied by the cold transcript of them given by the old dervise; and she is apparently about to suggest to her

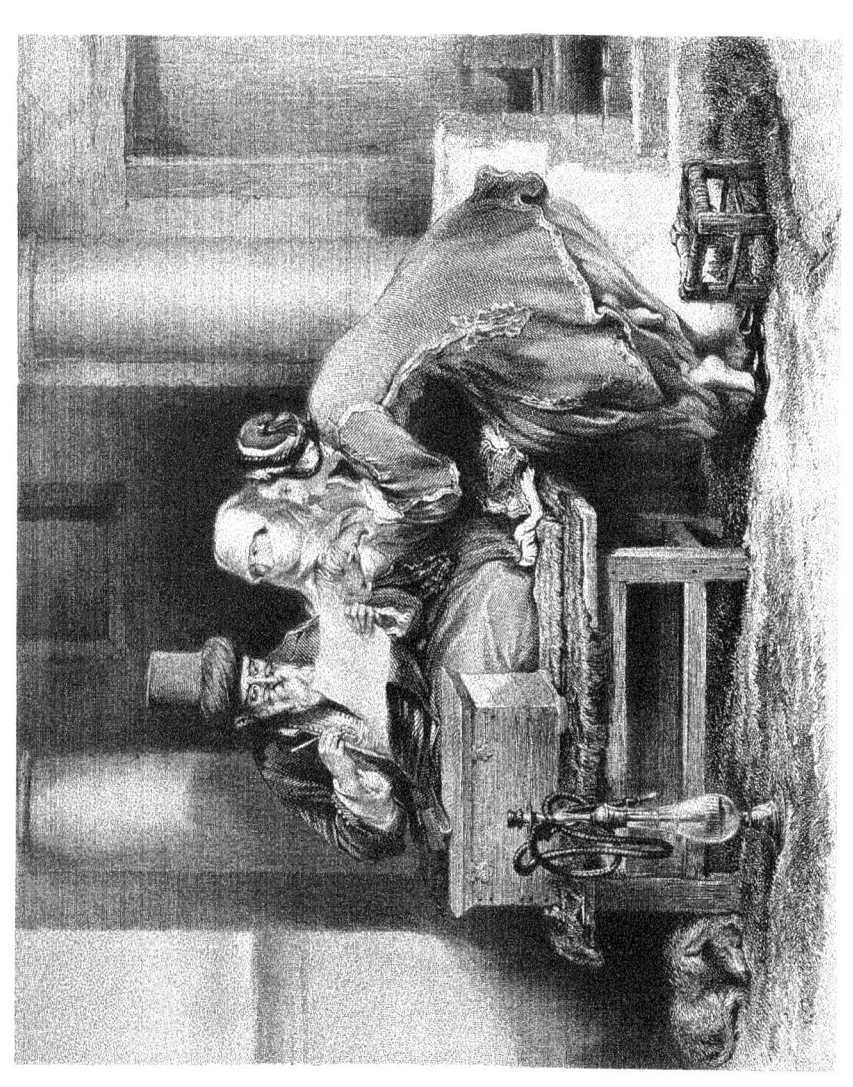

amanuensis some more impassioned additions, which seem sorely to perplex him. This Turkish lady is drawn to the very life, although the eye is not, to our thinking, so expressive as we can remember to have seen it, glancing from beneath the muslin "yashmak," or veil, worn indiscriminately by Turkish and Armenian ladies, who are not a little coquettish in the manner of wearing it, so as to set off their charms. It is certainly a contrivance which defeats its own object of veiling beauty, which, in fact, it rather heightens, by throwing *all* the expression of the face into that orb, which, in the East, is almost universally fine, and also, perhaps, by concealing sometimes, as a Christian lady at Pera once maliciously remarked to us, on our praising these Turkish beauties, "la bouche qui est mauvaise, les dents qui sont horribles." Lord Byron was greatly struck by the peculiar effect of the Oriental eye, heightened in its expression by the dyeing of the lashes with henna; and his description of it is as truthful as poetic:—

> " Her eyes' dark charm t'were vain to tell;
> But gaze on that of the gazelle,
> It will assist thy fancy well:
> As large, as languishingly dark,
> But soul beamed forth in every spark,
> That darted from beneath the lid,
> Bright as the jewel of Giamschid:—
> Yea, *soul!* and should our prophet say,
> That form was nought but breathing clay,
> By Alla! I would answer, Nay."

The exclusion of the Turkish women from Paradise, he tells us in a note, " is a vulgar error, since the Koran allows at least a third of Paradise to well-behaved women; but by far the greater part of Mussulmen interpret the text their own way, and exclude their moieties from heaven. Being enemies to Platonics, they cannot discern any "fitness of things" in the souls of the other sex, conceiving them to be superseded by the Houris." This speaks volumes for the low and dishonourable estimate of women, which is the result of a false religion. Among the Arabians, however, with whom poetry and science were honoured, it was not unusual for women to exhibit many accomplishments, as we may learn from the Arabian Nights. But among the unintellectual Turks it is otherwise; and the sole education of the sex now consists in such voluptuous accomplishments as may tend to heighten the effect of their personal charms.

Few sights in the world can be prettier than the "Valley of Sweet Waters," as it is called; a spot in the environs of the city, where the Turkish ladies are in the habit of repairing on certain days in the week, with their servants and children, to spend the day under the branching plane-trees in eating sweetmeats, gossipping, and listening to musicians and story-tellers. No member of the male sex is ever known to intrude upon the privacy of these open-air re-unions, unless some adventurous Frank, who steals unobserved into the circle, at the risk of expulsion, and a summary castigation by the cudgels of the 'cordon' of male servants who keep watch over these sequestered beauties, and are only to be propitiated—and that not always—by a liberal donation of piastres.

The accessaries to this pleasing picture are very correct. One of these is the "narghileh," a pipe in which the tube passes through water, with a flexible handle, and amber mouth-piece. Last, but not least,—the dog. This is a perfect representative of the tribe which serve as scavengers to the dirty metropolis, and are even sometimes piously provided with bread by the bequests of some charitable Mussulman—we have seen it so distributed. They are a vile, unsightly, wolfish breed, wandering about the city, without settled owners, impudently stretching themselves upon the pavement, or crouching in holes and corners, or howling in concert at the sight of a hat. In remote provinces they would almost tear a Frank to pieces; but they are less annoying in Constantinople than they used to be. As in Cairo, every quarter has its own set, and they pounce upon any intruder, and remorselessly tear him to pieces, unless he is lucky enough to get out of their bounds.

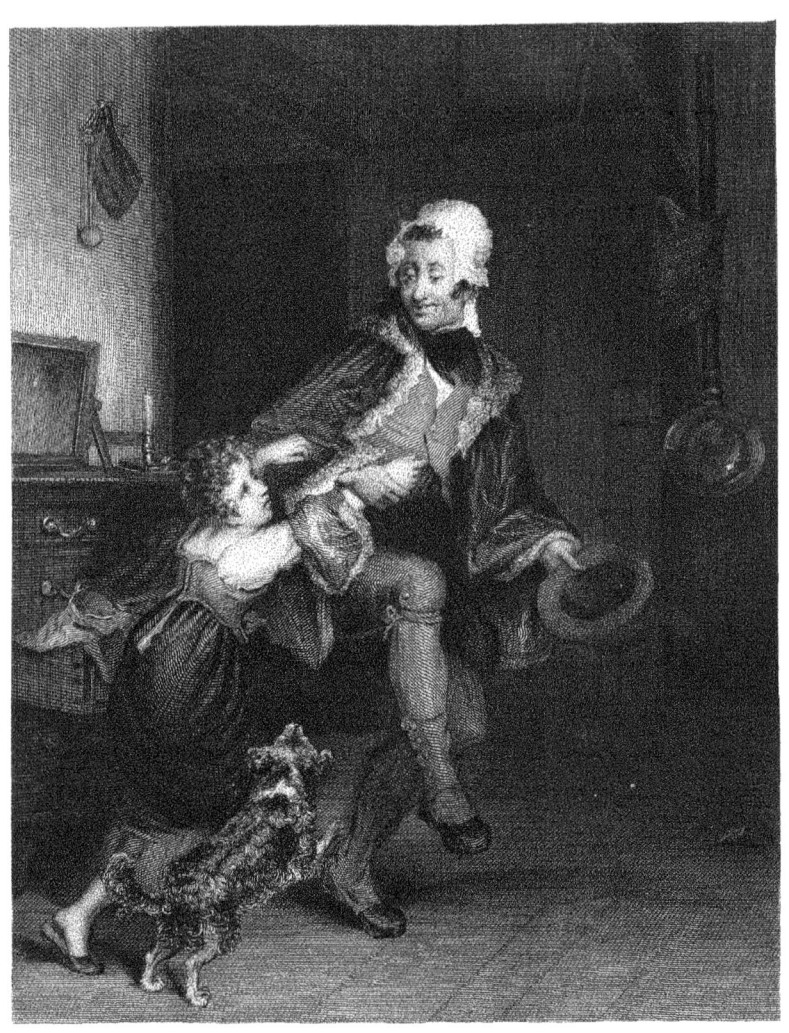

THE WARDROBE RANSACKED.

THE picture from which this engraving is copied, has the curious distinction of being the only one of Wilkie's which was disapproved of by the "Hanging Committee" of the Royal Academy, and by them recommended to be withdrawn, as unequal to the former efforts of the painter, and indeed unworthy of his high reputation. There are numerous notices of its origin, progress, and final destiny, in the painter's journals. He appears to have taken it up as a relief from the more elaborate and arduous picture of the "Village Alehouse." The first we hear of it is in his entry of Feb. 12, 1810 :—" Was employed most of the day in making the sketch on a panel of 'The Man with a Girl's Cap on,' (The Wardrobe Ransacked,) and afterwards in trying different arrangements in the sketch of my large picture." Next follow certain entries respecting its progress. From the first it seems to have puzzled and divided the connoisseurs, who differed widely in their estimate of its merits. Hayden thought it too trivial and unsuitable for exhibition, whilst Seguier encouraged Wilkie to proceed with it for that purpose. Such as it was, however, the picture seems to have cost no little time and pains, and to have been wrought up almost entirely from living models. The painter appears to have been a little perplexed himself as he proceeded with his eccentric subject, and to have altered the composition from time to time. When the picture was at length completed, the next puzzle was, what name to bestow upon such a curious "*jeu d'esprit.*" Sir George Beaumont suggested the appropriate title—"No Fool like an old Fool;" but Wilkie, more modest and literal, contented himself with calling it, "A Man teasing a Girl by putting on her Cap," and then left it to take its chance at the exhibition of the Royal Academy. Not long afterwards he received a note from Sir George Beaumont, desiring to see him about a matter of importance. On calling, he was informed that the President West had expressed a wish that the picture should be withdrawn from the exhibition, being generally considered inferior to Wilkie's other works. Vexed as he was, and sensible of the mortification of withdrawing a work which he had deemed worthy of his credit, the artist determined to abide by the judgment of his friends in the council. On learning that their prevailing opinion was unfavourable, he at once bowed to their decision, and sent for the picture. He now, at the suggestion of Seguier, bestowed additional labour upon it, altered it in effect and colour, and introduced more subject. A great improvement, in his opinion was the putting a black silk cloak upon the man. The picture was not destined, after all this trouble, to go a begging.

Lord de Dunstanville purchased it for a hundred guineas, and other patrons it would seem were also desirous of possessing it.

The conduct of the Academicians upon this occasion gave rise to as much controversy as the picture itself. Not a few deemed their conduct vexations and unwarrantable, and Wilkie himself afterward appears to have regretted his facility in yielding to their dictum. But we must confess that we can see no ground whatever for imputing to them any jealous hostility to the accomplished painter, upon whom all eyes were at that time fixed, but on the contrary believe them to have been actuated by a nice regard to the maintenance of his high and deserved reputation. How far they may have erred in judgment is another question.

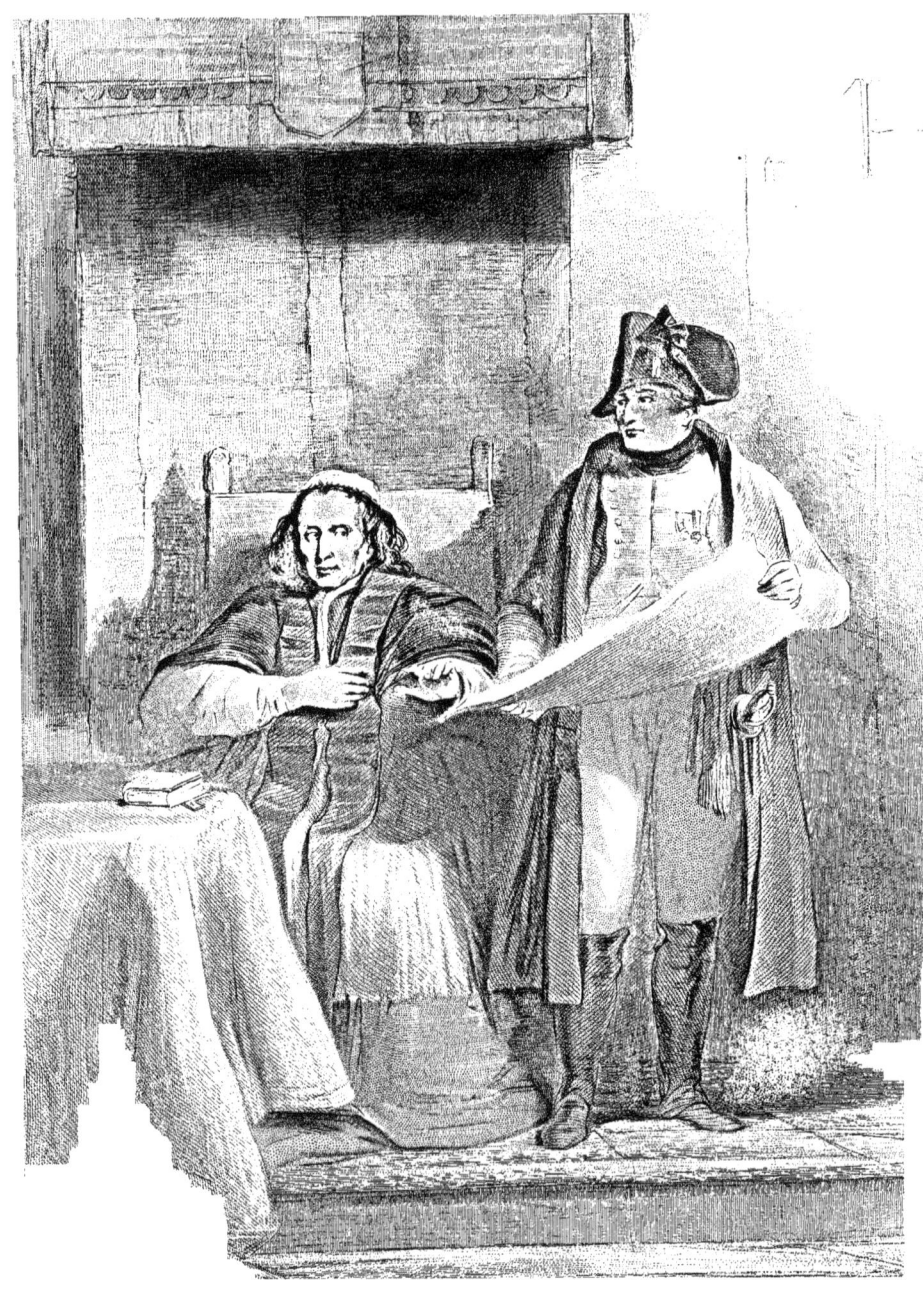

NAPOLEON AND THE POPE AT FONTAINEBLEAU.

THE dispute between Napoleon and Pius the Seventh originally arose out of the refusal of the latter to alienate any of his secular dominions at the demand of the all-grasping emperor. His holiness had in consequence been forcibly carried off from Rome, removed to Grenoble, and then brought back to Savona in Italy, where, says Sir Walter Scott, he was confined until June, 1812. In the meantime, a deputation of the French bishops was sent with a decree by Napoleon, determining that if his holiness should continue to refuse canonical institution to the French clergy, as he had done ever since the seizure of the city of Rome and the patrimony of Saint Peter, a council of prelates should be held for the purpose of pronouncing his deposition.

On the 4th September, 1811, the holy father admitted the deputation, listened to their arguments with patience, then knelt down before them and repeated the Psalm, *Judice me, Domine!* When the prelates attempted to vindicate themselves, Pius VII., in an animated tone, threatened to fulminate an excommunication against any one who should attempt to justify his conduct. Then, instantly recovering his natural benignity of disposition, he offered his hand to the offended bishops, who kissed it with reverence. The French prelates took leave sorrowfully, and in tears. Several of them showed themselves afterwards opposed to the views of Napoleon, and sustained imprisonment in consequence of their adhesion to what appeared to them their duty.

The chemists of our time have discovered that some substances can only be decomposed in particular varieties of gas; and apparently it was in like manner found that the air of Italy only confirmed the inflexibility of the Pope.

His holiness was hastily transported to Fontainebleau, where he arrived the 19th of June, 1812. The French historians boast that the old man was not thrown into a dungeon, but, on the contrary, was well-lodged in the palace, and was permitted to attend mass—a wonderful condescension towards the head of the Catholic religion. But still he was a captive. He abode at Fontainebleau till Napoleon's return from Russia, and it was on the 19th of January, 1813, that the Emperor, having left Saint Cloud under pretext of a hunting-party, suddenly presented himself before his venerable prisoner. He exerted all the powers of influence which he possessed,—and they were very great,—to induce the pontiff to close with his propositions; and we readily believe that the accounts which charge him with having maltreated his person are not only unauthenticated, but positively false. He rendered the submission which he required more easy to the conscience of Pius VII., by not demanding from him any express cession of his temporal rights, and by granting a delay of six months on the subject of canonical instalment. Eleven articles were agreed on, and subscribed by the Emperor and the Pope.

In regard to the report which has charged Napoleon with offering personal rudeness to his prisoner, it is but just to quote the statement of Louis Buonaparte:—" I knew Pius the Seventh from the time of his journey to Paris in 1804; and from that period until his death I never ceased to receive from the venerable pontiff marks, not of benevolence only, but even of confidence and affection. Since the year 1814 I have resided at Rome; I have often had occasion to see him, and I can affirm that in many of my interviews with his holiness he assured me that he was treated by Napoleon in every personal respect as he could have wished. These are his very words :—' I had nothing to complain of personally : I wanted for nothing ; my person was always respected and treated in a way to afford me no ground of complaint.' "

Few subjects could have been better chosen to display the powers of a great painter. The meek yet firm manner of the imprisoned and suffering pontiff, as he refuses to sign the document forced upon him by his imperial jailor, finely contrasts with the haughty and almost insulting demeanour of the latter. It is the contest between the two great powers, the spiritual and the military, which then divided between them the empire of Europe. That poor old man, a helpless captive in the hands of the victor of a hundred battles, yet feels himself possessed of a far mightier influence than that of brute force—a power over the hearts and consciences of millions—a power which will subsist after the changing tide of fortune shall have swept away the temporary glories of his imperial persecutor. The painter has finely diffused over the features of the venerable pontiff this sense of inward dignity and power, as well as depicted the baffled and irritated look of Napoleon, encountered by a spirit as resolute as his own, against whom his menaces are powerless; who may be deprived of liberty and stript of temporal sovereignty, but whose spiritual dominion can only acquire an increased influence over the affections of his people, through their sympathy with sufferings he has been called upon for conscience sake to endure.

This picture has an additional interest, as being among the first fruits of Wilkie's residence in the Eternal City. He was struck with everything he beheld—the red-legged Cardinals, with their splendid equipages; the regiments of priestly personages, in black and other colours; the bare-footed monks, " white, black, and gray, with all their trumpery;" the wild, picturesque-looking peasantry from the Campagna and the Appennines; the endless processions and festas out-of-doors, and the gorgeous ceremonial of Catholic worship within. He took care to be present at the washing of the pilgrims' feet, and watched the Contudini, as they went about the city, chanting hymns to the Madonna at every corner of the street. With memorials of these spectacles he stored his portfolio, and as his shattered health allowed him, worked up his materials into pictures, in which he sought to embody all the results of his recent study of the great Italian masters.

HEBREW WOMEN READING THE SCRIPTURES AT JERUSALEM.

How powerfully Wilkie's mind was impressed by everything he saw at Jerusalem, has been already mentioned in the preceding memoir. But nothing struck him more, both as solemn and affecting in itself, and as affording a fine subject for his art, than the spectacle at the "Jews' Place of Wailing," This is a secluded nook beneath the shadow of the great wall which surrounds the enclosure of the Mahommedan Mosque of Omar, generally considered as identical with that of the Temple of Solomon. The lower courses of the masonry are much larger than the superincumbent mass, and have indeed every appearance of being a portion of the actual stonework of the original Jewish wall; and their preservation is easily accounted for, as they form the external support of a terrace upon which the Temple platform is raised, and which it was not the object of the victorious Romans to destroy. After the taking of Jerusalem by Titus, and the subsequent revolt of the Jews in the time of Adrian, they were forbidden to enter the city of their forefathers; but after a long period had elapsed they were permitted to return, though subject to every indignity and outrage. They were also allowed to purchase the right of assembling together in this hidden corner beneath the ruins of their Temple, to bewail the sins which had caused the desolation of Israel, and to read those prophecies that foretell her final restoration. The sight is an affecting one: here, every Friday, may be seen a small cluster of the fallen people, crouching beneath the massive memorials of the former pride and splendour of their race. In the city which was once the seat of their power, they are now as exiles—other religions and other races have usurped their dominion: they are treated with contempt both by Christian and by Mussulman, and exposed to the insults of both. But the hearts of this people, wherever they may be scattered, are still turned with longing to the soil of their forefathers, and to the ruinous walls of their beloved Jerusalem; and though subject to every injury, and even compelled to subsist on the precarious resources derived from such alms as their wealthier brethren may furnish, they still repair, even from distant lands, to the Holy City, there to wear out the remainder of their days, and to die and be buried in the Valley of Jehoshaphat.

Few indeed of the group who assemble at the "Place of Wailing" appear to be in prosperous or even decent circumstances. Their looks are worn and poverty-stricken; their garments threadbare and sordid; and they implore with earnestness the charity of the stranger. The women are generally better clad, and enveloped in white veils. As they

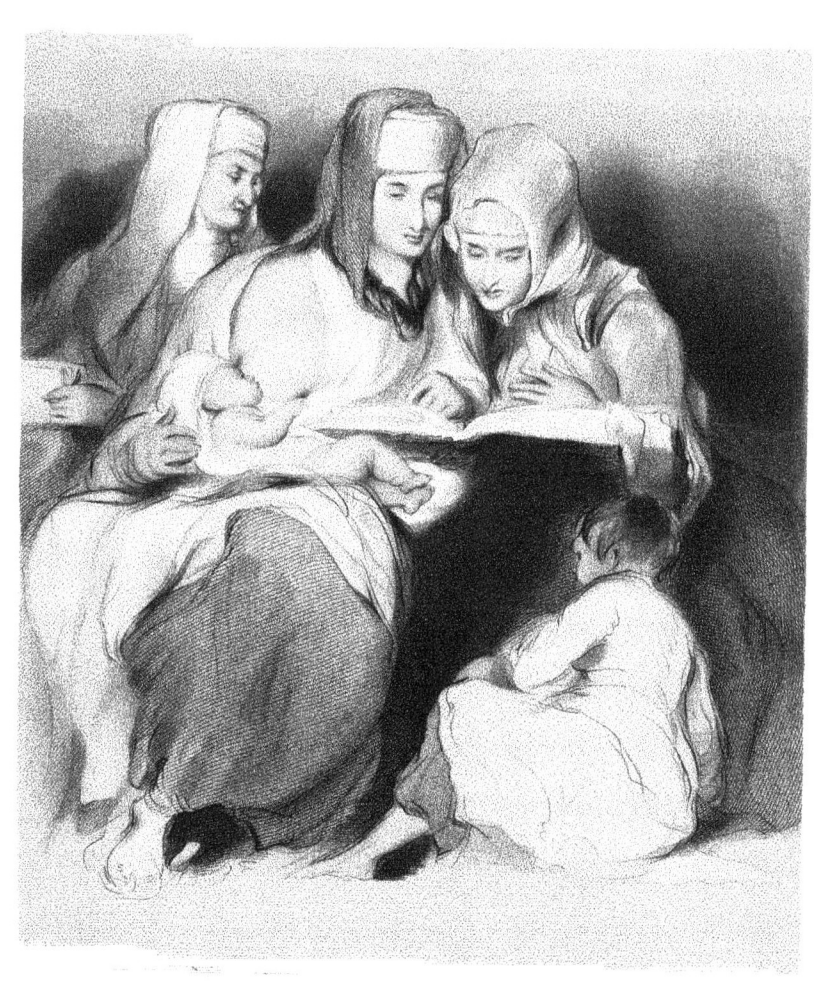

SKETCHED BY SIR DAVID WILKIE R.A.

enter the small enclosed area in front of the ancient wall, they "kiss the stones thereof," and breathe through the ruinous chinks and fissures a prayer for the restoration of Judah. In the shadow of the wall are to be seen groups of venerable men and women reading the book of the law, and meditating upon its consolatory promises of forgiveness, after the allotted measure of their sufferings shall be fulfilled.

Since the dedication of the Temple of Solomon, in the midst of a grateful and adoring people, what changes, what revolutions, has this spot witnessed, perhaps beyond any other upon earth!—The power of the Jews soon followed by rapid decline, caused by internal dissension;—we see their Temple prostrate, and the people led away into captivity, till, after a long interval of foreign servitude, a returning colony of exiles, with arms in their hands, build up again the holy walls in the midst of peril and discouragement. Following the varying fortunes of the Temple, we behold it profaned by Antiochus, purified by the Maccabees, stormed by Pompey, pillaged by Crassus, till a prince of foreign race, the gorgeous Herod, restored it to more than pristine splendour, soon to be followed by a complete and final overthrow. We mark in idea the triumphant entry of Jesus; his purification of the desecrated courts; the wonder of his Galilean disciples at the enduring splendour of the fabric, built as if for eternity, and hear them listening to the terrible prediction of its impending overthrow. Then follow the awful scenes of Calvary, and the persecution of the scattered followers of Jesus. The undaunted apostles are seen preaching the new religion even in the Temple courts, where we witness the narrow escape of Paul from the attack of the infuriated Jews. And now rapidly hurries on the last fearful siege, terminated by the destruction of the Temple, and the dissolution of the Jewish state in fire and blood. Again the site is long left desolate—a pagan temple on the Holy of Holies;—the very *name* of Jerusalem forgotten. Then follows the establishment of Christianity. Justinian, in building a church to the Virgin, with a holy horror of the Divine judgment, leaves the site of the Temple covered with rubbish. Next come the followers of the Prophet; and the Caliph Omar, conducted to this spot by the Christian patriarch, removes the filth, and founds upon the site a magnificent Mahommedan mosque. See that again and again change masters; the Crescent give place to the Cross, the Cross to the Crescent, which even now is waning to no distant change. In revolutions such as these three thousand years have passed away, the Jews have been scattered over the face of the whole earth, they have been exposed to every extremity of illtreatment. Is it not then affecting, even wonderful, to see a handful of this scattered and persecuted people (the subsistence of whose nationality, through long ages of convulsion that have fused together the blood and the manners of so many other races, seems little less than miraculous) still lifting their prayer, amidst the memorials of their glory and their guilt, to the Great Being who was once their tutelary guide, when the world around them lay sunk in the darkness of polytheism? May it not well seem as an earnest of their final restoration to the land of their forefathers?

HEBREW WOMEN READING THE SCRIPTURES.

In the sketch before us, Wilkie has finely seized the expression of sadness which is characteristic of the fallen remnant of Israel. We may also remark the noble cast of their countenances. The changes that have failed to obliterate the Jewish race, have modified to some extent its appearance. In Western lands the Jewish face would not be selected as the type of form; but judging from the specimens we have seen in the East, the original stock is distinguished for personal beauty. Nowhere have we found finer or fairer faces than among the Oriental Jews. We need not descant on the beauty of grouping and expression in this fine but hasty production: they show the mind of Wilkie, and the extent of his powers, and in some degree what might have been expected from him had he lived to realize his favourite dream of a new and scriptural style of painting.

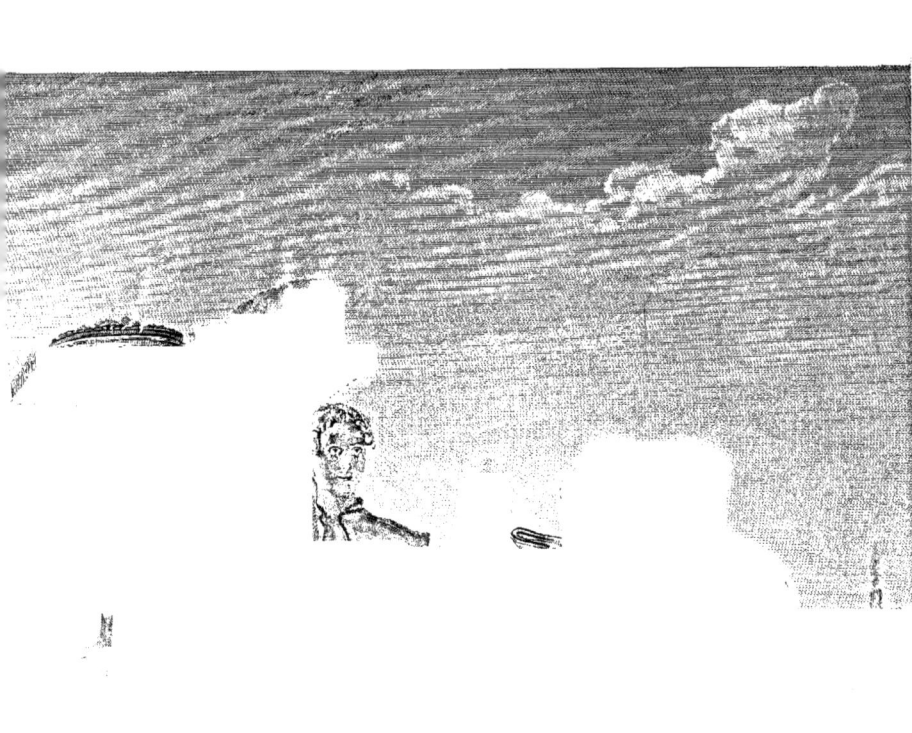

READING THE NEWS.

The first notice we find of this picture is in a letter from Wilkie to Sir G. Beaumont, in which he tells him, "We are all in this part of the world preparing for the exhibition. I shall have two small pictures, one of which, 'The Newsmongers,' is for General Phipps, a subject of his own suggestion." It does not appear that the picture, on its being exposed to public criticism, made any very lively impression, even if it were not considered to be somewhat below the average of the painter's works. In sober truth, we cannot regard it as one of his most felicitous specimens: the subject was none of his own choosing, and he seems to have been somewhat at a loss how to give point to it. A group of rustic figures are assembled together to listen to some very engrossing news, though of what nature there is nothing in the picture that can lead us to divine:—it may, for aught we know, be the intelligence of a battle or a coronation, or some such wonderful event; but more probably a piece of information more especially interesting to the villagers themselves. Whatever it be, it creates evidently no small sensation; the porter has stopped his wheelbarrow, and is staring with all his eyes—the baker's man has come to a standstill, oblivious, in his eagerness to drink in the important information, of the dishes of baked meats and pudding of which the hungry owners are impatiently awaiting the arrival, and which are meanwhile undergoing an unsatisfactory process of refrigeration—even a little urchin, whose growth outruns his garments, has stopped his hoop to listen, and the little housewifely creature, who is nursing "baby," is learning betimes to gratify the darling passion of her sex. These materials, it will be conceded by the artist, are skilfully grouped, and there are many admirable traits of expression, with a bold and rich treatment of light and shade and colour—yet the entire effect is, to our thinking, comparatively deficient in interest.

It is in truth but rarely that an artist works out well the suggestion of a patron—better far leave him to his own untrammelled fancy for the choice of a subject. Much of Wilkie's admirable genius was thus diverted from its proper and natural channel. Portraits, both single and family, historical incidents, or courtly scenes, without the least regard for the bent of his genius, were ruthlessly inflicted upon him, to his own infinite vexation and loss of fame, and the no less injury of the public and posterity. How many admirable artists in our own day are thus compelled to toil for subsistence, and to exhaust their powers over a class of works of which the judicious critic cannot but regret the production!

READING THE NEWS.

There has been, indeed, considerable difference of opinion as to whether Wilkie acted wisely in ever stepping beyond the line of Scottish or at least of British character. His biographer, Mr. Allan Cunningham, with that almost idolatry of his friend which runs through all his work, and colours his estimate of Wilkie's productions, regards his last performances as rising not only in the scale of subject, but also of execution, above those by which he first gained his fame. This estimate is one which very few of his admirers will feel able to agree with. Some, indeed, of his later works, and among these, unfinished as it is, we are inclined to place the one before us, may challenge a comparison with the finest of his contemporaries in the same walk of art; but the public, we fear, will always look back to his earlier productions, with the feeling that they are altogether unequalled in their own distinctive originality, and with the regret that he was not enabled to add a larger number to these few and precious chef-d'œuvres of our national art.

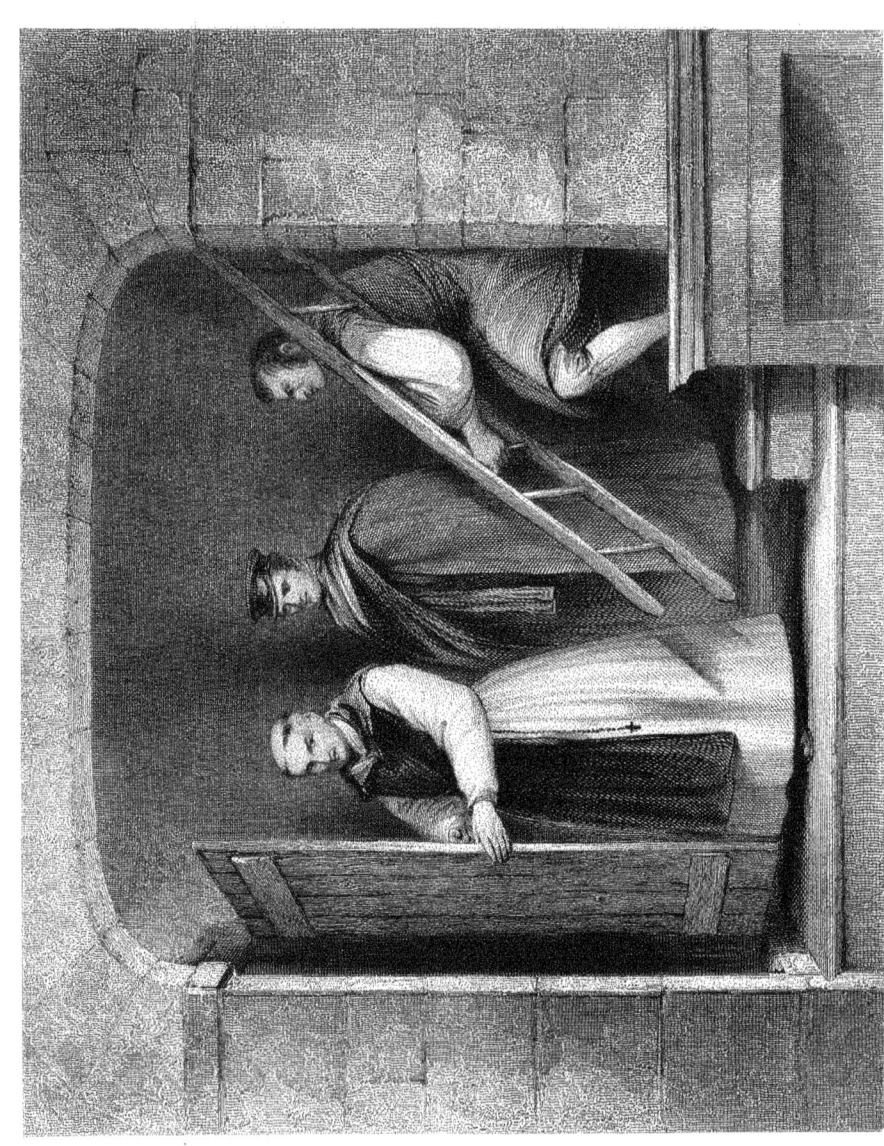

WILKIE IN SEARCH OF MURILLO.

WILKIE, in a letter to a brother painter, describes Spain as "the wild unpoached game preserve of Europe, in which he has had six months freedom by himself alone." His journals and correspondence contain numerous notices of the treasures of art over which he thus ranged unrestricted. Velasquez and Murillo were his favourites, and he thus contrasts their different styles. "Velasquez is a surprising fellow; he may be said to be the origin of what is now doing in England. His feeling they have caught without seeing his works, which here seem to anticipate Reynolds, Romney, Ræburn, Jackson, and even Sir Thomas Laurence. Murillo, though of the same school, and of nearly the same time, is a painter opposed in almost everything to Velasquez: if not greater in point of talent, his subjects are more elevated; his painting and colouring more general and abstract at the same time. No painter is so universally popular as Murillo: without trick or vulgar imitation, he attracts every one by his power, and adapts the higher subjects of art to the commonest understanding." In the Escurial, and numerous private collections, Wilkie found many specimens of this master, but he made a journey to Seville expressly to see the collections of his works said to exist there; nor was he at all disappointed in his search. In a letter to Prince Dolgorouki, he says that the "Capuchin convent contains about fifteen of his productions; they were once more. You have, no doubt, been struck with that quality or power in Murillo that makes him admired by the unlearned as well as the learned in art. Being a favourite in all countries, it is not surprising that he should be so in Seville. Here, even among the lower classes, he is venerated as if he were the patriot and benefactor of the city; his name is with them synonymous with all that is excellent—a term, which makes in their eyes every beautiful picture, painted by whom it may, a Murillo."

The following biographical sketch of this great painter is extracted from Mr. Stirling's admirable work, "Annals of the Artists of Spain."

"All that is known of the personal history of Murillo tends to the advantage of his fame. Gifted with much energy and determination of mind, and great powers of application, he obtained, by his amiable and attractive manners, a considerable influence with his fellow-men. His character bears so strong a resemblance to that of Velasquez, that the great court-painter may have been his model, both as a man and as an artist. Discreet and conciliating towards friends and rivals, both of these celebrated sons of Seville seem to have been free from that proneness to boasting and self-glorification, the besetting vice of Alonzo Cano, and one generally inherent in the oriental blood of Andalusia. The early history of the Sevillian academy affords evidence of the good sense of Murillo, and of the moderation of his temper. Cean Bermudez records a happy reply made by him to his fellow-painter Valdes Leal, a man too arrogant, he was accustomed to say, to admit of rivalry. This haughty antagonist having one day condescended to ask Murillo's opinion of a work which he had just finished, and of which the principal feature was a rotting corpse, the painter—who had probably not yet given an opening for a retort by painting the Tinoso—replied, ' Compadre, it is a picture which cannot be looked at without holding one's nose.' Cean Bermudez was doubtless repeating the tradition of Seville when he relates that the scholars of Murillo found him in all things the opposite of the testy Herrera: a gentle and pains-taking master, and in after-life a generous and fatherly friend. . One of them attended him in his last moments, and Meneses Osorio, Marquez Joya, Antolinez, and others of less distinction, lamented his death as if they had been his children. The friend of good Miguel Manara, and the votary of the holy Almoner of Valencia, he practised the charity which his pencil preached; and his funeral was hallowed by the prayers and tears of the poor who had partaken of his bounties. His story justifies the hortatory motto graven on his tomb; he had lived as one about to die. Like Velasquez, Murillo enjoyed a high contemporary reputation. The invitation to court was not the most signal homage paid to his genius. He had the pleasure of reading his own praises in the Memorial of the festivals held at Seville on the canonization of St. Ferdinand, one of the most beautiful books of Spanish local history. In that work Don Fernando de la Torre Farfan proclaims the renown of Murillo's name, and the 'learning' of his pencil; he asserts that he was 'a better Titian,' and that Apelles might have been proud to be called the Grecian Murillo; and he remarks of one of his beautiful delineations of the Immaculate Conception, 'that those who did not know that it had been painted by the great artist of Seville would suppose that it had had its birth in heaven.' Murillo was probably better known abroad than any other Spanish painter except Ribera and Velasquez."

We have preferred to give this sketch of Murillo as being intimately connected with Wilkie's journey to Spain. There is some doubt, however, whether the title of this plate is not a misnomer, and whether it should not rather be "Wilkie in search of Corregio," than of Murillo, since he tells us that he had to make use of a ladder in the course of his examination of the pictures in the Escurial, near Madrid, which stupendous palace he likens to Hampton Court and St. Paul's together—palace, convent, and church in one, full of neglected treasures of art.

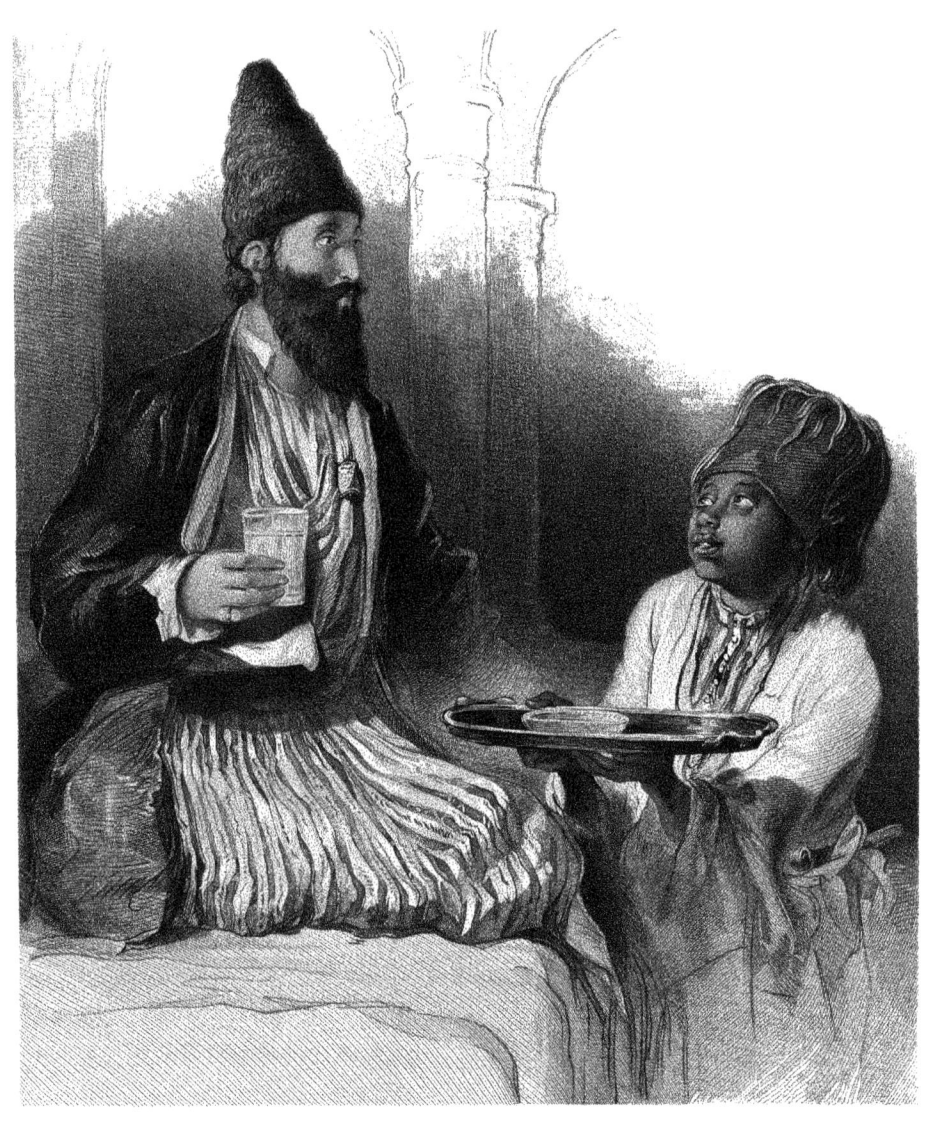

HIS SLAVE HIM SHERBET.

BY SIR DAVID WILKIE R.A. — ENGRAVED BY H. ROBINSON.

A PERSIAN PRINCE,

HIS SLAVE BRINGING HIM SHERBET.

THIS is one of the boldest of Wilkie's Oriental sketches. Among the personages whom he had the opportunity of painting when at Constantinople, was the Persian Prince, Hallicoo Mirza, at that time a resident in the city, and we find in his Journal the following entry respecting him:—" Went to the Prince Hallicoo Mirza in a carriage; found him at home at ten; after a time, was led through the garden into a street, to a distance, then to a house, and on going up stairs he showed me into a room with a divan, where was a little girl very young—she was placed on the ottoman. I made two drawings from her; one for the prince and one for myself. She was white, but had a little colour, full eye and lip, very long hair, and rich dress; she had no expression, and was perfectly silent. It was not explained what she was; perhaps she might be a slave, a Circassian slave. There was an elderly black in the house, who looked much like an eunuch; there was a young black girl, a slave, and a white woman, a Turk, in the house: altogether it was a singular and characteristic scene."

It is not unusual to see a few Persians among the mixed crowd of foreign merchants in the bazaars of Constantinople. Their physiognomy and costume are perfectly distinct from the Turkish, the Armenian, the Jewish, and other classes of the population. Their features are longer and more delicate, and their dress generally is tighter to the person, and yet remarkably graceful and elegant. The distinguishing peculiarity, however, is the head-dress, which, in striking contrast to the voluminous turban, consists of a high and conical-shaped cap, of the finest black wool. The style and shape of this cap is doubtless of very ancient origin: the sculptures representing the kings of Persia and of Nineveh, have head-dresses very similar in general appearance.

It would be difficult to select two forms of our species more distinctly contrasted with each other, than this elegant and noble-looking Persian prince and his negro slave; types, respectively, of the Asiatic and African families; of the Caucasian and the negro. In the first we see form and expression at the same time so commanding and beautiful that Wilkie is said to have selected it as furnishing him with the best ideal of our Saviour; while the second verges upon positive deformity. The painter has, however, thrown into

A PERSIAN PRINCE, HIS SLAVE BRINGING HIM SHERBET.

the eyes and countenance of the negro boy an expression of gentleness and kindliness which they very often wear, especially in the East, where the treatment of slaves is comparatively humane and paternal. Torn from the interior of Kordofan or Sennaar, and brought from Egypt into the slave-market of Constantinople, it would seem to have been the good fortune of this poor negro lad to have acquired a good and feeling master. The manner in which the painter has treated this head shows how art can detect the beautiful beneath the mask of external ugliness, bring out latent expression, and render predominant traits which escape the vulgar observer. There are few of Wilkie's sketches from nature, masterly as they are, which surpass this of the negro boy.

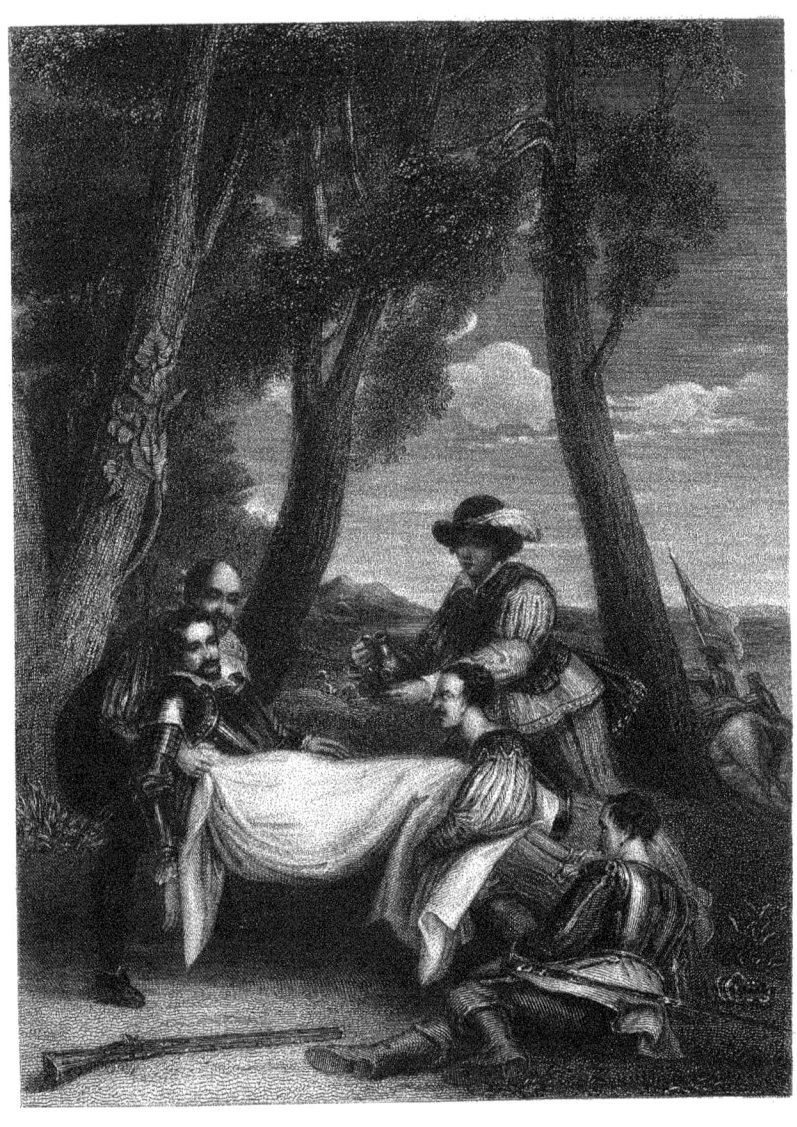

THE DEATH.

PAINTED BY SIR DAV.D WILKIE, R.A — ENGRAVED BY W. GREATBACH

DEATH OF SIR PHILIP SIDNEY.

THIS picture, one of the smallest ever painted by Wilkie, originated in the request of Mr. Dobree, for whom " The Letter of Introduction" was painted, that he would give him his assistance in a work he had long contemplated, intended to commemorate the dying scenes of remarkable men. As in the case of his commission to paint Alfred the Great in the Neatherd's Cottage, Wilkie, as well as certain of his more enlightened patrons, felt that he was labouring in a walk unfitted for him—so here, too, he appears to have been reluctant to undertake the desired task, and recommended his friend Stothard, whose reading, and whose elegance of taste and design, would, as Wilkie suggested, "fit him better than any other artist for illustrating the incidents in the lives of great characters gone by." Eventually, however, he produced the picture from which this engraving is taken.

The life of the gallant and accomplished Sir Philip Sidney hardly need to be recalled to our readers. He was the ornament and delight of the English court; the ideal of a perfect gentleman, and although few are now found to read his " Arcadia," he was distinguished in his day as a poet of no mean accomplishment. The circumstances of his death, which this picture was designed to commemorate, are also generally known, and require but brief mention, for they have achieved universal renown.

Suffering under the agony of his wounds he called for water, but on seeing a soldier carried by in a state of still greater prostration—looking wistfully, perhaps, on the precious cup he was about to carry to his lips—Sidney commanded it to be given to him, with the remark, " This man's necessity is greater even than mine." Such a death was worthy to close a life of high chivalrous feeling, of true nobility of nature, and of the ideal of Christian knighthood.

At Penshurst in Kent, the family seat of the Sidneys, are many interesting memorials of Sir Philip. There is the tree planted at his birth—a portion of his shaving-glass—his sword—his portrait when grown up, and another as a boy, grouped with his brother Robert. " The picture is tall and narrow in shape, representing the youths with their arms linked affectionately together. Their likeness to each other is striking. Philip's taller stature reveals the elder brother, as does also his manly firm-looking position, with the right arm a-kimbo, and the hand upon his waist, reminding us of a taper lady's of the present day, for it contrasts with the swelling drapery about the hips. There is something touchingly beautiful in the nestling sense of security, which seems to have impelled the younger brother, Robert, to his side, and from whence he now looks abroad upon the world. It was to this son that Sir Henry Sidney, the father, wrote the letter in which he thus spoke of the other : " 'Follow the advice of your most loving brother, who in loving you is comparable with me, *or exceedeth me.* Imitate his virtues, exercises, studies, and actions. He is a rare ornament of his age, the very formula that all well-disposed young gentlemen of the court do form also their manners and life by. In truth, I speak it without flattery of him or myself, he hath the most virtues that I ever found in any man.' Next to the being the son thus spoken of, who would not wish to be the father that could thus speak ?"*

* Penny Magazine.

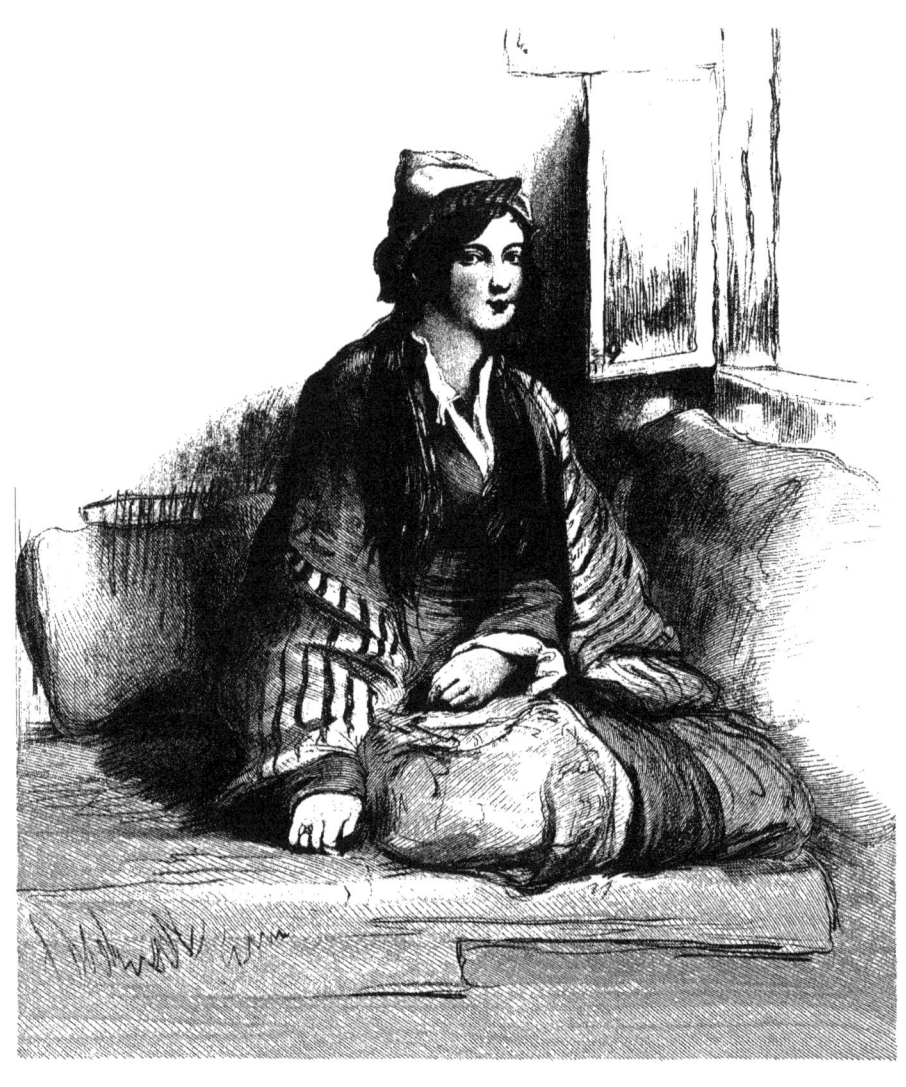

A CIRCASSIAN LADY.

SKETCHED BY SIR DAVID WILKIE, R A -- ENGRAVED BY H. ROBINSON

LONDON PUBLISHED FOR THE PROPRIETORS, BY GEO. VIRTUE, 26, IVY LANE.

A CIRCASSIAN LADY.

THIS should more properly have been entitled—a Circassian *Slave*, belonging to the Persian Prince Hallicoo Mirza, of whom there is a portrait in this collection, accompanied by an account of Wilkie's visit, and of his making also the annexed sketch. Everybody has heard of the far-famed Circassian beauty, and bestowed sympathy upon the wretched girls who are sold by their heartless parents into slavery, to become the mistresses of Mussulman magnates. " It is, however, but fair to add," says a recent reviewer of the excellent work of Herr Wagner on the Caucasus, " that the odious character of the trade is somewhat mitigated, when we observe the hardships on the one hand to which the Circassian women are condemned in the precarious life on the mountains, and on the other, the condition of the slave-girl in the harem of the wealthy Turk, such only being able to indulge in the luxury of Georgian or Circassian handmaids. It may also be said, that the Mohammedan virgin has in no case the disposal of herself, and that, as far as her reception of a husband is concerned, the choice must be tolerably indifferent between one stranger and another of the same religion. Still, however we may soften it down, the feature is revolting, and quite incompatible with any notion of true heroism in the people among whom it is found."

Herr Wagner describes the Tscherkesses (our Circassians) as a most splendid race. But even here, he observes, " whoever expects to find pure specimens of the ideal of manly beauty in any great number amongst the people, will be strangely disappointed, for even in Tscherkessia the great mass is composed of the descendants of many different races, of the serfs and vassals of the nobles, whose origin is not certainly known, but who most probably are sprung from prisoners of war or subdued aboriginal tribes. The nobles, i. e. the *Works* or knights, form at the most a fifth part, or, according to the belief of many well-informed Russians, perhaps but a tenth of the whole people termed *Adigles*. These *Works* alone, and the still more aristocratic branches of the princely families, fully justify the far-spread reputation of Circassian beauty. The Tscherkassian nobleman intermarries only with families of equal birth, and thus he preserves the purity of the stock, the nobility in blood and person, the beauty of feature, the knightly haughtiness in bearing, and a peculiar elegance in his motions, manners, and mode of speaking."

In regard to the attempt of Russia to subjugate Circassia, Herr Wagner, who was intimately acquainted with all its details, concludes, "that the power of resistance is very far indeed from being yet exhausted in the defenders of the vast natural fortress of the Caucasus, and that all the might which Russia could bring against it, will not be able to effect any speedy conquest, so long as they retain the indomitable spirit and the rooted abhorrence of Muscovite slavery that now certainly animates them."

To turn to the sketch before us. Few of our fair countrywomen, we think, will be disposed to admit the superiority of Circassian beauty from the lady here placed before us. A specimen of almost doll-like prettiness, with the listless languor of mental vacancy—she seems a toy to amuse the leisure hours of a sultan, rather than a companion for an intelligent man. Torn at an early period from home—transferred to the slave-bazaar, and thence to the harem of her purchaser, she looks like one who would gladly bask awhile in the passing favour of her master, and then as contentedly give place to a new favourite. Incapable of the darker passions of jealousy and revenge, which have sometimes wrought such terrible effects in Oriental harems, she is quite a personation of the gentle "Dudu" of Lord Byron.

We have more than once visited the slave bazaars of Cairo and Constantinople, in the expectation of seeing some of these vaunted Georgian and Circassian beauties, but were destined to be disappointed. They are kept very close, and rarely shown, unless to expected purchasers. The price is often very high, and when we add the expense of their dress and maintenance, none but the wealthiest can afford to indulge in such costly luxuries. In general the Mussulmen, contrary to the common belief, have but one wife. The intermarriages with Georgian and Circassian women has much improved the beauty of the Turkish race. Slaves of both sexes, in Eastern lands, have often, even from Joseph's time, attained the highest honours, and sometimes become possessed of sovereign power; as witness the Tartar and Circassian Memlooks in Egypt. The story of the beautiful slave, Shegeret-ed-Door, who, after getting her husband murdered through jealousy, was killed herself by the *pattens* of his women, is a remarkable incident in the history of that period. The son-in-law of the late Sultan Mahmood was a slave.

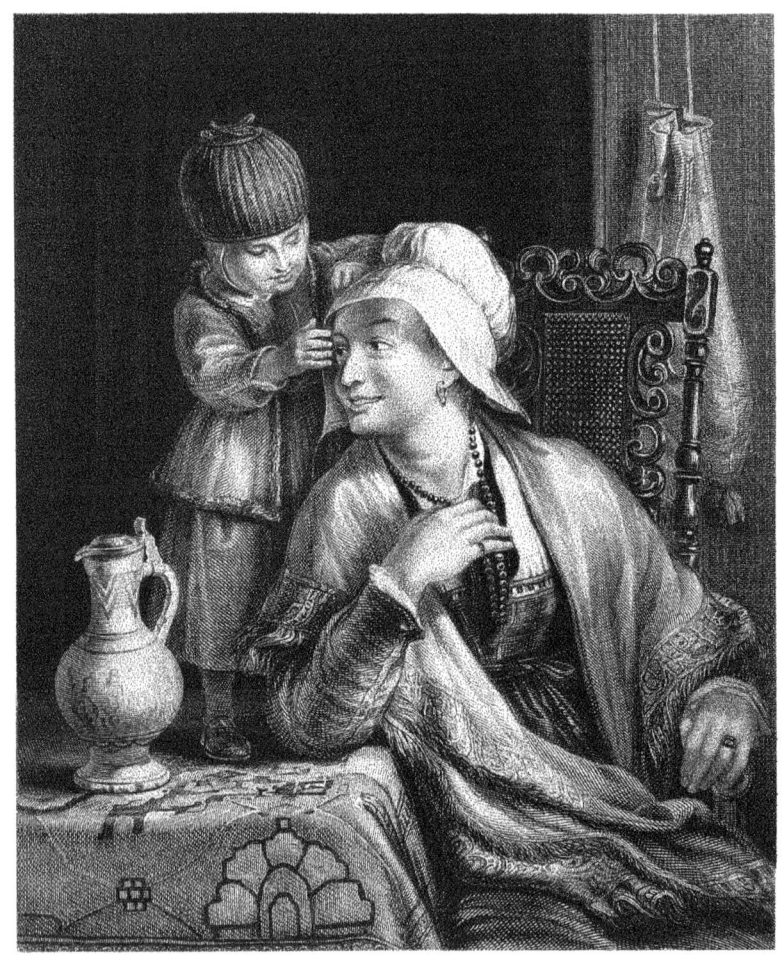

MOTHE AN CHI

FROM AN ETCHING BY SIR DAVID WILKIE, R.A.; ENGRAVED BY J C ARMYTAGE.

MOTHER AND CHILD.

WE must confess ourselves rather at a loss with reference to this subject, of which we can find no notices in Wilkie's "Life and Letters;" unless, indeed, it be, as we incline to believe, the "Spanish Mother and Child," painted for Sir William Knighton. This picture, exhibited at the Royal Academy in 1834, excited very general admiration, and attracted the notice of royalty, King William the Fourth, especially, admiring the expression of the child. Many were desirous of becoming purchasers of this picture.

As to the subject itself, it is one of that simple class which requires but little to be said of it, depending as it mainly does for its attractiveness upon the consummate skill of the painter. It is as eminently natural and pleasing in expression as it is powerful and brilliant in execution. We have before had occasion to remark that Wilkie is unusually successful in his portraiture of childhood. In modern times no painter, except Sir Thomas Lawrence, has left us such charming representations of its impulsive joyousness and engaging archness. And yet, oddly enough, both painters were destined to live and die bachelors. Sir Thomas had more than one narrow escape; but we hear of only a single instance of Wilkie's being at all seriously affected by female charms. This was at the period of his visits to Chelsea, when engaged upon his great picture of "The Pensioners." At the house of a physician, upon whom he was in the habit of calling on his way, he met with a young and beautiful lady, whose attraction, as it would appear, did for a while somewhat disturb his otherwise exclusive devotion to his art. He might, perhaps, have been tempted to think of changing his condition, but from nervous apprehension that his addresses might not be encouraged by the fair object of his admiration. This characteristic prudence obtained an easy victory over a feeling which could never have amounted to passion; and the painter, with a passing sigh, returned to devote himself to his beloved pursuit, which henceforth never knew any rival in his affections. He may be cited as another illustrious instance corroborating the remark of Lord Bacon :—" Certainly the best works, and of the greatest merit for the public, have proceeded from the unmarried or childless men; which both in affection and means have married and endowed the public ;"—a saying perhaps more verified in the case of painters than of the members of any other profession.

If Wilkie was not, however, destined to be exercised in that "discipline of human nature"—the care of a family, nor to labour for their well-being, a labour, which, according to Burns, constitutes the " true pathos and sublime of human life."—no man was in his nature more affectionate, or more generous in assisting his friends or relatives. His piety towards his parents, his kindness to his brothers and sisters, the sacrifices he submitted to and the cares he took upon him on their behalf, present us with a beautiful example of warmth and truthfulness of heart. Few feelings in his life, as we learn from his private journal, were equal to that in which he beheld his widowed mother, seated as the mistress of his house in London, and rejoicing in the fame into which her partial encouragement of his boyish inclinations had so remarkably ripened. Here was, indeed, a domestic scene surpassing all the brightest visions ever created by his pencil—a genuine and affecting picture of " The Mother and Child."

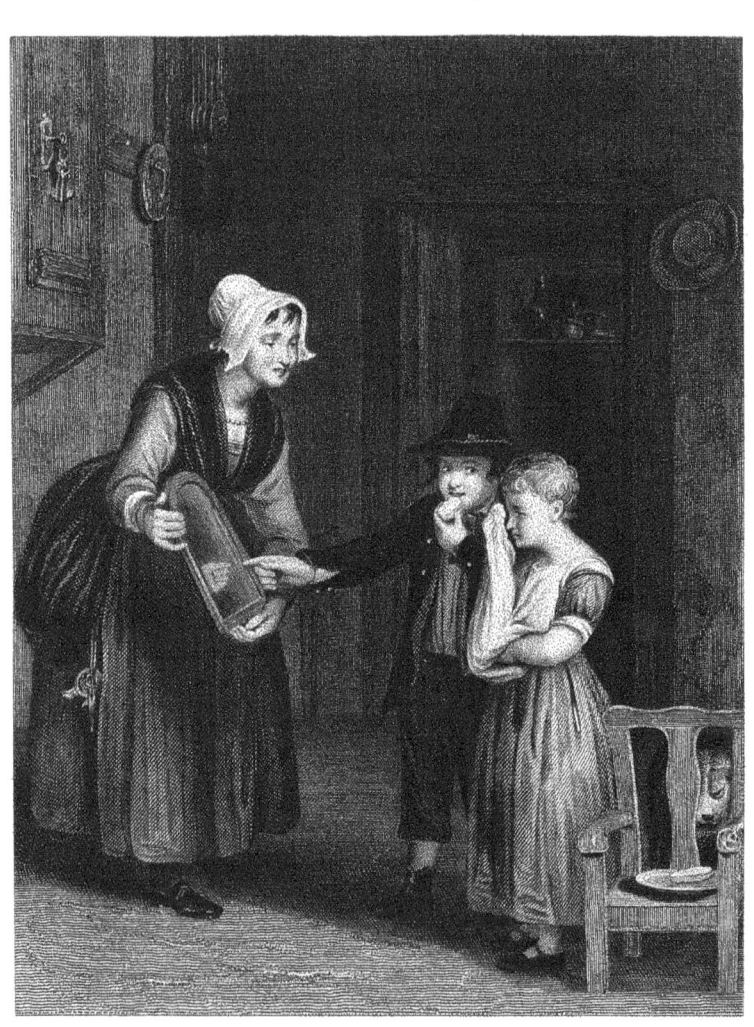

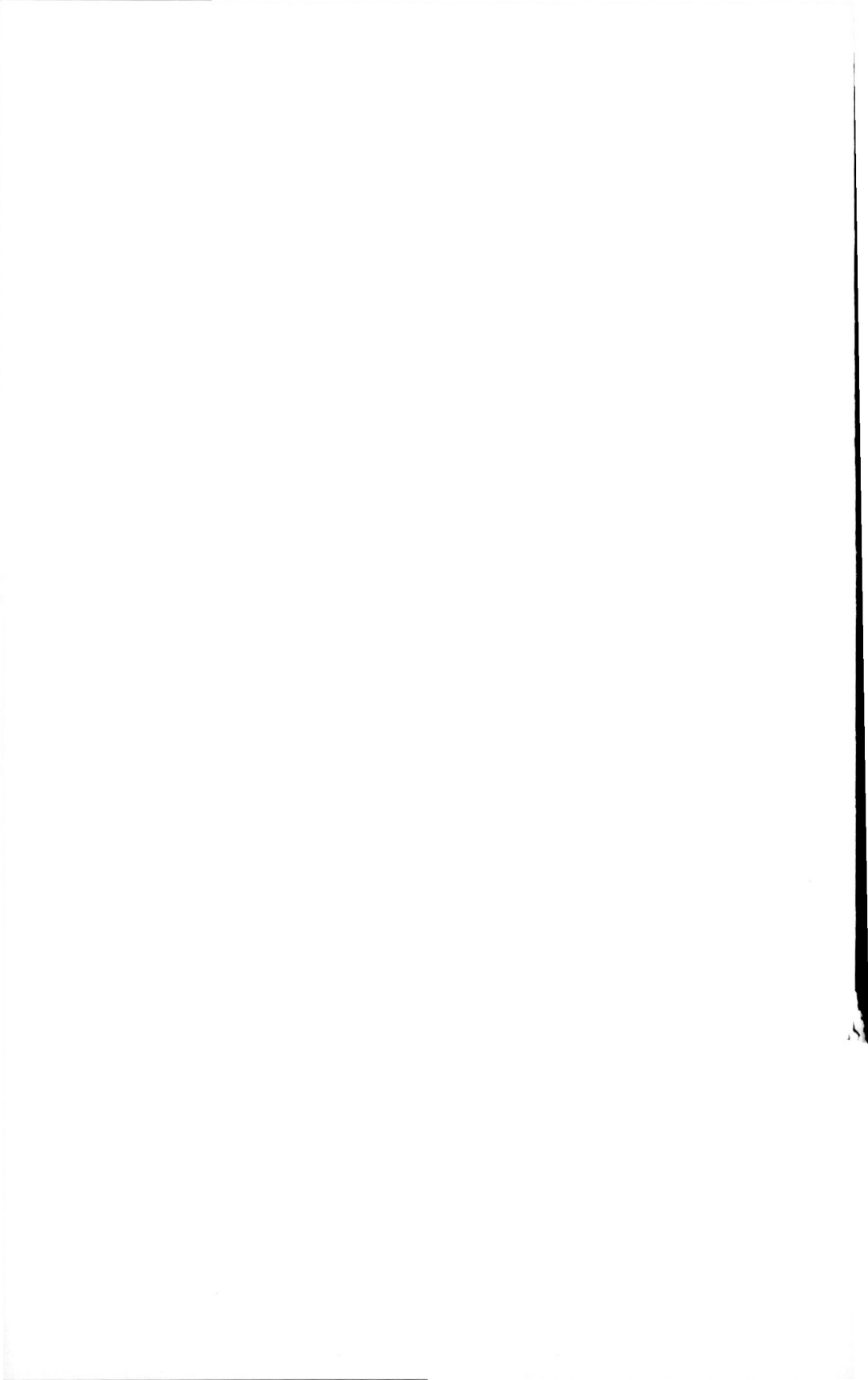

DORTY BAIRN.

WE are at a loss as to when and for whom this picture was painted, but it bears the unmistakeable stamp of Wilkie. It is one of the same family of domestic subjects by which he has immortalized himself—ascending from such minor incidents as the present—" The Cut Finger," " The Jew's Harp," and " The Rabbit on the Wall," to the more pathetic circumstances of the " Reading of the Will," or the " Distraining for Rent." Wilkie was the painter, " par excellence," of household life, in all the varieties of its characteristic amusements and peculiar trials; and as such his works must ever be cherished by a people whose joys centre in the sacred retirement of home.

The incident chosen by the painter carries us back to our childish days, when the first impulse of nascent enterprise led us to dash delighted through every puddle, and to wade through every stream, and the organ of "constructiveness" was developed in piling up " earth-mounds " and pyramids of dust, like rude aboriginal attempts at architecture, or making " dirt pies," built up with clay crust, or to fit out armaments of stick and paper boats; the whole to the no small detriment of clean pinafores and snowy stockings. There is a little " ne'er do weel," who has been engaging in these or similar amusements, and her tidy mother is endeavouring, by a moral process to which we have all been subjected when in the tantrums, to awaken a sense of shame. There is something intensely comic in the whole business. The delinquent blubbering through all her dirt, is compelled, *nolens volens*, to regard herself in the glass; and with averted look is trying, to adopt the words of the poet,

" The struggling pangs of conscious truth to hide,
To quench the blushes of ingenuous shame."

There is, however, we fear, far more of rage than of remorse, in that dogged, sullen visage; a rising against this unjustifiable curtailment of natural liberty, an indignant sense of violated right. The amusingly grievous and wrathful expression thrown into the girl's face, is heightened by the sly mischief in the countenance of the boy, who was probably both instigator of the offence and also informer against it. While this scene of domestic discipline is proceeding, there is a little episode going forward in the corner. The girl has been obliged to lay down her bannock upon a low chair while she is subjected to the penitentiary process; and " a very sly dog," profiting by the abstraction of all around, is evidently calculating whether he can insinuate his head through the bars of the chair far enough to accomplish the capture of the cake; the loss of which will cap the climax of correction, and aid in producing a permanent and salutary impression upon the infant mind.

BENVENUTO CELLINI AND THE POPE.

BENVENUTO CELLINI was one of that wonderful galaxy of men who flourished at the most palmy period of Italian art. He was, as Vasari tells us, a citizen of Florence, and cultivated the art of carving in gold and silver, in which branch he had no equal; his diminutive figures showed such a play of fancy, as well as such admirable workmanship. He was patronized at Rome by Pope Clement VII., after whose death he returned to Florence, whence he visited the court of Francis I., and at length returned to his native city, which he adorned with the fine statue of Perseus, in the Piazza del Gran Duca. After a very stirring and eventful life he died at Florence on the 13th of February, 1470, in the seventy-first year of his age.

"Though I might enlarge," says Vasari, "on the productions of Benvenuto, who always showed himself a man of great spirit and vivacity, bold, active, enterprising, and formidable to his enemies, a man, in short, who knew how to speak to princes as to exert himself in his art, I shall add nothing further, since he has given us an account of his life and works, with more art and eloquence than it is possible for me to imitate." This same piece of autobiography is one of the most interesting that has come down to us. It presents us with a perfect picture of the man and of the age in which he flourished, when art grew up in the midst of strife and convulsion, when its professors were as familiar with the rapier and stiletto, as with the painter's crayon or the sculptor's hammer. Benvenuto was as much of a soldier as an artist, altogether as fiery, daring, and unscrupulous, and we may add superstitious,—a true type of the Italian of his age. Although he stabbed or killed in the duello more than one of his rivals, when thrown into prison he tells us that he was visited and comforted by the Virgin Mary. When the Constable Bourbon took Rome by assault, it was no other than Benvenuto, if we are to believe himself, who picked him off as he was advancing to the attack. While shut up with the Pope in the Castle of St. Angelo, he performed an almost Munchausen exploit: "Perceiving a Spaniard at no great distance, I fired off the gun," he says, "and hit the man in red exactly in the middle. He had arrogantly placed his sword before him in a sort of Spanish bravado; but the ball of my piece hit against his sword, and the man was seen severed into two pieces." Falling on his knees, he entreated his holiness, who was delighted with this exploit, to absolve him from the guilt of homicide, as likewise from *all other crimes* he had committed in that castle in the service of the church. "The Pope, lifting up his hands, and making the sign of the cross over me,

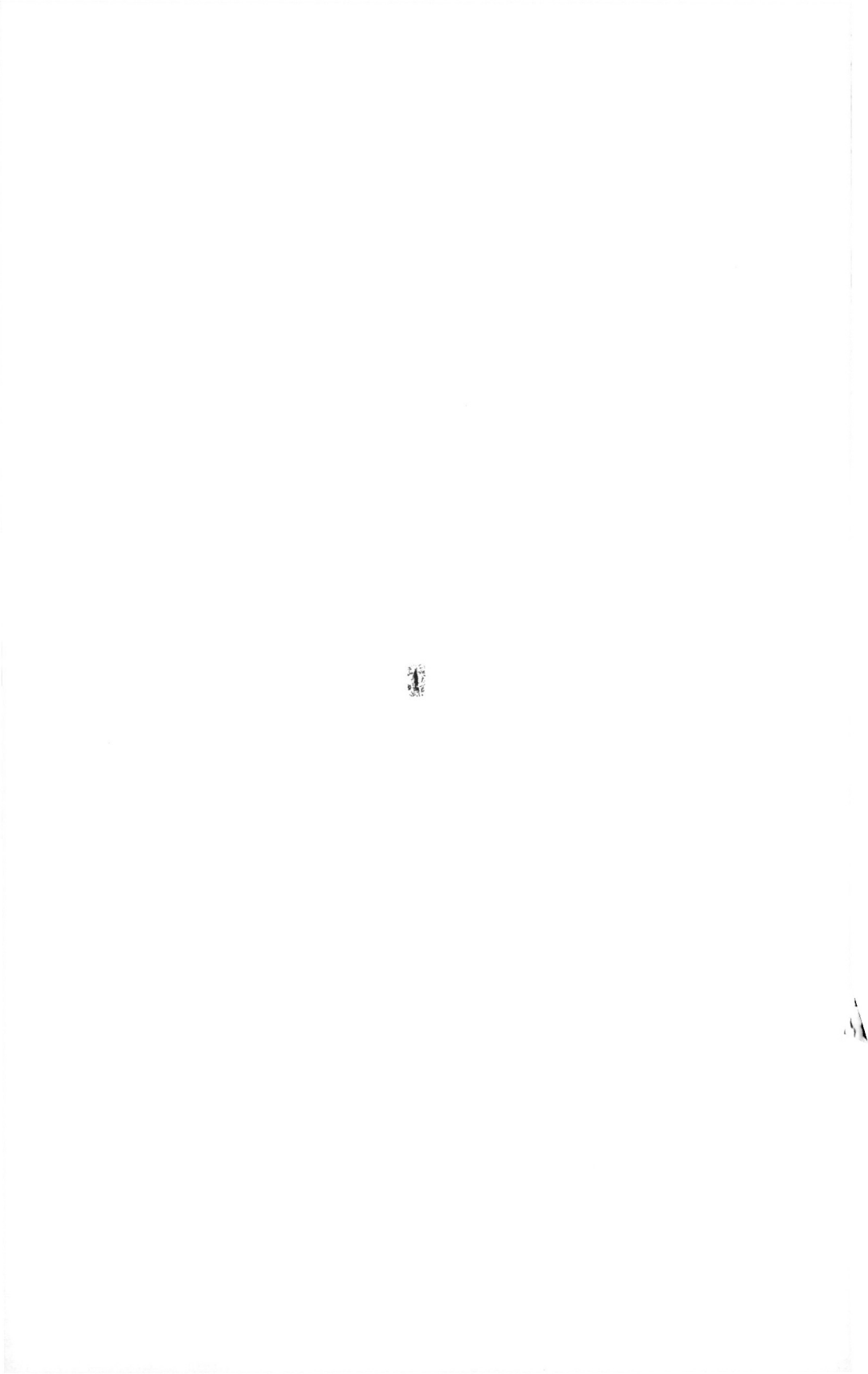

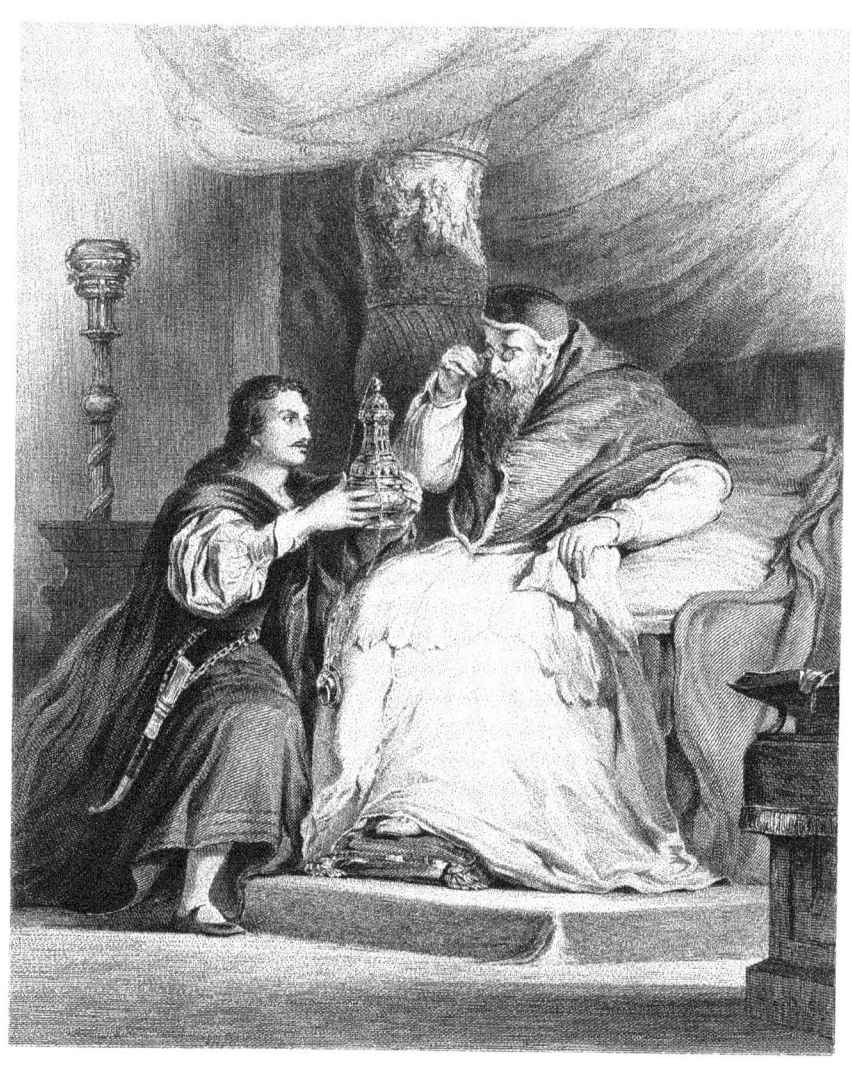

said he blessed me, and gave me his absolution for all the homicides I ever had committed or *ever should commit*, in the service of the church."

The fiery and impatient humour of Benvenuto was perpetually involving him in quarrels. His reverence for the Pope was profound; but this did not always extend to the Cardinals, who interfered with him and gave him a great deal of trouble. On one occasion when the Pope had ordered him to proceed with a chalice, the annoyances of one of these "foolish Cardinals," as he calls them, had, it seems, prevented his completing it, at which the Pope was greatly enraged, and a violent scene took place between them.

"In my way to the palace, I meditated within myself," he says, "an excuse for discontinuing the work; and thought, that whilst the Pope was considering and examining my performance, I might acquaint him with my case: but I was mistaken; for as soon as I appeared in his presence, he said to me with great asperity, 'Let me see that work of yours; is it finished?' Upon my producing it, he flew into a more violent passion than before; and said, 'As there is truth in God, I assure you, since you value your living soul, that if a regard to decency did not prevent me, I would order both you and your work to be thrown this moment out of the window.' Seeing the Pope thus inflamed with brutal fury, I was for quitting his presence directly; and as he continued his bravadoes, I put the chalice under my cloak, muttering these words to myself: 'The whole world would prove unable to make a blind man proceed in such an undertaking as this.' The Pope then, with a louder voice than before, said, 'Come hither! What's that you say?' For a while I hesitated, whether I should not run down stairs. At last I plucked up my courage, and, falling on my knees, exclaimed aloud in these words, because he continued to scold: 'Is it reasonable, that when I am become blind with a disorder, you should oblige me to continue to work.' He answered, 'You could see well enough to come hither; and I don't believe one word of what you say.' Observing that he spoke with a milder tone of voice, I replied, 'If your Holiness will ask your physician, you will find that I declare the truth.' 'I shall inquire into the affair at my leisure,' said he. I now perceived that I had an opportunity to plead my cause, and therefore delivered myself thus : 'I am persuaded, most holy father, that the author of all this mischief is no other than Cardinal Salviati; because he sent for me directly after your holiness's departure; and when I came to him, called my work a fantastical piece, and told me he would make me finish it in a galley. These opprobrious words made such an impression on me, that through the great perturbation of mind I was in, I felt my face all on a sudden inflamed, and my eyes were attacked by so violent an heat, that I could hardly find my way home: a few days after, there fell upon them two cataracts, which blinded me to such a degree that I could hardly see the light; and since your holiness's departure, I have not been able to do a stroke of work.' Having spoken thus, I rose up and withdrew. I was told that the Pope said, after I was gone, 'When places of trust are given, discretion is not always conveyed with them : I did not bid the Cardinal treat people quite so roughly;

if it be true that he has a disorder in his eyes, as I shall know by asking my physician, I should be inclined to look upon him with an eye of compassion.'" Benvenuto was soon restored to the favour of his Holiness.

In this beautiful picture, Wilkie has well hit off the elegant and fiery young Florentine, who presents a piece of his workmanship to the pope, who is evidently enraptured with its design and execution. There is great breadth and richness in the style of the drapery: the introduction of the twisted and decorated column, similar to that in St. Peter's, as well as the ornamented candelabrum, are characteristic and appropriate, and add to the richness of the composition.

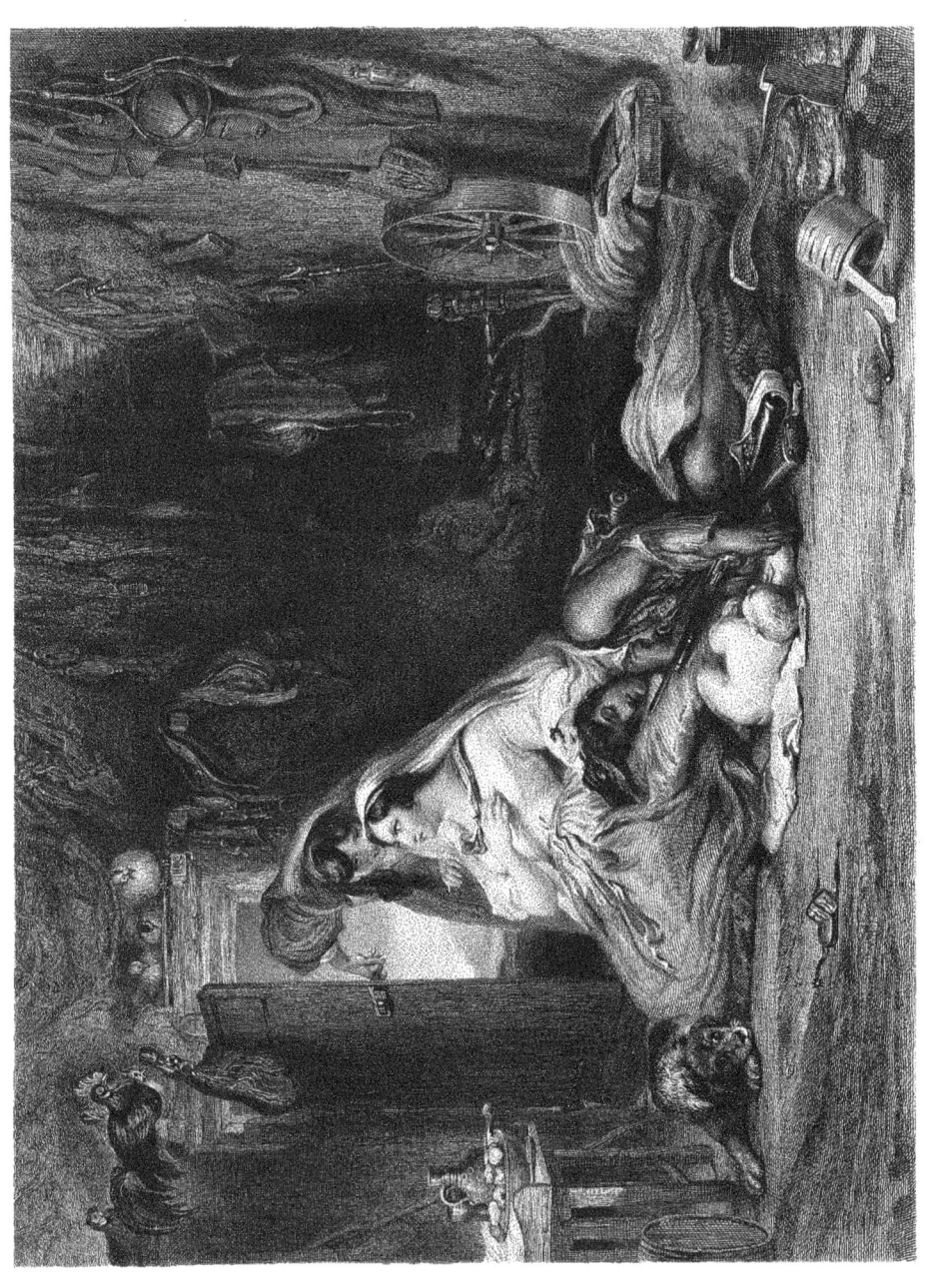

THE PEEP-O'-DAY BOY'S CABIN.

It having been represented to WILKIE, when in search of subjects, that Ireland was yet a mine unworked, in which he could not fail to labour to advantage; he set off in 1835 on a tour through that island. He was exceedingly delighted with a country in which, as he observes, "Velasquez, Murillo and Salvator Rosa would have found fit subjects for their study," and he was surprised at the Spanish and Italian look of the people. The whole economy of the people, he might well say, furnishes the elements of the picturesque. They build their own cabins, fabricate their own clothes, dig their own turf, catch their own salmon, and plough their own fields; bringing into their confined dwelling a confused variety of implements not to be described.

However he might have appreciated the qualities of his subject, few will be of opinion that WILKIE has added much to his previous reputation by his Irish performances. Miss Edgeworth, a great admirer of his character and talents, was compelled to remark, when the sketch of the above picture was placed before her, that neither the dress nor the expression were characteristically Hibernian; and although the picture corrected many of the defects of the sketch, it cannot be compared with Wilkie's Scotch subjects for expression and character.

The picture is so well described by Allan Cunningham, that we cannot do better than quote from him. "The Peep-o'-Day Boy represents a fine vigorous young man lying asleep in a rude wigwam or cabin, among hills less rude than his home; weapons are within reach of his hand; a naked child, lately nestled in his bosom, lies in slumber behind him; while his faithful wife (a young and lovely creature) sits listening lest some hostile foot should escape the keen eyes of a handmaid, who watches the dawning daylight on the neighbouring mountains, and seems fearful lest it should, as it increased, remove the veil of night from armed bands who seek the life of him whom she served." It is a forcible representation of the misery of a course of lawless rapine; but grand as is the general effect, its details are deficient in that inimitable truthfulness to local character, which throws such a charm over the Blind Fiddler and the Distraining for Rent.

During his short stay in Ireland, Wilkie appears to have regarded the condition of the people rather with the enthusiasm of a painter in search of the picturesque, than with the eye of a politician conscious of the defects of their social condition. He notices, in regard to costume, the curious distinction, that while in Dublin the lower classes wear only the cast-off clothes of their superiors, adorning themselves with faded swallow-tail coats and seedy hats, in Connaught and Connemara the clothes, particularly of the women, are the work of their own hands, and the colour they are most fond of is a red they die with madder. A petticoat, jacket, and mantle, brighten up the landscape like a Titian or Giorgione.

We must not omit to notice the singular ability with which the engraver has seized the peculiar tone of the original picture, as well as copied its most minute details.

Lightning Source UK Ltd.
Milton Keynes UK
UKHW012017211118
332759UK00017B/1447/P